Create Space

D0279376

Derek Draper has worked as a leadership consultant, business psychologist and executive coach for nearly fifteen years. He is the co-founder and CEO of CDP Leadership Consultants and was previously Managing Consultant and Head of Business Development for the UK and Europe at the global consultancy YSC.

He has assessed and developed senior business people in around twenty FTSE 100 companies and in some of the largest privately held companies in the world. As well as working in the UK he has worked with businesses in Germany, the Nordics, Russia, Saudi Arabia and Africa.

Prior to this he worked in politics, as chief aide to Peter (now Lord) Mandelson, and was the founder of Progress, the centre-ground think tank. He was also an entrepreneur in the marketing and communications sector helping build and sell a public affairs consultancy to Omnicon and then co-founding an advertising agency which was sold to Cello.

Today, as well as leading CDP he has a small psychotherapy practice in Bloomsbury and is a Governor of the Tavistock and Portman NHS Trust. He is an active member of the Association for Business Psychology (ABP). He lives in London with his wife, the TV and radio presenter Kate Garraway, and their two children, Darcey and Bill. He tweets @derekdraper and you can sign up to receive his regular newsletter at www.derekdraper.net/signup.

This is a stimulating, thought-provoking and valuable guide for those who are serious about 'being the best they can be'. It blends research, considered insights and storytelling to offer a very practical framework to take control and make space for reflection, learning, possibilities and being. It will act as a useful 'coach' in all aspects of one's life and at all stages in one's career.

Valerie Scoular, former Group HR director at Barclays,
British Airways and Dentsu Aegis Network

What I most like about *Create Space* is the twelve stories at the heart of the book. They bring to life the ideas within it in an engaging and entertaining way. Whether you are at the start of your career, enjoying your first management responsibilities, or sitting in the C-suite, this book has lots to offer. I highly recommend it.

Henry Birch, chief executive of the Rank Group plc

Create Space is coming at the right time. Leaders today are always on, and operating in environments which are rapidly changing. So figuring out how to get the space to think, learn, decide and grow is a very high-leverage piece of help.

Austin Lally, Group CEO, Verisure

This book sets out in a very well researched, practical way how you can create the physical and mental space to make better decisions, build deeper professional relationships and get the things that really matter done. Whether you work in business, the public sector or the third sector, if you aspire to master the art and science of leadership, this is a great guide.

Gavyn Davies, chairman, Fulcrum Asset Management,
and former chairman of the BBC

No matter how busy you think you are, find the time to read this book. Packed with far-reaching insights and simple steps for wresting back control of your diary and your career, *Create Space* is a must-read for thoughtful leaders looking to take their performance – and the performance of their teams – to the next level.

Sarah Wood, founder and non-executive chair,
Unruly.com (part of News Corp)

Derek Draper will do something for you that no politician can; he will help you take back control.

Robert Peston, ITV political editor (former BBC business editor)

I'm moderately successful but permanently playing catch-up. I'm late for everything. I struggle to prioritise, and even to catch my breath. I juggle with only mixed results. I'm glad I stepped back and created enough space to read Derek Draper's original, clever, practical book. Space to think is the most basic necessity. Draper has shown me, for the first time, where I can find it.

Euan Rellie, co-founder and senior MD,
BDA (Business Development Asia)

I see loads of business books and they can often be one idea stretched out to fill a book and a little bit too 'ivory tower'. This book's different. Each chapter takes a vital skill and digs deep to really understand it, through very lifelike and funny stories. There's then a tonne of practical suggestions that will resonate with anyone who works in business. If you're serious about your career, grab this now and get reading.

Ian King, business editor, Sky News

Create

How to
Manage Time,
and Find Focus,
Productivity
and Success

Space

DEREK DRAPER

P

PROFILE BOOKS

First published in Great Britain in 2018 by
Profile Books Ltd
3 Holford Yard
Bevin Way
London WC1X 9HD
www.profilebooks.com

A CIP catalogue record for this book is available from the
British Library.

ISBN 978 1 78816 048 3
eISBN 978 1 78283 447 2

Text design by sue@lambledesign.demon.co.uk
Typeset in Dante by MacGuru Ltd

Printed and bound in Great Britain by Clays Ltd, Elcograf S.p.A.

FSC
www.fsc.org
MIX
Paper from
responsible sources
FSC® C018072

To my wonderful wife Kate, who created the space for me to come truly alive, and Darcey and Bill who fill our space in such captivating, joyous and hilarious ways.

Contents

Acknowledgements

This book is entirely built on the experiences I have had working with hundreds of talented people from a large number of UK and global businesses. I thank them, their colleagues, their bosses, and their HR partners. It was a pleasure and an honour to work with every one of you.

I wouldn't have found my way into leadership consulting if I hadn't met Gurnek Bains. He became my boss, my inspiration and my friend. To make a good living doing something so inherently interesting and worthwhile is a blessing. I thank him and his then business partner Ken Rowe for welcoming me to YSC.

There I met some great people. Early readers of my drafts included Kylie Bains, Rani Bains, Francesca Elston, Anita Kirpal, Georgia Samolada, Jane Anderson, Jonathan Bloom, Nik Kinley, Georgina Cavaliere, Kevin Bright, Emmett Gracie, Chris Rawlinson and Stuart Schofield. In particular Susannah Yule, David Longmore and Lara Menke have become close friends and each contributed a great deal to my thinking.

I left YSC to set up CDP and my partners Sarah-Jane Last and Paul Jeffrey, along with Joanna Floyd, Rob Davies, Gerard de la Garde, Susie Orbach, Juliet Rosenfeld, Susan Kahn, Orla Coughlan and the rest of our Associates deserve thanks for putting up with me being distracted from our new business for the best part of a year. Our UCL based researchers Alex Farcas and Felix Schmirler provided valuable research help in the early days. Thanks also to the CDP designer Mike Hughes, our finance manager Chriss Goodey, our accountant Marc Jason, our lawyer James Harman at Simkins and my Executive Assistant Claire Acfield.

My leadership consultancy rests on the foundations of the psychology I learned at the Wright Institute in Berkeley, California and at the Tavistock Clinic in London. My erstwhile US psychotherapy supervisors Jessica Broitman, Laurie Case, Peter Silen and Mike Rubino, and my UK ones, Brett Kahr and Susie Orbach, but above all my psychotherapy patients, have over the years enabled me to develop the capacity for the deep psychological thinking that informs my corporate work today. As did my US BFF Caroline Date.

My CDP colleague Elloa Atkinson was actively involved in the final stage of the project and her research, ideas and drafting were vital to the book being completed. She was a joy to work with and it's no exaggeration to say that certain sections of the book are as much hers as mine.

Ed Docx deserves special thanks as he worked with me in the early stages of the book to make the theme clear and compelling. He is an amazing writer, teacher and friend. Others who read and commented on versions of the manuscript include Henry Birch, Rowenna Davis, Richard Hawkes, Darren Watmough, Nick White, Anton Fishman and my in-laws Marylyn and Gordon Garraway. As always Ben Wegg-Prosser was a true adviser, ally and friend throughout.

Andrew Gordon at David Higham Associates took the book under his wing and there surely can't be a more pleasant, thoughtful, committed agent. His comments on the book altered its structure fundamentally and improved it significantly.

Louisa Dunnigan, my editor at Profile Books, cajoled and challenged me until the book was the best it could possibly be. She was penetrating, thorough and always right. I can't thank her enough. My copy editor Joe Staines made some typically understated but excellent suggestions, all of which were gratefully received.

Of course, final thanks and acknowledgements go to my parents Ken and Chrina and to my own wonderful family, to whom the book is dedicated.

Introduction

T HE TWO IDEAS at the heart of this book came to me during two very different afternoons.

One was spent hiking up a mountain in Kenya; the other in a noisy works canteen off a ring road on the outskirts of London. Oddly enough, both took place while I was working for the same client, a FTSE 100 giant, whose products fill aisles in every super-market in the world.

A couple of years ago I was sent to Africa to work with some of the company's local business leaders. After a few days, I had an afternoon off and hired a driver to take me to a nearby national park, close to the Serengeti and the Great Rift Valley. As I hiked up Mount Longonot with a guide, a herd of wild giraffe strolled across our path. Luckily, that day, no lions. Half-way up we stopped and surveyed the surrounding landscape. The dusty valley seemed to go on forever. Vast swathes of green, brown and yellow scrubland rolled on and on to an eventual horizon marked by dark, jagged mountain-tops. The only visible signs of humanity were a few indistinct clumps of grey, marking out various hamlets and small towns. I was struck dumb by the stillness and grandeur spread out before me. I had never before experienced such a sense of limitless, almost entirely empty space. What a contrast to my usual hectic existence.

This land was where our ancestors first walked the earth. Roughly 200,000 years ago the first recognisably human figures had spread across this part of Africa, and every single one of us alive today has DNA that can be traced back to that group – some scientists argue to a specific man and woman. About 75,000 years ago these slender, graceful, large-brained *Homo sapiens* began to journey slowly out of Africa. Over the next tens of thousands of years they settled pretty much everywhere on the planet, displacing several other hominid species, such as the Neanderthals, along the way. Just 30,000 years ago 'we' became the only humans. The world was our oyster.

For roughly a thousand generations afterwards, life remained essentially the same. Yes, language, tools, rituals and art became more sophisticated, but day after day our forebears awoke to see boundless land and skies all around them. One imagines a typical day would have involved a bit of conversation, undoubtedly some loving, maybe a little fighting, certainly some hunting or gathering, but there wouldn't have been much to 'do' in the modern sense. For tens of thousands of years we humans weren't focused on 'doing' but simply 'being'. We were surrounded by space and we could never have dreamed, in any sense, of filling it. Then something astonishing happened. Imagine an old-fashioned movie projector suddenly breaking and speeding up, frames rushing by until, finally, the film bursts into flames.

If the whole of human history were represented by one human life of eighty years, the first seventy-five years would have been spent in small tribes, hunting and gathering in ways wholly recognisable to those who first walked the savannah. At age seventy-five, people would have started coming together in larger tribes, some nomadic but most setting up the first small farming communities. Only in the last year of this symbolic eighty-year-old's life would people have been settling down in the earliest cities and inventing such basic foundations for civilisation as the wheel and writing. Just a few months before the person's death, the invention of the printing press would have meant pamphlets and books becoming available to more than just a tiny elite. The industrial revolution wouldn't occur until the final month or so; TV in the last week; mobile phones in the last few days; Google, Facebook, the iPhone, VR, AI pretty much in the last hours, or even minutes, before death.

Suddenly we have gone from existing within limitless space to living in an age where, in every sense, the space around us is

indiscriminately filled multiple times over. Huge numbers of us –
and more and more each day – live in high-rise cities, commute to
work in cattle-like conditions, and feel harried and overwhelmed. We
are bombarded daily with thousands of sounds and images, and gaze
for hours at a time at one screen or another. With just a few taps of
our fingers we are able to conjure up almost every major piece of
writing, thought or work of art that has survived in those previous,
long, slow 200,000 years.

When I was a child, if I wanted to read a book I had to walk to
the library and check it out; our typical family holiday was in the
Lake District fifty miles away; a new kids' film at the local cinema
was a twice-yearly event; and two (out of a total of three) channels
provided an hour's worth of children's TV each evening. Filling time
and space required effort. I had fallow periods where I had to think
about what I wanted to do. I then had to expend time and effort to
make those things happen.

My children, on the other hand, are immersed in a tablet world
with instantaneous access to a limitless array of videos, reading and
games. They can talk to virtually anyone and see virtually anything
in the world. They can fill all the space they have with just a few
clicks. They don't ever really have to think about what to do. They
never have to wait. Their minds need never be empty. They can be
passive consumers of whatever is tantalising and easy to reach.

My parents had jobs that involved turning up, doing their work
and clocking off. There were no emails to catch up on in the evening,
no Facebook to check. Colleagues and bosses never telephoned.
Actually, I think it happened once in all my childhood when my dad's
foreman called to say there'd been a power cut at the factory and
not to come in that day. Today, for almost all professionals, setting a
boundary between home and work is a constant struggle, one often
lost. We are confronted with texts, emails, messages, which come at
all times of the day and night. While we might stress about our kids
spending too much time on their screens, we invariably admonish
them while pausing only briefly from scrutinising our own.

This is a wholly new situation for humankind and one we simply aren't 'wired' for. The several millions of years of hominid evolution that resulted in *Homo sapiens* shaped us to roam the African plains, not the World Wide Web. This crowded, rushed, overwhelming world is undoubtedly our destiny; but we aren't in control of it.

Only a Luddite would claim this is all bad. The possibilities for progress, learning and pure enjoyment are legion. The benefits and costs, long-term consequences, and what comes next can be debated. Already the gurus at Google are forecasting that by 2030 our brains will effectively be wired to the Cloud.

My interest, though, on that warm evening back in my hotel on the outskirts of Nairobi, was not in futurology or even philosophy, but in the immediately practical. How can we reinstate some of that sense of space that I had felt on Mount Longonot back into our busy, modern lives? How can we step back and regain some control? If we don't, our time and energy will be increasingly taken up dealing, almost unconsciously, with a deluge of information, stimulation and demands over which we effectively exert little choice.

I went to bed with all these thoughts swirling around my mind. In the morning I woke up and turned to a new page in my notebook. I wrote down what was to become the first key insight of this book:

> *We have become the first generation in one thousand generations of human beings who, rather than having the need to fill space, have the need to create it.*

*

A few weeks later, in a glass-walled office block on the edge of London, I was working with Katya, who was high up in the same company's supply chain function, the unglamorous but crucial part of any complicated global business. I was coaching Katya as part of an initiative involving 150 high-potential managers, out of which I had been allocated half a dozen to work with personally. It was our first meeting, and she had flown over from Moscow where she was based. Unfortunately, the business was launching a new product that afternoon and their HQ was heaving, with all the meeting rooms overbooked. Even the café, where we decided we'd have to make do, was crammed with people. Eventually we managed to find two seats. Around us 200 office workers chatted over lunch, some shouting to colleagues on other tables, others gesticulating as they spoke on their mobiles, cutlery and crockery clanging around us.

Katya was understandably distracted. She hoped to use the trip to touch base with lots of people and her phone kept pinging. She carried a massive pile of papers and a scribbled to-do list that she kept glancing at anxiously. I wondered whether she felt she had much better things to do than talk to me. Gradually, though, she focused her attention on my questions and she began to tell me about the challenges she faced making the company's supply chain more efficient.

Katya had all of the traditional hallmarks of a rising business leader: she was smart, personable and driven. But she found it hard to find the time to do the deep thinking her job required. She also struggled to connect on more than a superficial and transactional level with the people she needed to work with. In meetings she could be dominant, despite the fact that she knew that this discouraged others from contributing.

As we discussed all this, I had to struggle to hear her above the hubbub of the canteen. We were also interrupted a couple of times as her colleagues came over to say hi. At one point, as she began to open up more about her own weaknesses, someone came and squeezed in next to us and started talking loudly on his phone. As he manspread she shifted uncomfortably towards the edge of the bench.

I sighed and looked up to the polystyrene ceiling, studded with over-bright spotlights. Suddenly I had a memory of the stillness and space of that African valley. Then two thoughts hit me one after the other. Prompted, no doubt, by the lack of physical space we had been struggling with all afternoon, I realised that space, in its widest conceptual sense, was exactly Katya's problem when it came to her work. Furthermore, there was a connection between the vastness of the African valley and the cramped canteen, and how the sense of space of the former needed to be somehow re-created in the latter. Not literally, but psychically.

I'd spent the last decade working as a business psychologist and leadership consultant helping businesses audit and develop their leaders, teams and organisational set-up and culture. Up until then I'd seen the issues that I dealt with as disparate problems, requiring distinct interventions. For some reason, that day, I began to see them for what they were: symptoms.

I now felt that there might be a common theme underpinning the hundreds of assignments I had worked on over those years. After I'd arranged to visit Katya in Moscow a few weeks later and bid her farewell, I spent that evening jotting down my thoughts:

○ Modern life, particularly work, fills any space indiscriminately

○ This means most leaders feel overwhelmed and not masters of their own destiny

○ A leader must, therefore, consciously push back and create space

Such space is vital for:

○ Deeper self-insight and sense of purpose

○ Better strategic and creative thinking

○ Richer relationships

○ Delivering what really matters

Therefore:

○ You can't deliver your best or really grow as a leader unless you first create space

As the next few months unfolded I saw this lack of space everywhere. I avoided talking about it in coaching sessions while my ideas continued to form. Again and again, though, it seemed to be the issue that lay underneath the surface.

A YouGov survey commissioned by Virgin found that 51 per cent of employees have experienced anxiety or a sense of burnout in their current role, with 65 per cent of employees reporting that their manager expects them to be reachable outside of the office. A 2015 survey of UK GPs, who you'd think would know more than the rest of us about maintaining good physical and mental health, found that three-quarters of them were emotionally exhausted. Another study found that 92 per cent of us feel stressed all or a lot of the time. The incessant demands of the modern workplace, and our own unhelpful working habits, place a glass ceiling on how far we can grow. To shatter that we have to make a fundamental reorientation of how we interact with the world.

What I was beginning to realise was that creating space isn't just one way of becoming more successful, it actually underpins such growth and success *per se*. It is the prerequisite for being able to really change. Because before you can develop and grow, you first have to create the space to allow you to think, feel and act differently. If you simply try and bolt on some behavioural change or developmental goal to how you operate now, it may have some effect but it won't be truly transformative. This thinking led me to the second insight that underpins this book:

> Before you set out to grow as a leader, you must first create the space that you will grow into. Creating space is the a priori task that unlocks optimal personal performance and development.

★

The idea and meaning of space has long been a topic of exploration in philosophy, going back to Plato and Socrates. Later, space became an important idea in the work of thinkers as diverse as Kant and Einstein. In 1781 Kant wrote that, 'Space is not something objective and real ... instead, it is subjective and ideal.' While complex, Kant's theories open up the idea that space is not a constant and that we can influence how much space we feel we have through our mindset (see Part 5). Meanwhile, Einstein's theory of relativity unpacked ideas of time and space, and revolutionised our understanding of these concepts and the relationship between them. His theory states that both space and time are relative, dependent on the motion of the person observing them. Again, our relationship to space changes it. Somewhat echoing Kant, Einstein demonstrated that space is neither fixed nor static. Both of these thinkers helped inspire the notion of 'psychic space' that is interspersed throughout this book.

On a practical level these notions help explain why people have such different attitudes to space. Some people feel overwhelmed and hemmed in when the objective pressure they are under is relatively low. Others seem to handle huge competing pressures with grace and aplomb. This is partly down to the latter using similar approaches and tools to the ones in this book, and partly due to traits like intellectual bandwidth, energy and resilience. But it is more than that. These people's relationship to the world around them, their place in it, and therefore the space they feel they have is quantitively – and qualitatively – *different* from those in the first group. Hence the old aphorism, 'if you want something done, give it to a busy person.'

The question of space also surfaces in classic psychoanalytic literature. The renowned post-war psychoanalyst D. W. Winnicott writes about 'potential space', while contemporary Californian analyst Thomas Ogden builds on this idea in his description of 'the analytic space'. I will return to these later.

The seminal work by French philosopher Henri Lefebvre elucidates three types of 'space': the physical (nature, the cosmos); the mental (including logical and formal abstractions); and the social. For me it was the contrast between two manifestations of the first type of space – the vastness of the African landscape and the claustrophobia of Katya's office canteen – that had set off my thinking in the first place. But Lefebvre shows that there is more to space than just what we see. His second type – the mental – relates to that unique, subjective sense each of us makes of physical external reality. This idea is linked to a concept I will explore later, that of the 'inner world'. The final type of space – the social – is the space between ourselves and others, the space we create with each other. Again, this is something I explore later when I explain the concept of 'third space'. All these different types of space interact with each other in complex, infinite ways – where we are, who we are with and what we perceive of the situation. Lefebvre's three-part definition helps clarify that space is not just another way of saying 'time', linked and important though that is. It also gives depth to the notion of 'creating space'. We aren't just creating space to 'fit more in', we are actively creating our own personal *version* of space: the place(s) within which we live.

An interesting side note is how we relate to space for our possessions. The UK alone uses 37.6 million square feet of storage space, the equivalent of 268,500 removal vans. Just as we are drowning in information and tasks, we are also drowning in stuff.

*

The need to create more space seems virtually ubiquitous in our modern, busy world, and applies in all areas of our lives: to our relationships with our wives, husbands, and significant others; to our friendships; to our roles as parents; to how we relate to – and look after – ourselves. It is also a need keenly felt in that most busy arena of our lives – the world of work.

My interest in space had been initially triggered by my work as a leadership consultant, and I found myself fascinated by how these ideas had the possibility for creating profound change in my clients. So my thinking about space began to focus on what the phenomenon meant for the world of work, and in particular, for people aspiring to be leaders in business. The model for 'Creating Space' which I went on to develop, maps onto Lefebvre's descriptive definitions though it is more behavioural in its orientation, with four overarching dimensions:

1. Space to Think
2. Space to Connect
3. Space to Do
4. Space to Be

Space to Think is about having the intellectual and psychic freedom to think in a deep way about yourself and the world. **Space to Connect** involves having the emotional capacity to share what you have to offer with others, and accept what they have to offer you. **Space to Do** relates to prioritising and then having a productive impact on the world. **Space to Be** requires us to step back a little and ensure that we are building the kind of life we really want to have.

While I was developing these ideas, I was working with a global leadership consultancy and I wanted to see if their data backed up my thinking. The company had assessed around 50,000 leaders over the last twenty-five years and had a database of the results which enabled people to be benchmarked against others in similar situations. But their framework, understandably, didn't draw out space as a discrete area. Instead it looked at more traditional leadership capabilities, such as strategic thinking and influencing. So I had to go back to the raw data – the assessments themselves. I examined 1,000 random reports that had been written by around fifty consultants from all over the world, about leaders in every region – Europe, the Americas, Africa, Asia and the Middle East – within the previous five years.* As well as containing a psychological profile of the anonymous assessee, each report contained approximately half-a-dozen strengths and roughly the same number of development areas. I sat for several days reading them, noting where any report's development areas contained words and phrases relating to space. These included the word 'space' itself but also related concepts such as 'stepping back', 'making room to...' and so on.

In total the reports contained more than 4,500 development areas. You can read more about the analysis in the Appendix (on p. 282). Suffice to say here that an examination of the data led me to conclude that the issue of 'space' is an issue across all types of businesses and in every culture. Indeed, virtually all – 93 per cent – of those assessed appeared to have a development need that related to

---

*I am grateful to the then Chairman of YSC, Gurnek Bains, for allowing me access to the reports he had analysed for different reasons in his own book, *Cultural DNA: The Psychology of Globalisation*.

creating space in some form or another. The number of people with
at least one development area relating to each theme broke down
as follows:

Theme	Percentage of Reports highlighting this area
Space to Think	46%
Space to Connect	75%
Space to Do	32%
Space to Be	11%
None of the above	7%
At least one of the above	93%

So three-quarters of all global executives assessed – and by
implication, global executives *per se* – need to create more space
to connect. Nearly half need to create more space to think, a third
space to do, and roughly 10 per cent need to create more space to be.

★

On the next page is the full model with its twelve constituent parts.
It encapsulates the key areas where I have found people most need
to create space, and expands on those four key aspects that I outlined
earlier: to think, connect, do and be.

A leader who hasn't created such space for herself will be operating in a way that is primarily about responding to what is happening
around her. She will be working hard, but in a way shaped by exter-
nalities, not herself. She will feel she has little or no space and is far
from being in command of her own life.

A leader who consciously and consistently creates space, on the
other hand, takes decisive control over her working life. She creates
space so that she can think through and decide her own priorities
and then have the space to work on these. She constantly creates
and manages space rather than falling victim to a lack of it. She pro-
actively chooses how to fill the space she creates rather than letting
it be filled by events or the demands of others. This is much more

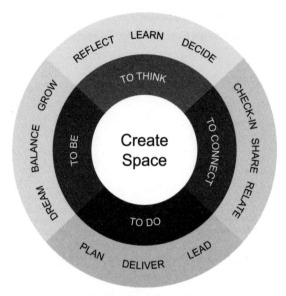

Create Space model

than just a question of time, or even energy, although it is certainly those things, it is primarily a state of mind. She becomes the master of her destiny.

When I first created this model, I presented it at the Association for Business Psychology Annual Conference and asked the attendees to fill in a 'space inventory' to explore their own relationship to the idea of creating space. This provided evidence that backed up my ideas. Almost everyone there desired more space in their working lives and, on average, only had 70 per cent of the space they wished for. You can take the same BETA version of the inventory at www.derekdraper.net.

★

Enriched through this practical research and study, the two core ideas that drive this book have nonetheless remained the same as they were at the end of each of those two very different afternoons:

*We have become the first generation in one thousand generations of
human beings who, rather than having the need to fill space, have the
need to create it.*

*Before you set out to grow as a leader you must first create the space
that you will grow into. Creating space is the* a priori *task that
unlocks optimal personal performance and development.*

If you want to be a real success at work with all the excitement, satisfaction and rewards that entails, you must step back and
embrace the idea of 'first creating space' as the animating idea and
organising principle of how you approach your working life. This is
the key to unlocking your true potential and becoming the biggest
success you have it in you to be. Each decision, every action, all your
plans must begin with the creation of the space into which they will
be realised.

Gone are the days when the leader is the man in the corner office
on the top floor. You are a leader. Even if you are only the leader
of yourself – though that 'only' is misplaced. As the Roman philosopher Seneca the Younger wrote, 'to rule oneself is the ultimate
power.'

In most modern workplaces power is shared and diverse. Leading
is a more ambiguous, fluid phenomenon. It is often more a question
of influence than authority. Making things happen requires working
with others to achieve a particular goal. Sometimes we are leaders,
sometimes followers, and sometimes we are out on our own.

So the notion of Creating Space applies to everyone's working
life (and beyond), whether they are a CEO, an individual contributor,
or a graduate recruit. But if you are a senior leader, or aspire to be, it
is worth noting how closely the 'Create Space' model maps the leadership frameworks used by the world's leading leadership firms and
global companies. I carried out an analysis of over fifty different leadership frameworks, including those of various FTSE 100 and Fortune
500 companies, and of organisations such as the British Civil Service
and the US Army, which shows this alignment clearly. On the right
of this table you will see the key elements from these leadership

frameworks (they tend to be, unsurprisingly, pretty similar) and how they fit under each element of the 'Create Space' model.

Create space to ...	Is linked to these leadership capabilities ...
Think	Decision making, problem solving, strategic thinking, creativity, innovation
Connect	Collaboration, inspiring, motivating, developing, influencing, connecting, self-awareness, self-satisfaction, EQ, teamwork
Do	Executing, mobilising, high performance, managing change, transformation, delivery
Be	Better work-life balance, personal meaning and purpose, sustainability, resilience

This table illustrates how important creating space is to succeeding as a leader. Most business people want to get better at the capabilities listed in the right-hand column. Indeed, it is estimated that companies spend nearly $50bn a year trying to help their employees get better at these. However, unless you create the space to do the things on the left-hand column you will not have freed yourself up to grow the capabilities on the right-hand side. Again, creating space comes first. The development this unlocks then follows.

The next twelve chapters take each of the elements of the model and bring it to life through a case study based on actual coaching and development work that I have done with clients (though all the clients depicted are composites and identifying details have been changed). Each story is followed by an exploration of the themes and the wider issues raised, followed by a more practical section. So, to take the example of the chapter on Delivery: first you will read a story about someone struggling to create space to deliver, then you will read about what delivery is and why it's important, followed by a concluding third section containing practical suggestions that you can try out for yourself.

You may want to read through the chapters in order or turn to an area that is most relevant to you right now. Each chapter stands alone, but are all connected to each other, especially within each Part. The final Part pulls together some of the key lessons from Parts 1–4 and summarises the three fundamental foundations needed to create space – setting your strategy, raising your productivity and adopting the 'space mindset'.

However you decide to approach the book, I hope that you will find yourself engaged and challenged. Most importantly, I hope it inspires you to identify where *you* need to create more space, and provides some guidance to help you do so.

PART 1

Create Space to Think

T HE THINKING WE DO, the ideas we have and the decisions we make are the prerequisites for taking effective action – and in order to deliberate properly we need to have some dedicated time and a clear mind. If we rush, or try to think in a pressured, distracted environment, the quality of our reasoning will suffer. We won't come up with the best ideas, we won't have fully thought things through and we'll make poor decisions.

Yet many of us don't feel we have the time and space to do the deeper contemplation that our complex, high-responsibility jobs require: There are three elements we need to address to create the space for such high-quality thinking:

First we need to **Create Space to Reflect**. This is what psychologists call 'meta-cognition' or 'thinking about thinking': being able to mull things over and test our conclusions. We need to do this before we make decisions and afterwards, so that we can constantly improve the quality of our thinking. Raku, in our first story, feels a pressure to take action quickly, but in doing so short-circuits the examination that is required before she rushes forward.

Second, we need to **Create Space to Learn**. In a world of uncertainty, change and endless innovation, we can't rely on what we already know. We need to learn new things and make new intellectual connections. We'll meet Rachel, who doesn't want to look foolish or make herself vulnerable, so she fails to learn the things that are required for success in her new role.

Finally, we need to **Create Space to Decide**. We must eventually let our reflections and learning inform a clear goal that we are going to aim for. This requires a deep understanding of the business context we operate in and the resources at our disposal. Deciding is the act of turning your internal thoughts into an action that will impact on the external world. In Hans's case he doesn't have the confidence and inner freedom to take this final, crucial step.

In all three stories we will see how a failure to create space to think can cripple people's ability to perform well and succeed, and how creating space to think provided the means for Raku, Rachel and Hans to get moving again. It gave them a greater understanding of themselves and the world, and they felt more certain of their opinions and decisions. In short, their minds had been opened up, rather than being prematurely closed down. The depth, breadth and quality of their thinking had improved and that became visible for all to see.

CHAPTER 1

Space to Reflect

Raku and Her Sister's Ghost

LESSON: *If you make the space to reflect on your decisions, and explore more carefully what you are doing and why, you will free yourself to contribute to the very best of your ability.*

RAKU WAS A GENERAL MANAGER for a pharmaceutical company. Originally from Japan, she had excelled at science in school and had initially started her career in the lab of one of her current employer's main competitors. Her ambitions extended far beyond being a research scientist. She had always harboured the desire to go into general management and, with a combination of persistence and the MBA she'd got under her belt from Stanford, she had finally made it.

Raku had been used to getting virtually top marks all her life (she'd even been in the top 3 of her MBA class) so she had been mortified when she sat down with her manager Greg and received an annual performance rating of just 3 out of 5. After leaving the meeting visibly upset, she had asked to see Greg again the next day. Would he consider changing the rating, she asked, listing the things she'd achieved that year. He held fast, explaining that at present she was making decisions too quickly, even rashly, was too fixed in her mindset and wasn't really listening to her team. She had been in charge of a project that had got into a mess and he'd had to step in to get it back on track. She recognised all this, of course, but her response was to grow sullen and withdrawn. He had then suggested that she meet with a coach to think through what was going on and why she had been given such a poor rating.

I had coached Greg for different reasons a couple of years before, and so he'd called to ask if I would coach Raku. He told me in confidence that he'd known he was being a little harsh by awarding her a 3 but explained that he wanted to shock her into some changes. Raku arrived early for her appointment, and when I came out to meet her in reception she jumped up from her seat and greeted me with a nervous smile.

Once we had settled into my office she was pleasant and forthcoming. After I explained a little about how I worked, I asked her to tell me her story. She began with her first job – in the research lab. I gently stopped her and asked her to start earlier, with her earliest memory.

This is something I always stress to my clients – I work in business but I am a business psychologist. The type of psychology I practise holds that our early years affect how we turn out as adults. When I assess people for recruitment, internal promotion or development I take a full life history. I always tell each one: 'If I am going to get to know Jo the professional, I have to know Jo the woman and, as a psychologist, I believe that part of what made Jo the woman was what happened to Jo the girl.' Another one of my stock remarks is: 'When I ask you, in a moment, to tell me your story, you should start not with your first job, but with your first breath.' Most people take this in their stride, some are surprised but OK with it; a few show some resistance. I assess and coach people all over the world, and in some cultures (such as those in Russia, Africa and Saudi Arabia), the resistance can seem greater. Actually, once people, whatever their background, feel they are with someone they can trust, they invariably open up and share some deeply personal experiences – even those who initially most baulked at the idea. Indeed, often initially the most reluctant end up sharing more than anyone.

Raku definitely fell into the category of more resistant. Indeed, she questioned the purpose of talking about her childhood at all. I explained that, not always, but time and again, I find that the fundamental development areas that someone has, have their genesis not in recent events, or even early career experiences, but in what happened earlier on, within the family, as they first formed their assumptions and attitudes about the world. There is a famous psychoanalytic paper called 'Ghosts in the Nursery' and I suspected that Raku, like most of us to one degree or another, was haunted in some way by a figure or figures from the past. The fact that she was resistant to talking about her early experiences, I'm afraid, just made me more suspicious.

Luckily, the scientist in her was intrigued by the hypothesis that there could have been factors from the past influencing her today.

'OK,' she said, 'let's give it a go.'

She started to tell me about what sounded like a pretty normal childhood on the outskirts of Kyoto. Her parents were very typical of their generation, low key and deferential. Her mother worked part-time in a flower shop while her father was a 'salaryman' for a big corporation. They both wanted her to do well but didn't overly push her. Then she said something surprising.

'What would have been the point anyway, my sister was the clever one.'

I often find clients do this, they will say something offhand, almost flippantly, that jars a little. I don't always explore it there and then but store it away for later. Raku went on to tell me about school, university, being awarded her PhD and getting her first job. Just as I felt she was relaxing and I was getting to know her a bit, she abruptly changed her tone.

'Can we get on to our plan now?' she asked.

It was the first sign I'd had of her being a bit pushy, even impatient. Sometimes when this happens I intentionally act in a way that aims to surface what I suspect are underlying feelings and frustrations.

'Oh, we'll get to that,' I said, in a laconic tone. 'There's no rush.'

As I went on to ask about what she thought her co-workers made of her, I could see that she was distracted and kept looking at the clock.

'Is there something wrong?' I asked.

'We have twenty minutes left,' she said, 'are we going to end today without a solution?'

I asked Raku if she felt rushed.

'Yes. Always,' she replied.

This would have surprised most observers, as she initially appeared to have such a gentle, calm manner. I was to learn that she was like the archetypal swan – graceful and elegant on the surface, but paddling furiously underneath.

'Do you know why?' I asked.

'Why what?'

'Why you rush?'

She answered straightaway. 'No idea, it's a busy world, right?' She laughed.

'OK,' I said. 'I'm going to ask you again. This time, don't answer straightaway. Sit with the idea, see what comes to mind.' I paused. 'OK, why do you rush?'

She sat, looking at me with a frown on her face. I waited. Her brow furrowed further.

'Just say the thing that's on your mind, even if it doesn't seem to make sense,' I said.

'For some reason I am thinking – to catch up. But that makes no sense, right?'

'Who are you trying to catch up with?'

'No idea,' she shot back.

'Again, pause and let the notion sit in your mind a bit.'

She sat quietly, again, looking unhappy. I waited. Eventually, she repeated what she'd said before: 'No idea.'

'OK, let's come back to that,' I said.

I had begun to put together what I call my 'formulation'. It simply means my sense of what was going on. What were the underlying dynamics driving the problem I was being asked to help with? What was Raku's Core Pathogenic Belief?

Core Pathogenic Beliefs (CPBs)

This is a clumsy phrase (I haven't been able to think of a better one) that just means a belief or assumption we have about ourselves that is inaccurate and harmful, hence pathogenic, or diseased. It is a concept that appears in various forms of psychology. In Cognitive Behavioural Coaching, people are asked to keep a thought record of how they are thinking, feeling and behaving, in an effort to identify what some Cognitive Behavioural Therapy practitioners call a 'schema'. My colleague Paul is involved in an organisation called Clearmind International Institute where they call it 'Suspicion of Self' or 'SOS', and I know of a couple of people who call it, informally, your 'SMB' – 'Shitty Mistaken Belief'. I first came across the phrase 'core pathogenic belief' when I lived in California and was briefly involved with the San Francisco Psychotherapy Research Group.

It doesn't really matter what you call it, so long as you work on identifying it. Psychodynamic Leadership Consulting, which is what I practise, believes that our past affects our present, and therefore our future. The experiences we have early in life lead us to form assumptions about ourselves and the world that become a set of core beliefs. We usually only have a dim sense of what these are, as they have been woven into our psyche and are largely unconscious. Even if we are aware of them, we don't necessarily see their influence on us or how they colour our approach to almost everything, it's just how 'we see the world'. It's like someone who is colour blind and can't differentiate between red and green: they could go through life blissfully unaware of their condition – until they first come across some traffic lights!

It is vital to bring core pathogenic beliefs to consciousness, to articulate them, name them and face them. As fantasy author Terry Pratchett says: 'as every wizard knows, once you have a thing's real name you have the first step to its taming.'

Core beliefs become pathogenic when they are out of kilter with reality; become extreme, or too fixed; or when they suited past circumstances but are now outdated. The psychoanalyst and writer

Stephen Grosz explains it well when he says: 'Experience has taught me that our childhoods leave in us stories – stories we never found a way to voice, because no one helped us to find the words. When we cannot find a way of telling our story, our story tells us – we dream these stories, we develop symptoms, or we find ourselves acting in ways we don't understand.'

A simple example would be if you grew up with parents who let you down and couldn't really be trusted. You would very likely have inculcated a suspicion of people and whether they could be relied on. The ordinary misunderstandings and mistakes people make would take on a more ominous meaning. The psychological idea of confirmation bias would come into play and you'd only notice the times when things went wrong, further confirming your CPB. This could affect how easily you made friends, how you handled romantic relationships, and how you treat your co-workers, or, if you are a manager, your team. As one client I worked with told me, 'I do trust people but I set the bar very, very high – and people don't get a second chance.' Imagine how enjoyable it is working for him.

Identifying and transforming your CPBs is vital if you are to develop on a fundamental level. As psychoanalyst Carl Jung wrote: 'Until you make the unconscious conscious, it will direct your life and you will call it fate.'

*

I was beginning to have a sense of what Raku's core pathogenic belief might be, but I wanted to gather some more evidence. At our next meeting I asked her to do two short self-assessment questionnaires: the first was an online resource developed by Lawrence Wilkes that rates the degree to which you use reflective practice. Raku scored in the mid-range of this, which for someone of her intellect (and scientific background) was surprisingly low.

I also asked Raku to do a short questionnaire that is based on Kolb's Learning Styles (which look at the interplay between experience, reflection and experimentation). This results in a circle with two axes: the vertical one is a continuum between 'Intuition' and 'Analysis' and looks at *how* we make decisions; the horizontal looks at what we *do* when we've made a decision, and ranges from 'Action' to 'Reflection'.

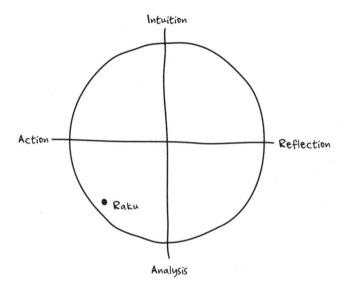

Raku, as I'd suspected she would, came out in the bottom left-hand corner, showing that she was highly analytical, not that intuitive, very action-oriented, and with little tendency to reflect. To my surprise she looked impressed.

'What are you thinking?' I asked.

'Well, I'm surprised. Nine short questions and you get a pretty good picture of me. It's almost scientific. Unless,' she added with a mischievous glint in her eye, 'it's just a fluke.'

'Well, either way, if it feels right to you, let's reflect on the consequences. What might this mean for how you are at work? What comes to mind?'

'Actually, it's interesting, you know,' she replied. 'What comes to mind isn't here but my time back in the lab, in my first job. My old boss, he would say, "Raku, stop charging ahead like a bull". He said I needed to stop starting new experiments without thinking through the implications of the results I already had.'

'And that feedback reminds you of what?' I gently prompted.

This time she didn't blurt out an answer. I waited.

'It's kind of like what's happening now, what Greg is going on at me about.'

'OK,' I said, 'we're going to do our own experiment now.' Her eyes lit up.

'I am going to get us some coffee, and in the ten minutes or so I'll be away I want you to sit still and reflect on just one question ... What is going wrong for Raku and why? Don't write the first thing that comes to mind. Try and think a little more deeply, and also try and tap into your feelings – in other words don't ...'

'... rush!' she said, finishing my sentence.

I smiled. She smiled back, looking straight at me for the first time since we started talking and holding her gaze.

'OK, here are some pens, there's the flip chart.'

When I came back with the coffees she was sitting still, looking at the flip chart. On it were written a few words and phrases:

I rush
I don't stop to think
I want to get on to the next thing
I leave people behind
This is EXHAUSTING

I passed over her drink.

'One other thing,' she said. 'I worked out who I am trying to catch up with.' She looked at me.

'You know, don't you?'

'I think so,' I replied but kept quiet.

Then she confirmed what we were both thinking.

'My sister.' She paused, seeming lost in thought. 'Still, after all these years.'

'And when you look at your management colleagues, all of whom have more experience than you, and have been managers for almost the whole of their careers, you want to catch up with them too.'

She nodded. 'But the more I rush, the less well I do!'

This is the power of a core pathogenic belief. It works below the surface. Usually you're not even conscious of it, or, if you are, just barely or fleetingly. Raku's was: 'If I don't rush and do lots quickly, I will not catch up.'

The trace of that childhood trauma, of being incredibly clever but still not quite as clever as her sister, was being projected on to her situation today. It made no logical sense, but it was driving her to act in a way that was harming her.

The rest of the coaching was spent exploring what a new, more reflective style would look like (drawing on some of the ideas I outline later). Back in the office she was taking time to listen, digest and reflect on what she was learning. She had managed to wean herself off her rush to rush, conscious now that rushing wasn't the means of catching up but the barrier to doing so. The feedback from Greg and her colleagues was good. One of them summed up the change when she said, 'It's like we're getting all of Raku now, whereas before we were just skimming the surface.'

*

Don't Rush: Creating Space to Reflect

'In order to understand the world, one has to turn away from it on occasion.'

Albert Camus, from The Myth of Sisyphus and Other Essays

Raku's story is one of rushing. She was driven by an unconscious need to catch up with those she perceived as being ahead of her. Projected today on her more experienced fellow managers that need was actually, it turned out, a replaying of a much earlier psychological dynamic – the desire to match the accomplishments of her gifted older sister. This early experience left an imprint on Raku's psyche that was triggered whenever she had a feeling of being behind. Without knowing it, she would slot into a familiar track of behaviour.

One manifestation of Raku's rushing was a lack of reflection. She didn't take the time to stop and think through her actions, either before she acted, or afterwards. This led to her making mistakes and alienating her team. Ironically she wasn't using one of her key strengths – her strong, logical intellect – to its full advantage, squandering it by not thinking deeply or richly enough about what she and her team needed to do. My experience of working with hundreds of business leaders convinces me that Raku is far from alone in this.

At its core, self-reflection is being able to think in a careful and considered way about ourselves, our work and our relationships. It empowers us to pause in the middle of the chaos, to zoom in or out, as needed, in order to get a deeper understanding of a situation – untangling the various thoughts, feelings and observations we may not immediately have been able to make sense of. The philosopher and psychologist John Dewey wisely wrote: 'We do not learn from experience; we learn from reflecting on experience.'

Reflective practice is just a modern fancy phrase for something that humans have done since the beginning of history. In the 5th century BC, the Chinese philosopher Confucius wrote: 'By three methods we learn wisdom: First, by imitation, which is easiest, second by experience, which is the bitterest and thirdly, by reflection, which is the noblest.' About a century later, Socratic thinking – critical, deliberative self- questioning – was developing on the other side of the world, in Greece.

Since then, definitions of 'reflective practice' have embraced ideas such as 'deep consideration', 'quiet contemplation', 'standing outside of oneself', and 'challenging conventional wisdom' – especially when it's *your* conventional wisdom. It requires a spirit of inquiry and a radical curiosity. It is about trying to take as objective a view as possible, analysing the situation around you, and interrogating your view of things to see what you might have missed, or what other possibilities exist.

The former US Defence Secretary Donald Rumsfeld was once

mocked for talking about 'unknown unknowns', but he was actually saying something very profound:

'... as we know, there are known knowns; there are things we know we know. We also know there are known unknowns; that is to say we know there are some things we do not know. But there are also unknown unknowns – the ones we don't know we don't know.'

So reflective practice is thinking about thinking and knowing about knowing – so-called meta-cognition. Psychoanalytic writers have variously called it 'the ability to see oneself from the outside and others from the inside' and 'thinking about feelings and feeling about thinking'. For that reason it requires honesty, vulnerability, a lack of defensiveness and a high sense of accountability. At its core it is simply an ongoing, meaningful conversation you have with yourself.

Reflecting, however, is far from just an intellectual exercise. It has very practical, tangible benefits. First, the quality of your decision-making will improve. This was Raku's big lesson. You'll make fewer mistakes and learn from the mistakes you do make more quickly. Because you have heightened your questioning of yourself and your observation of your impact on the world, you will grow in flexibility and agility – able to seize opportunities and change course when necessary. Moreover, you will also increase your self-awareness, a key element of your emotional intelligence and therefore your ability to build relationships, collaborate and influence others. You will also have more clarity about what you are doing and why – those bigger questions that underpin our professional lives but are often repressed or neglected because we don't make the space to think about them. All this accelerates your self-development as a leader. (In Chapter 12 I outline a practice I call 'Your No.1 meetings', which shows how you can do all this systematically.)

Counterintuitively, taking time to reflect increases productivity. By pausing to reflect you actually get more done, not less. The authors of a Harvard Business School study conducted in 2014 define self-reflection as 'the intentional attempt to synthesize, abstract, and articulate the key lessons taught by experience.' The research found that when people added fifteen minutes of reflection into the end of their work day, as opposed to working an extra fifteen minutes, their productivity increased by nearly a quarter in just ten days; and when reassessed a month later, that spike in productivity had stuck. The authors argue that, 'Once an individual has accumulated a certain amount of experience with a task, the benefit of accumulating additional experience is inferior to the benefit of deliberately articulating and codifying [or in other words, reflecting on] the experience accumulated in the past.'

Other research backs this up. One study of UK commuters found that those who were prompted to use their commute to think about and plan for their day were happier, more productive and less burned out than people who didn't.

Reflecting matters perhaps more than ever in the VUCA (volatile, uncertain, complex and ambiguous) environments, which have become the norm in the last few decades. Yet it's all too easy to lose touch with the ability to do what the behavioural economist and Nobel Prize Winner Daniel Kahneman describes as 'slow thinking'. This involves reflectively examining underlying thoughts and beliefs, challenging assumptions and identifying connections between seemingly disparate pieces of information. This is in contrast with lazier, more automatic and shallower 'fast thinking'. If you've ever spent a morning churning through one email after another in your inbox and then trying to turn your attention to a task which requires you to focus more deeply, you'll understand the difference between slow and fast thinking. Even the most senior of leaders are at risk of becoming over-reliant on fast thinking, unless they deliberately carve out white space in their day, and they may even find that their ability to think reflectively and strategically begins to atrophy. Without a pause for reflection you run the very real risk of constantly working from a place of reactivity instead of creativity.

To make matters worse, even when we see its value and strain to practise it, self-reflection is often the first thing to drop off our agenda when things get busy or stressful. Collectively, we are addicted to the illusion that the busier we are, the better. We mistake activity for productivity, failing to acknowledge that productivity actually requires reflection, as those Harvard researchers found. Since so many of us work in the knowledge economy, the most valuable asset we have is our attention, and – like a battery on a smartphone – it gets depleted fairly quickly. The onslaught of demands and information that comes our way every day via emails and social media alone are actually reason enough to turn off the noise and give oneself enough space to be able to hear oneself think.

Collectively, however, we have a long way to go if we are to see a tangible change in the culture of the modern workplace: A 2015 Harvard study found that CEOs typically have less than 15 per cent of their working week available for solo work. Moreover, most of these few precious hours are consumed by reviewing information and dealing with urgent issues, rather than in taking 'quiet time' to do the reflective work that is so critical. Further down a company, the demands on people are often no less intense.

Consciously cultivating a reflection-ready mindset and attitude requires commitment and application. If you attempt to plough your way through self-reflection, as Raku initially did in her coaching session with me ('Why do I rush? It's a busy world, right?'), you won't reap its many rewards. Being reflective, by its very nature, has a different cadence and rhythm to it than most of our working day, which is exactly why it enables us to see things differently and to think new thoughts. Eventually you might even begin to enjoy – perhaps even relish – this opportunity to slow down. Most people I work with do, even those who are most 'busy'.

Finally, be aware that we all have an inbuilt psychological barrier to self-reflection because it will sometimes make us feel bad. We will discover that we have been short-sighted, foolish or inconsiderate. We need the self-confidence and resilience to embrace this rather than live in a fugue of comforting self-delusion. Urging deep, profound self-reflection is a little like asking Superman to take off his cape and confront the frailties that lie beneath. It takes a true superhero to do that.

For that reason, and because of the relentless demands the modern world makes on our time, self-reflection isn't always easy. But the more you do it, the more you'll see the truth of that feedback from one of Raku's colleagues: 'It's like we're getting all of Raku now, whereas before we were just skimming the surface.' Without creating the space for regular, rich self-reflection you are operating as a shallower version of yourself. By creating that space you give yourself – and offer the world – a richer and deeper you.

The Reflecting Cycle, square breathing and other practical tools to help you create the space to reflect

So how do you build reflective practice into your life? About the past (what has happened); the present (what you are trying to make happen now); and the future (what you want to happen next).

The simple model of reflective practice – the 'Reflecting Cycle' – that I use with clients looks like this:

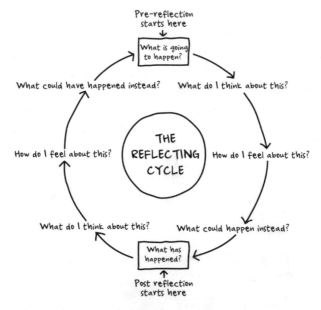

The Reflecting Cycle

The idea is that you constantly recycle your experiences – before and after they happen – asking yourself three key questions:

1. What do I *think* about this?
2. How do I *feel* about this?
3. What could happen/have happened *instead*?

This draws on Kolb's learning cycle, which inspired the second test that I asked Raku to take:

1. I had an experience
2. I reflected on it to evaluate what went well or badly
3. I considered some ideas and options for change
4. I planned a different action

What might this look like in practice? You could use your reflecting time to mull over any projects or concerns that have been nagging at you. If you have encountered any challenges in communicating with your colleagues, clients or stakeholders, explore the possible assumptions, biases or expectations that might have played a part in you misreading or misunderstanding the situation. You could do a 'post-mortem' on a project, analysing what went well, observing your own reasoning processes, articulating lessons learnt and identifying problem areas and errors in judgement or flaws in the decision-making process. You can also do this in advance of an upcoming project, in which you aim to identify all the possible pitfalls and failures, and put the relevant contingency plans in place.

ASK YOURSELF: *Do I understand what reflective practice is? Do I know how to follow this or some other model? Have I committed to being more reflective?*

To develop and really embed your reflective practice, there are four aspects that require attention:

1. **The temporal space** – How do you make time to reflect?
2. **The physical space** – Where should you reflect?

Keeping a Reflections Journal

Research shows that when we write down our thoughts and feelings it underlines their meaning to us. Noting things down also gives us a record to look back on. The act of re-reading what you wrote yesterday, last week or even a year ago is, in and of itself, reflective practice. Your notebook becomes a treasure trove of ideas and insights that you can return to time after time. If you're new to journalling, or sceptical about it, I would suggest the practice of 'one thought journalling': writing just one thought that you have had every day. It's remarkable how powerful reading the accumulation of such jottings can be after only a few weeks. Eventually, you may start to write more. I offer every client an A5 moleskin journal that contains some key models and inspirational thoughts, and most take it and make use of it. Others opt for keeping notes on their phone or laptop – whatever works for you.

3. **The relational space** – Who can help you?

4. **The psychic space** – What internal resources do you need?

The temporal space – how do you make time to reflect?

This is the *sine qua non* of your reflective practice. You might really 'get it' and be good at it, but if you don't actually do it what's the point? Carving out time is essential for reflective thinking, particularly since it goes against the grain of our 'always on' culture. Before we look at how you might do this, we need to pause to look at a couple of prerequisites that will be required if you are to succeed.

I address wider issues of time management later. Here I just want to flag up the first prerequisite for making more time to reflect, which is that you are using the time you already have as efficiently as possible. In summary: are you focusing and prioritising enough? Are you delegating wherever you can? Are you accepting 'good enough' solutions when 'good enough' will do? Are you making full use of the time you do have (e.g. the early morning or your commute)? Or do you habitually waste time, the classic examples being spending too much time on Facebook, or surfing the web looking at funny but ultimately inconsequential videos.

The second prerequisite involves a shift in mindset: changing from a mindset that either neglects reflection altogether, or de-prioritises it due to 'not having enough time', to a mindset that puts it front and centre of your priorities during your day-to-day working life. Embracing this mindset – that reflection isn't a 'nice to have' but a 'need to have' – will be the psychological foundation of your efforts to carve out more space for it.

When working with clients I find that reflection is required on three overlapping levels:

1. The day-to-day or tactical (what should I say to Jane this afternoon about that issue that came up on the call?).
2. The big, strategic questions (am I even in the right career?).
3. The level in-between (who should we partner with to get this project done?).

This in turn informs the issue of having time to reflect. Often, people will assume that reflection requires large chunks of time to be set aside, but that is only half the story. As well as setting aside specific blocks of time to reflect, it is also important to incorporate reflecting into your daily *modus operandi*.

That is why I talk to clients about two types of reflecting: deep reflection and 'on the job' reflecting. The former requires setting aside blocks of protected diary time where the focus is on key fundamental questions. But, and this is a crucial point about reflective practice, it isn't only about the 'big things', neither does it necessarily have to take a long time, or need to be a discrete process quite separate from the hurly-burly of the everyday. There are degrees of reflective practice.

Certainly, when you are reflecting on the bigger stuff you need to make sure you won't be disturbed. Deeper reflection requires going under the usual surface patterns of thinking to draw on the more peripheral aspects of our intellect and emotions. Without uninterrupted time you simply won't get there. You also need time to stick at it. Even when you think you're not getting anywhere, keep going – don't pick up your phone or rush back to your inbox. Keep going because the light-bulb moment may just be another few moments of frustration away.

We usually organise our calendars to respond to the demands of others and the day-to-day pressures of work, and that way time for reflecting is squeezed out. This needs to be flipped around. For periods of deep reflection you need to build chunks of reflection time into your calendar and protect them as you would a crucial sit-down with your boss or a big client meeting. Obviously, in practice you may sometimes have to sacrifice this time, but at least start off with a commitment to the importance of time for you to think.

Sometimes clients tell me this is impossible, especially if they have calendars that are visible to everyone. I urge them to be bold and push back. Explain the blocks of time. You would be amazed what can be achieved by explaining what you need, and being tough about it. One client said his boss would never allow it, but when I persuaded him to try he came back to the next session and said, 'You know, I put those big green slots into my diary marked "thinking time" with a slightly sick feeling, and sure enough my boss emailed saying "what the hell is all that for?" I explained that this was how I wanted to work, and that it would lead to better decisions and more efficiency, and she replied, "OK, cool". I was gobsmacked.'

Such discipline is often a feature of the working routines of the world's top businesspeople. Jeff Weiner, CEO at LinkedIn, blocks between ninety minutes and two hours each day for reflection and describes these buffers as 'the single most important productivity tool' he uses. Yana Kakar, Global Managing Partner of Dalberg, reserves three, two-hour blocks of time for reflection each week. She makes a great point: 'Thinking is the one thing you can't outsource as a leader. Holding this time sacred in my schedule despite the deluge of calls, meetings, and emails is essential.' Others concentrate reflection in a single day. Brian Scudamore, the serial entrepreneur at O2E Brands, sets aside all of Monday for thinking and organising the rest of the week, which is filled with back-to-back meetings. He also creates a suitable environment for deep thinking by not going into the office that day. At AOL, Tim Armstrong has instructed executives to spend half a day of each working week on reflective thinking. However you decide to do it – by having a change of scene and/or blocking out time in your diary – actively creating space to reflect will reap dividends, as these business leaders testify.

While I was writing this, I was working with the newly appointed global HRD of a big tech company who was nominally responsible for tens of thousands of employees and was feeling swamped by the multiple demands on her time. 'I don't have time to stop and think,' she complained. After listening to her moan for a bit, I asked if we could go through that day's diary. By being very tough we managed to claw back two hours. Half of that time consisted of things that, on reflection, she realised could be delegated to someone in her team, or left for them to do alone instead of her feeling she had to ride shotgun. The other hour was the result of cancelling two 'get to know you' meetings. She really resisted this, feeling that she would hurt the people's feelings if she cancelled, and get the relationships off on a bad foot. In the end she sent both an email telling the truth: 'I feel swamped and need to create some space to think, so although I'm looking forward to meeting I'd like to do it in a few weeks rather than now. I feel rude doing this but hope it's OK.' She got two lovely, empathic emails in return, one even said, 'Good for you – I need time for that too and now I have an extra half an hour today to pause for a moment.' All too often we end up doing what we think we *should* do rather than what we have decided we *need* to do.

As I said earlier, as well as trying to carve out space for deep reflection you should also create space for 'in the moment' reflecting. If we are faced with a problem to solve or a decision to make, we will often feel rushed into a solution because we don't feel we have time. But rather than bang off an email with your instant response, try and find a short breathing space to reflect. I know of one executive whose every important email goes into her draft box before she then reads them again later and sends them off. She says the number of times she ends up changing what she wrote, or at least fundamentally finessing it really surprises her. After all, she says, I haven't really done any thinking in between. But of course she has – just unconsciously.

The idea of constant 'in the moment' reflecting was really brought home to me by a leader I worked with a couple of years ago. This often happens. While I spend my time trying to help others develop, they invariably end up developing me. I'm lucky to spend time with some very accomplished business leaders and receive an endless stream of such lessons. I always note these down afterwards and offer them as suggestions of possible best practice to others I work with. In this case, I was helping this guy with the restructuring of part of his business. After we had left a particularly difficult meeting, we strode to the lift in silence, then as we stepped in, and the doors closed, I tried to start a conversation. He smiled and held up his hand, signalling for me to be silent. He then spent our descent breathing deeply with his eyes nearly closed. When we reached the ground floor he turned to me and said, 'Sorry, I was just wondering if I could have handled that better. I do think we could have offered something and I'll need to send a quick email when we get into the car.'

I think someone else would have reached for their smartphone straightaway in order to move on from the downbeat mood of the meeting, or allowed themselves to get over-emotional and expressed some annoyance – what one psychoanalytic writer labels 'chuntering', filling up space with unproductive grumbling about something. Not this guy. He spent what could only have amounted to a minute or so checking in with his thoughts and feelings but in a focused, productive way. As I got to know him, I saw him do this dozens of times a day. Even sitting next to him in the back of a car, I'd see him end a phone call and stare into space, lips silently moving as he reviewed the conversation, reaching a conclusion about whether he could move on or should revisit some aspect of it. If the latter, he would scribble something down in the little notepad he always had ready in his inside jacket pocket. This way he didn't need to set aside a big chunk of time at the end of the day or week to review what had happened, it was a practice that he wove into his working day from dawn till dusk. He had grown accustomed to asking himself:

1. What sense do I make of what just happened?

2. What sense can I make of what will happen next?

So should you.

ASK YOURSELF: *Have I consciously thought about what time I have for reflecting, on the big stuff and the more day-to-day? If I need to create more time to reflect how am I going to do that?*

The physical space – where should you reflect?

There's an old saying where I was born in the North West of England – 'there's nowt so queer as folk.' It's a truism that can be lost in the coaching and development world. An American aphorism captures the same idea, 'Dif'rent strokes for dif'rent folks.' And the question of where you should reflect has as many answers as there are people who want to do the reflecting. The issue isn't obeying some writ handed down, it's discovering for yourself the environment that is most conducive to the deep, contemplative thinking that reflection requires.

I've had clients whose dedicated 'thinking space' is the closing moments before sleep, their morning shower, exercise routine, or their commute into work. I have worked with someone whose best environment for thinking is on long arduous bike rides, while another cycling fanatic said that his mind totally clears and he thinks of nothing as he speeds along (though maybe his unconscious is at work, who knows?). Several clients have told me they love to think while taking walks. This doesn't have to involve backpacks and mountains, it could mean a few leisurely laps around the block. I worked with one founder of a tech start-up who drew quizzical looks from new employees when he regularly left the office to stroll round the nearby park, until they interacted with him and realised that he would invariably return energised and full of fresh ideas.

Some people are great compartmentalisers. They can walk from a loud open-plan space into a conference room, take one breath and find themselves at peace and worlds away from the hurly-burly just a door away. Others take hours to decompress from what faces them on the computer at their desk. Some find the occasional day working at home is a great chance to step back and take stock, for others it's the last place they feel they can have profound thoughts about work. A 2013 Gensler WPS survey found that 16 per cent of employees believed they could focus most effectively at home against 73 per cent who said they preferred an office setting. Yet all too often working practices diktats are issued that apply to everyone, rather than allowing people to choose what they feel is best for them.

I coached one CEO from Italy whose company, just before she took it over, had decided 'democratically' to get rid of all individual offices in their Milan HQ and operate on one big open-plan floor. As an introvert she found such an environment uncomfortable, draining and actually psychologically hostile. She shared the story of a friend, a fellow CEO (of an Italian bank), who worked in similar conditions and had taken to sitting in a toilet stall for half an hour every day to get some alone time. This is utterly ridiculous. I reminded my client that she was, after all, the CEO, and she had the right to the working conditions she needed. Having explained her feelings to everyone in an all-company email, she brought in the carpenters the next day.

If you don't have that level of power, there are still things you can do. Think imaginatively about how you can create a space for thinking in such an environment. There are countless creative ways to communicate this to your colleagues. Elena Kerrigan, the Managing Director of productivity training company *Think Productive*, puts a china cat out on her desk to signal to colleagues that she is in a time of deep focus and does not want to be interrupted. Not that such tactics always work. In one firm I worked at I would put on some very large headphones when I didn't want to be interrupted. One old school colleague persisted in walking over to my desk and actually knocking on the headphones with his knuckles whenever he wanted my attention. Bless you Charles.

As well as thinking about physical space, you might want to consider other ambient issues. If you know that you can't think straight in complete silence, consider using an app that plays white noise or playing some music that aids self-reflection. Services like Spotify offer great playlists designed to support focus and concentration. As I write this I am listening – as I always do when writing – to a Spotify playlist called Baroque Study Music, created by someone called Bobby Kennedy. Cheers Bobby – I should probably have put you in the acknowledgments.

ASK YOURSELF: *What physical space is best suited to helping me reflect deeply? How can I spend more time in that space?*

The relational space – who can help you?

When working with clients, I try to help them work out the type of thinker they are. A question I often ask is 'if you have a problem to solve, how would you go about it?' I might then prompt them with some examples: Would you find a quiet room and shut yourself away with a notepad or a laptop? Would you crave a whiteboard and lots of coloured pens so you could sketch out ideas and images, a sort of 'mind-mapping'? Or would you want to call together a few colleagues and brainstorm together?

I am a more introverted thinker, but I recognise that others are different. The secret to collaborating is not to be judgemental. Picasso once remarked that 'without great solitude no serious work can be done.' This was true for him (and for me) but not, of course, for everyone.

I like to do my initial thinking on my own and then present my ideas to a few key people to get their feedback. I remember a colleague who was the polar opposite. She liked me to sit down next to her with the proverbial blank sheet of paper – or in this case screen – and start an open-ended, winding and (what seemed to me) unfocused discussion. I could literally feel my brain freeze and my capacity to think shutdown. When we discussed this she said that was exactly how she feels if she sits alone staring at blankness. I wanted to reflect *internally*, she had the need to reflect *externally*. There is no right or wrong way, what matters is that you are aware of your own style – and the needs of others – and are able to find a way of working that works for everyone, even if that requires a bit of give and take.

Incidentally, such insights are invaluable when building high per-forming teams. I have seen really harmful discord in teams caused by a lack of understanding of different team members' individual thinking styles. One team I worked with had built up a story about one member being aloof and withdrawn, but actually the issue was just her reflecting style. Once we identified what was going on, and the team recognised her need for some private thinking space before contributing in a group, they changed their ways of working (for example, distributing drafts and ideas in advance) and the person in question's contribution soared as a result.

Another team I worked with typified a different dynamic. In this case, a majority of members tended to pre-prepare everything and wanted short, sharp discussions that cut to the chase. The minority, who liked to reflect aloud, were seen as distractors and time wasters. Once their 'reflective styles' were out in the open they were more understood, and the team added on just ten minutes to the main agenda item so that a slightly more abstract unfocused discussion could take place. While this sometimes left the more introverted contributors being frustrated, they also admitted, when we reviewed things together a few months later, that certain useful ideas and insights had been expressed that wouldn't have been under their old way of working.

Some organisations actively try to create a relational, reflective culture. Ways of doing this include building in collective points of reflective inquiry. For example, asking a 'big question' of the whole company once a month, or encouraging an open, honest commu-nity blog.

Even if you are an introverted thinker, it may pay to involve others in your thinking. At NextJump each employee is assigned a 'talking partner' with whom to check in on a daily basis, venting any frustrations, exploring their weaknesses and devising the best way forward. Talking Partnerships are two-way coaching relationships where each partner helps the other to get to know their blind spots. Interestingly, the idea tends to grow on those to whom it didn't initially appeal.

Finding a balance between the two extremes is important. If you tend towards a more introspective style of thinking make sure you have a way of somehow getting the input of others, if you are more extravert make sure that you haven't just reacted to the input of others and have brought your own deeper thoughts to bear too.

ASK YOURSELF: *What's my way of maximising my own self-reflection while also getting the input of others to my reflective practice?*

The psychic space – what internal resources do you need?

Reflecting requires us to get into the right headspace, ideally entering a different level of awareness or consciousness. A simple, sure-fire method to do this involves taking a moment to centre yourself before you start reflecting. Inspired by Yoga techniques thousand of years old, US Navy SEALs use the technique of 'square breathing' or '4×4 breathing' to reduce anxiety on the battlefield. Hillary Clinton used it when Donald Trump goaded her during the 2016 US Presidential debates. But it is also useful in less dramatic situations, calming you down and allowing your mind and body to pause and re-centre.

1. Sit comfortably and take a deep inhalation through your nose, filling your lungs and expanding your stomach for around four seconds, 1, 2, 3, 4.

2. Hold that breath for the same time, 1, 2, 3, 4.

3. Then slowly exhale through your mouth, contracting your stomach until all the breath is exhaled, 1, 2, 3, 4.

4. Hold that empty breath for another four seconds, 1, 2, 3, 4.

Repeat the exercise a few times, until you feel your mind clear and your body relax.

Go on, stop reading and try it now. Feels good doesn't it?

As you can see a practice such as this doesn't require a huge amount of time, or a special environment. It is available to you every minute of every day, wherever you are in the world.

★

It's important when we are reflecting that we are not only drawing on the conscious but also the unconscious – the vast netherworld where connections and inspirations lie hidden. It is the workings of this unconscious that leaps into view when we feel we have our 'Eureka' moment of intuition.

There is a (possibly apocryphal) story about legendary adman Charles Saatchi. He was at lunch growing increasingly bored and restless as a prospective client laid out his problem – going in to some detail about his business, its marketing issues and the competitive challenges it faced. Finally, Saatchi interrupted him mid-flow and, as he called for the bill, scribbled out a slogan on the napkin. The putative client stared at it dumbfounded, eventually mumbling, 'But ... yes ... that's perfect, exactly what we need, you've cracked it!' 'Yes,' replied Saatchi, 'and that'll be £50,000 a month starting today.' 'But it only took you about ten minutes,' blustered the client. 'On the contrary,' retorted Saatchi, 'it took thirty years. Of reading, talking, learning and thinking.'

Saatchi knew that in order to excel at reflecting you need to feed your mind. This aspect of 'reflecting' takes us neatly on to the need to create space for learning that we'll be looking at in the next chapter. If your brain is just stuffed with quotidian low-level stuff, you will only ever have that to draw on. Make space to read beyond your day-to-day work, and/or attend events and conferences. This is less about 'keeping up to speed', though that is useful, and more about broadening out and opening up your mind to new ideas and influences. This intellectual nourishment shouldn't just draw on business material – history, novels even poetry can all become threads that our unconscious weaves together and that one day may present us

with an 'obvious' answer. As one rather forbidding boss put it to me
once: 'What you're saying is the next time I catch a junior Associate
with his feet up on the desk reading the *Economist* I should say "well
done" rather than give him a bollocking'.

He looked sceptical, but – within reason – exactly.

ASK YOURSELF: *What do I do to feed my mind? How can I do more?*
Can I commit to doing ONE thing now that would enrich my knowledge
and experience?

CHAPTER 2

Space to Learn

Rachel and Her Need to Go It Alone

LESSON: *In today's fast-changing world you must operate with genuine humility and create the space to be curious and open to learning*

RACHEL IS A HIGH-FLYER in a global snacks business. She joined her company as a graduate trainee and excelled at the various internal placements that were part of that programme. After two years she had been asked to choose a specialism and had found that hard. Eventually, after dithering between finance, marketing and Human Resources she'd chosen the latter. Over the next decade she had enjoyed HR and was a particularly commercially minded HR Business Partner, but that hadn't proved to be satisfying enough for her. For the last few years, like Raku, she had yearned to move more into general management.

The company had seen her potential and hadn't wanted to lose her to a rival, so she had been given a chance to prove herself in a commercial trouble-shooting role, reporting jointly to the HR Director and Finance Director. During this time she had shown herself to have sound commercial judgement and an ability to work at pace and deliver results. She had therefore just been handed one of the most sought after roles in the business – running the company's account with one of the UK's major supermarkets. It was a key role, as so much business was done through that route to market. There had been heated debate about whether the appointment was wise given her lack of experience, but in the end she had been given her big chance.

Sadly, about four months into the job, it seemed that the gamble hadn't paid off. For the first time in her glittering career Rachel was failing. Such is the importance of the retailer to the business that even the CEO got involved in the debates over Rachel and whether the company should pull the plug on what was always an audacious, even risky, appointment. The business ran on a strict quarterly rhythm and she had about six weeks to show she had rescued the situation. I had been called in to see if, with extra support, Rachel could somehow save the day.

She turned up for our first session ten minutes late. It isn't always the case that such behaviour is a sign of something deeper (as Freud put it 'sometimes a cigar is just a cigar'), but often it is. She wore classic business attire and clearly took a lot of care with her appearance. Her lateness, coupled with her distracted air, made me wonder what she felt about the coaching, so I asked her.

'It's fine,' she replied. 'Good, helpful.'

Sometimes as a coach you have to back your gut and be bold. I went with what all my instincts were telling me.

'I don't believe you.'

For the first time she seemed properly to pay attention, but stayed silent. I waited.

'Don't believe what?' she asked.

'That you really want to be here.'

She grimaced but, again, kept quiet.

I went on, 'or at least part of you doesn't.'

'That's right actually, part of me doesn't.'

'How come?'

'Well, I know I need help but this is the kiss of death isn't it?'

'The kiss of death?'

'Yes, the final sign that Rachel has failed and is on her way out.'

'News to me,' I said. 'I'm here because Mark and Charlotte (the

HRD and FD) want to support you and make you the success they know you can be.'

'The success I used to be you mean,' she said quietly and I could see how upset she was underneath her mask.

'What's happening is really, really hard for you.'

She looked at me directly for the first time.

I continued, 'Upsetting on a very deep level.'

She had a fleeting look of what I took to be confusion, an expression that I guessed sprang from surprise that somebody seemed to understand what she was feeling, and was saying it out loud. Eventually she said simply,

'It is, yes.'

This exchange led to her opening up a bit and she talked about her fear that she had really messed up her career. Already there was a tenor to her remarks that made me wonder whether she was indulging in catastrophic thinking. This is a relatively common cognitive distortion, a psychological term for an exaggerated or irrational thought pattern. These are often the ramifications of the person's Core Pathogenic Beliefs that make it to the surface. In her case Rachel seemed to feel that a negative event – however insignificant – would lead to absolute disaster.

We then talked about her fear that the coaching was a sign that she had already failed, rather than a genuine attempt to help her not fail. Despite my reassurances, she seemed highly sceptical. I suddenly had an idea, one that would take a bit of manoeuvring to make happen. While I mentally filed it away, Rachel began to tell me the background to the situation she was in. There is always a balance between knowing enough about a client's situation to understand what is going on and trying to understand it too much. Usually people's issues aren't to do with the technical details of their job but rather what are called 'softer skills' – the way they think about things in a general sense, or relate to people. This is just as well, or in any given month I might have to be an expert in retailing, digital advertising, private equity and oil trading!

As the session came to an end, I thought that she seemed more relaxed and had accepted the coaching as a positive. As she left the room I said,

'See you next time.'

She replied, just as the door closed, 'Yes, if I'm still here.'

I decided that she clearly needed a bit more convincing that the coaching was not a portent of doom, and I went to work on the idea that had occurred to me earlier.

Consequently I found myself a week later standing at reception in the company's soaring glass atrium, its award-winning advertising silently displayed on large screens all around me. I waved over to one of my colleagues, hoping that we'd pull off our carefully planned choreography.

Luckily things went like clockwork. Just as Rachel stepped out of one elevator Jorge, the company's charismatic CEO, stepped out of the other. I could see Rachel clock this and hesitate. As the big boss strode through the parting throng, she followed in his wake. He greeted my colleague and then turned, feigning surprise at Rachel's appearance behind him.

'Ah! It's Rachel isn't it, how are you? Let me introduce you to Kylie, my coach.'

She blushed and looked at me. He waited.

'Umm ... this is Derek, he's uh ... my coach.'

'Good for you!' he exclaimed, 'I have always had a coach, some say it is the secret of my success.'

I swear he gave her an almost imperceptible wink.

We all shook hands and went our separate ways. When we sat down in our room she looked at me with a grin.

'You set that up didn't you?'

'Busted,' I replied.

'OK, I get the message,' she laughed. 'To be honest it's less Jorge having coaching, though that was a surprise, and more the fact that he would spend time sneaking around playing games to make the point – that means that they must want this to work, I guess.'

From then on she seemed more able to embrace coaching as the support it was rather than the stigma she feared. As we settled into the session I asked her to share her life story.

'Really?'

'Yes, it would help me really understand you.'

'OK, but it's no fairytale, let me tell you,' she replied, her face hardening.

She had grown up in a single-parent family and her mum had been pretty directionless, never sticking at jobs and eventually ending up long-term unemployed. She'd clearly been depressed but never received treatment. With tears in her eyes and a great sense of shame, Rachel admitted that when she was at university her mum had spent some time homeless and sleeping rough.

Sometimes we have thoughts that seem to come from deep within us. We feel we know something in our bones. When that happens in a session, I believe that such insights don't really come from me at all, but from some connection between me and the coachee – part of what psychoanalyst Carl Jung called the 'collective unconscious', or what I refer to as 'the third space' (see p. 205). When this happens I have learnt not to repress the thought but save it up to ponder on later or – if it seems really powerful and pressing – to offer it up there and then, taking the risk that it may not be appreciated and even be completely rejected. It's extraordinary how often it is actually accepted as a deep if unwelcome truth.

I had such an instinct about what Rachel was saying.

'You feel that if you don't keep pushing, keep succeeding, that you'll end up like your mum?' I ventured.

She looked straight at me, with a startled expression.

'That's my dream, I literally dream it and then wake up and lie there picturing it. Me, homeless, without Neil [her fiancé], without our flat, in the park, on my own, in rags.'

We had stumbled on Rachel's core pathogenic belief. It was directly linked to the catastrophic thinking I'd spotted earlier. This is how she articulated it for herself later in the session:

If I don't keep excelling all the time or make any kind of mistake

*it will start a slippery slope that will end with me losing literally
everything.*

That's quite an exacting and terrifying standard to hold yourself to. But while fear of failure is quite common, what Rachel
was experiencing was extreme and it highlights an important point
about pathogenic beliefs. Most people have them and – to a limited
degree – that's fine. A little self-doubt or performance anxiety can be
a motivating force. But taken too far such feelings become distinctly
unhealthy. There is a world of psychic difference between wondering
if your work on a project will mean that you will get your hoped for
promotion and believing that even the smallest dip in performance
will mean you end up destitute.

As we discussed the extent of Rachel's own fears she began to
make a flurry of connections between her professional and personal
life. She had always felt a low-level anxiety, even when things were
going well, which had skyrocketed in the last few months. She admitted she had been to her GP and was taking anti-anxiety medication.
She hadn't even told Neil about this. As she confessed this she gave
a sardonic laugh.

'Oh my God,' she said, 'it's Neil's nickname for me – "worry
wart", that's what he calls me!'

I let the thought sink in.

'Wouldn't it be nice if some of that worry went away,' I asked.

'God, yes. Yes please.'

We spent our next session unearthing the more realistic, healthy
belief that could guide her going forward. The mantra she eventually came up with was:

*It's OK to fail, it won't be the end of the world, I will survive
and do OK.*

Pretty simple and obvious to most of us but a revelation to her,
who had been semi-consciously behaving as if the opposite was true.

However, as in many coaching assignments, there was more than
one factor at work, what Freud called over-determination. The other

surfaced from the feedback calls I did with the people she worked with. Whenever I can, I do these after the first or second session, asking the client to nominate around half a dozen people who know them at work. I will then phone each one, spending half an hour or so, in confidence, asking about the client's strengths and weaknesses as they see them. I then synthesise these into a few themes and share these with my client. The list of those approached should be a diverse one: the client's boss and a couple of other senior stakeholders, some peers, some direct reports. I always push to have so-called junior people included in the list, and it was Rachel's PA and the youngest commercial guy in her team who shed most light on what was going wrong. During our chat they both used exactly the same expression: 'She won't admit what she doesn't know.'

Again, her childhood story held the key. With her mum proving so erratic and unable to cope, Rachel had taken on the role of looking after her younger brothers and sisters. In the psychological jargon she had been 'parentified'. This can have positive consequences – such children are often high achievers, able to take on responsibility and deliver, but the phenomenon also has a less healthy shadow side.

In Rachel's case she had been terribly worried, anxious and frightened, but hadn't been able to show it – to her mum, her siblings, or even herself. So she had developed a way of reassuring herself that she could cope. She knew everything. She didn't need help. As we discussed this together, it emerged how this underlying need to project absolute confidence and competence was negatively affecting her. We were able to see that her second core pathogenic belief was:

If you ask for help, the whole world will come crashing down, and you won't get the help anyway.

We spent a while talking about vulnerability, something she'd never felt able to show growing up, and together we watched the TED talk on 'The Power of Vulnerability' in which Brené Brown, a research professor at the University of Houston, describes how we have to dare to be vulnerable in order to fulfil our in-built drive for connection. One of the key findings from Brown's extensive research is that people with a strong sense of love and belonging also have a strong sense of their own worthiness, and are courageous and embrace vulnerability in spite of any feelings of shame or fears of being seen. The result is what Brown calls a 'wholehearted' life, full of gratitude, connection, compassion and meaning.

I became convinced that allowing herself to show vulnerability, and then being open to getting help would be the key to Rachel's success. But that was a big ask. Her pronounced fear of failure and inability to seek help were the twin dynamics that were driving her towards the very failure she dreaded. Like a small plane plunging, helter-skelter, towards the ground, we had to yank the controls hard and get her up and out of her nose-dive.

The breakthrough came as we chatted one day. She had been opening up more and more, and as she talked about what she might do differently she suddenly said:

'You know, Derek, I don't really understand how it's supposed to work, not like I did when I was doing HR.'

She stared off into space, seemingly weighing up something in her mind. Her gaze shifted and she locked eyes with me.

'How about this for vulnerability?' she lowered her voice and whispered, 'I don't know what the fuck I am doing.'

She seemed surprised to hear herself saying this out loud but, of course, it was just the echo of what her PA and colleague had said a few weeks ago.

Sometimes, if I feel the need to say something – what, in psychoanalysis, is called an interpretation – I don't. Often the person will say it for me. I felt that the answer to Rachel's woes was on the tip of her tongue. That her brilliant mind was ready to knit all our insights together and arrive at the one thing she had to do. She didn't disappoint.

'Why don't I just bloody ask?' she said. She looked deep in thought for a moment and then caught my eye again and laughed.

'Why don't I just bloody ask?!' she repeated.

The answer to this deceptively simple question was that her twin binds of being petrified of failing – and being seen to fail – and her reluctance, even phobia, about asking for help, was why she hadn't. But our work had loosened these binds and, together, we had created the psychic space for her to think differently.

The next fortnight was a whirl of activity as she went round telling people that she'd gotten things wrong and needed their help. She asked the right questions, truly listened and synthesised everything into her own solutions. She paid particular attention to people on the 'coal face', mining them for information. This reminded me of something Carolyn McCall did regularly when she was CEO of easyJet. She would get out of her office and spend a day behind the check-in desks or assisting a flight crew, believing that if you aren't listening at that level, you'll never really know what's going on. The Japanese have a word for it – going to the *gemba* or 'real place'. In Rachel's case, by the end of the fortnight even people at the big retailer whose account she handled were enlisted as her 'teachers'. It might have been a risk to show vulnerability to people she had a tough commercial relationship with and had to better in negotiations, but she went ahead and did it anyway.

Once she'd freed herself from her core pathogenic beliefs Rachel found herself flourishing again. Her strengths – her intellect, creativity and ability to get on with people – asserted themselves once more. This is the pernicious thing about CPBs, they are 'the enemy within'. Like the foulest weeds in a garden, they slowly strangle all that is healthy and good until we can barely see what once was there and what might, with work, be seen again.

It actually took another six months until Rachel's big account was really back on track, and the company, to their credit, stuck with her on that journey. As she showed she was now approaching things with a wholly new mindset, it allowed them to relax their own fear of failure a bit too.

*

Opening your mind: Creating space to learn

'Live as if you were to die tomorrow. Learn as if you were to live forever.'

attributed to Mahatma Gandhi

Rachel's tremendous fear of failure and inner paralysis around asking for help greatly inhibited her in her new role. The heightened sense of responsibility she had carried with her from childhood into adulthood, while an asset in many ways, did not allow her any capacity to be vulnerable, to admit what she didn't know or ask for help. She developed a persona – a 'pseudo-self' – which she carried with her into adulthood in order to cope with the challenges of her childhood. Masked by this persona, she presented herself to the world as permanently capable and independent, but this came at a high price as it also shut out any opportunity for her to learn more about herself. We don't all need to have had a homeless mother to have this CPB. In 2015, a survey in the US found that one in three Americans were scared of failure, with millennials more likely than any other age group to have this fear. Another study found that people tend to deal with the idea of failure in four ways: success-oriented people see failure as an invitation to improve rather than a reflection of their worth; over-strivers are so afraid of failing that they go over and above what's needed to make sure they don't fail; failure-avoidant people tend to procrastinate, make excuses or avoid setting stretching goals; and finally, failure-accepting people have so internalised the expectation that they will fail, that they do not even bother to try. This final group is the hardest to motivate.

What we seem to have forgotten is that as children we failed *all the time*, and that these failures were an essential part of learning and developing. People with a growth mindset (see p. 64) challenge the idea that failure is final and something to be ashamed of, instead they see it as a learning experience rather than a reflection of who they are as people. Babe Ruth, the famous US baseball player, scored a record-breaking 714 home runs in his career, which shifted the paradigm of what was possible within the sport – but he also had 1,330 strikeouts, which at the time was unheard of. The simple truth is that winners fail a lot, but they don't just flinch and do their best to bear it until it passes, they deliberately set out to learn and grow from their failures.

Worryingly, research is emerging that shows that fear of failure is something of a gendered issue; studies have found, for example, that while men will apply for jobs they feel 60 per cent qualified for, women only tend to apply if they feel 100 per cent qualified. A vast global study of female entrepreneurship found that in every country studied women had lower perceptions of their entrepreneurial capabilities than men – an idea that is not borne out by any objective reality.

As for Rachel, on a subconscious level, she had decided that making any space to learn – to discover something new about herself, her role or the world – would mean admitting that she didn't have all the answers, and doing that felt too risky given her childhood associations with that form of vulnerability. She couldn't untangle the past from the present, and it was only through coaching that she was able to admit that there were some significant (but, crucially, not insurmountable) gaps in her knowledge. It took a fairly dire situation to force Rachel to admit what her colleagues could plainly see – that there were a number of things she needed to learn.

There is a clear overlap between 'learning' and the reflection we discussed in the last chapter. But there is also a fundamental difference. When reflecting, you are focused on something that is happening or has happened (hence the suggested questions in the Reflecting Cycle on p. 32). You then explore your thoughts, feelings and behaviour in reference to that particular event. Learning, on the other hand, isn't necessarily about developing your own thoughts about something that has happened or will happen, but is a more general endeavour. André Gide called it the willingness to lose sight of the shore in order to discover 'new oceans'; and Marcel Proust wrote that it is a voyage of discovery that is less about 'seeking new landscapes' and more about 'having new eyes'. Learning is about the new *and* the familiar. It involves acquiring knowledge and skills, but it also entails a shift in perception. It is about the world, but, as in Rachel's case, it is also inevitably about us. There is a constant interplay – a dance – between two foci: learning about ourselves and learning about the world.

Let's take a look at the latter first. Rachel's fear of failure and sense of over-responsibility – which in her case were born out of her core pathogenic beliefs, but which are also engendered in many corporate cultures – essentially paralysed her ability to think clearly about what she needed in her new role (to learn what to do, seek feedback and ask for help). While some executives contend that stress stimulates them into doing their best work, and while there may be some benefits to working under pressure or to a deadline, the truth is that too much anxiety puts the body into fight or flight mode, Over time this may well create adrenal fatigue and burnout, and also inhibit our ability to learn. Rachel's fears hooked her into a 'fixed mindset' and prevented her from adopting a 'growth mindset', concepts developed by Stanford professor of psychology, Carol Dweck. A growth mindset is characterised by a belief that one's most basic abilities are not fixed or innate but can be developed. A fixed mindset, on the other hand, presupposes that talent is innate and that you are either good at something or not, leaving little room for humility, curiosity, learning or growth.

In her new role, Rachel succumbed to what Dweck calls 'fixed-mindset triggers', which for most of us are fairly similar – challenges, criticism, or performing below par or less well than others. When faced with these we can all too easily feel we are being attacked, and so get defensive and retreat to a more 'fixed' mindset and lose our learning orientation. These triggers can also easily stir up our core pathogenic beliefs, and unless we make a concerted effort to challenge and overcome these, we will usually find that insecurity and defensiveness are not far behind. Whatever your defensive behaviours – whether you shrink and blend in, become controlling, go off the radar or turn to a vast array of other responses, one thing is certain: defences definitely inhibit our ability to grow and learn.

Falling into a fixed mindset is perhaps one of the most insidious threats facing many talented, high-potential leaders. Admitting that you don't know everything, or that you still have room to grow, often feels too uncomfortable and too risky, especially in a demanding and competitive environment. Ideas may be the currency of the twenty-first century, but it is difficult to come up with good ideas if you do not give yourself permission to come up with bad ones. Creating the space to learn involves being willing to embrace our fundamental fallibility.

The paradox of the fixed mindset is that for Rachel, as for all human beings, learning and discovery are innate. We each have 100 billion neurons in our brains – the brain's building blocks – and each neuron has between 1,000 to 10,000 connections to other neurons. These connections are known as neural pathways. Every day, more electrical impulses are generated in your brain than in all of the mobile phones in the world!

Some of the pathways are extremely well trodden, which is why we can perform tasks like brushing our teeth or driving without having to concentrate on the motor skills we employ. This principle applies to our emotional and cognitive responses as well; the way we feel, think and react to certain events becomes second nature to us not because that is inherently who we really are, but because it is how we habitually respond to life. This then creates well-worn paths of least resistance for the electrical impulses to travel along in our brains.

Scientists used to believe that the brain was 'hard-wired', incapable of changing, adapting or reorganising itself. It was believed that once we reached adulthood no new neurons were produced and that the brain had little ability to create new neural pathways. It has since been discovered that the brain retains the ability to literally grow throughout a lifetime, although this does decrease somewhat as we age. The brain is, in fact, 'soft-wired', a term coined by renowned neuroscientist Dr Michael Merzenich. This ability to adapt is called neuroplasticity.

The implications are quite profound – we might have much more ability to transform aspects of our personality than we realise. We are not stuck with the brains we were born with and we're not trapped in patterns of thinking or behaviour, however ingrained they might seem. In other words, you *can* teach an old brain new tricks.

Kimani Maruge's story provides an inspiring example. In 2004, the 84-year-old Maruge entered *The Guinness Book of Records* by becoming the oldest person in the world to start primary school. He had never been to school but when the Kenyan government introduced free primary education, Maruge seized the opportunity, enrolled, and learned to read from scratch.

It's harder, maybe, if we come at this from a position of success or status. After all, while often exciting and expansive, learning can also be frustrating, anxiety producing and downright uncomfortable, particularly when our professional reputation or 'credibility' is at stake.

Insecurity, close-mindedness, arrogance and plain old ego can all shut down our space for learning. The shore of certainty is one of the most insidious obstacles standing in the way of new discoveries. We have to become willing to be beginners again, to 'lose sight of the shore'. Thinking that you already know everything you need to know greatly inhibits your ability to greet a familiar scene with fresh eyes. As unsettling as it may feel (especially to executives in senior roles), there is something to be said for the Zen principle of beginner's mindset, popularised by Shunryu Suzuki: 'In the beginner's mind there are many possibilities, in the expert's mind there are few.'

*

As well as creating space in our minds to learn about the world we also need to create space to become more self-aware. We all have behaviours, habits, blind spots, personality traits or tendencies that others can see but which we can't or are only vaguely aware of. Despite much of the current business and leadership discourse about how we all ought to concentrate on playing to our strengths, the truth is that our blind spots derail us from being able to fully leverage those strengths. They have the potential to undermine our best efforts and, as Rachel found, to cause real damage.

With clients I use a model of potential called DEEP, which delves into twelve qualities under the headings of Decision-making, Execution, Emotions and Motivation, and People skills. By breaking down the different elements that combine to predict high potential, it allows people to explore where they are strongest and weakest, highlighting areas they need to develop. Creating the space to identify our development areas and derailers, and acknowledging these to ourselves and others, makes us stronger not weaker. As Bryan D. Ungard of the Decurion Corporation memorably puts it 'Feast on your imperfections or starve on your ego.'

Yet we all have internal blocks and barriers to change. We are all tempted to live in our comfort zone. We all make errors, work less than efficiently and are unavoidably human. Leaders have to get comfortable being in metaphorical 'beta' mode all the time, more focused on becoming than buying into the illusion of completion. To coin another metaphor, as someone once said, a painting is never really finished; it simply stops in interesting places.

Today's best leaders possess open minds and are humble, they recognise that we exist in networks, and that in an increasingly complex world and marketplace no single individual will ever have all the answers. Google's Senior Vice President of People Operations, Lazlo Bock overtly looks for humility when hiring. 'Without humility,' he states, 'you are unable to learn.'

With some help from me, and the support of her bosses, Rachel was able to create the psychic space to learn some key *internal* things about herself that opened her up to learning the new, *external* things that she needed to know to really succeed at her job. Every one of us would prosper from admitting, as she did in the end, how much we have still to learn – in both of these important realms.

Growth mindsets, learning styles and other practical ideas to help you create space to learn

Creating the space to learn has much in common with creating the space to reflect. As well as a curious mindset and the discipline to prioritise more abstract things over the concrete demands that you face every day, the four aspects of space we looked at in Chapter 1 are all relevant. Let's revisit that section for a moment and think about how each impacts on your desire and ability to learn.

The temporal space – how do you make time to learn?

As in the last chapter, think about how you can make time to regularly and systematically build learning into your working life. It is interesting that many professions now expect people to have Continuing Professional Development (CPD) and that this is sometimes an actual requirement. It is for therapists, for example, and is becoming so for certain types of consultants. Yet most people who work in businesses don't have such a formal requirement to renew and refresh their learning. In the absence of anyone telling you to do this, you should adopt the mentality anyway and carve out some time each month when you will be carrying out your own bespoke 'CPD', even if you don't get a certificate at the end.

The physical space – where should you learn?

Think about where you are most comfortable learning? In the office with your headphones on? At home with your feet up? In a coffee shop? I worked with one executive who was a member of the London Library, a beautiful old institution in London's St James's Square. Whenever he could, he used to block out whole afternoons to stroll down from his office in Victoria and sit among the thousands of dusty volumes, the dozens of students and writers (some of them rather dusty themselves), and focus on whatever subject he was trying to master. When I last saw him he was grappling with AI

(Artificial Intelligence) and the potential effects of it on his industry. If he felt he'd made good progress he'd treat himself to coffee and cake, but if he felt he'd been a bit aimless or distracted he would forgo this pleasure and head straight back to the office ready to try again next time.

The relational space – who can help you learn?

If you're an introverted learner you will be happy on your own, in a quiet place with a book or tablet on your lap. If you're an extraverted learner, consider setting up a study group, or forum where people can present ideas and join discussions. One Global HR Director I work with asks her entire HR community (some 500 or so people) to join an hour-long webinar every week. Each quarter they do a quick online survey to discover what people want to learn about and who might deliver some interesting content. Sometimes it's one of the HR people themselves, sometimes an outside expert one of them knows, sometimes they even ask academics or authors to present. Recent subjects have ranged from 'What's the latest best practice in performance reviews?' to 'What is blockchain?', and they invariably get over a hundred people joining each week.

One obvious way of getting others to help you learn about yourself is to ask for feedback, but I am always amazed at how this powerful tool is usually only used irregularly and informally. Turning to a colleague after a meeting, or even conversation, and asking 'How did you think I did there?' could – and should – be a weekly or even daily occurrence.

I once worked with a business leader who had been highly successful, reaching the top level at companies such as HSBC and British Airways. He was a super smart, engaging individual, but he drove people hard and could be pretty direct. 'Sharp elbows' was his euphemism for it. However, he sometimes underestimated the impact of his style on certain people who were less robust. When, as part of a big transformation project, I undertook some stakeholder feedback calls, people actually talked about being frightened of him at times. He was genuinely surprised – and chastened – by this, and it allowed

Holding up the mirror: feedback from the company

It is also valuable for a leadership team to get feedback from the whole company. This 'holding up the mirror', as my old boss Gurnek Bains used to call it, is one of the most effective tools in a leadership consultant's toolkit. Gurnek would gather a group of relatively junior high-potentials in a business and take them through a process to articulate their view of the senior management team's effectiveness, most of whom the high-potentials hadn't even met. This would be supplemented by a gathering of quantitative and qualitative data – using a series of interviews, focus groups, surveys, group psychometrics and even a textual analysis of the company's internal and external corporate communications.

The high-potentials would then create an exhibition – using pictures, models, even play-acting – that the CEO and his or her C-suite colleagues would then experience. It was a process that was always incredibly eye-opening. Invariably the organisation's leadership had a distorted view of how people 'at the coal face' perceived them and the values and culture they were trying to create. Such a confrontation, if undertaken in a safe and managed way, allows deep learning to take place between both groups. One CEO that Gurnek worked with said it was the most useful two hours he had ever spent. Such an activity requires bravery and vulnerability, two of the perennial foundations of learning.

In an ideal world people wouldn't need expensive consultants to tell them what other people thought of them, they would simply ask. Creating a culture whereby the people you work with can respond with honesty and clarity to your request for feedback is one of the most difficult but profound things a leader can do.

him to see himself as others saw him. He put a lot of effort into recalibrating his interventions so that while he still challenged and pushed people, he didn't intimidate them – at least not too much. What he did was brave. We often shy away from feedback because it might be something we don't want to hear. But it often reveals things that we need to know, and provides the greatest raw material we have for learning about ourselves. I have also, incidentally, found that the mere act of *asking* for feedback can change people's perceptions of a leader.

Once you've sought feedback, you may find that someone has told you something you feel is wrong or unjust. If that happens the first thing to do is check whether you are being defensive, maybe ask others what they think. But it could be that the person concerned is misreading you, or basing their feedback on a misconception. In a really open feedback culture you could discuss this with them – give feedback on their feedback. Then they could give you feedback on your feedback on their feedback. And so on endlessly. I jest – but not entirely.

The psychic space – what internal resources do you need?

Before starting out on your own path to more learning, it is worth checking in to see the extent you are operating out of a growth mindset? Here is the schematic I have developed over the years for talking to clients about this difference:

FIXED MINDSET	GROWTH MINDSET
You think you already know what you need to know	You are hungry to know more and actively pursue new knowledge
You are wary of making mistakes and 'looking bad' (this often masks underlying insecurity)	You relish mistakes and see failures as learning opportunities and have enough self-esteem to be OK with these
You avoid hard challenges	You seek out challenges – the harder the better
You tend to give up easily	You persevere through difficulties and failures
You take the quick, easy route when you can	You put in the hard slog and don't cut corners

FIXED MINDSET	GROWTH MINDSET
You are defensive when given negative feedback	You seek out, embrace and learn from criticism
You mainly rely on yourself and don't want to appear vulnerable	You show humility and aren't afraid to ask for help
You resent and feel threatened by the success of others	You are inspired by and learn from the success of others

The key to developing a growth mindset is to become aware of your inner dialogue – the chat that goes on in your head between you and ... well ... you. Noticing and challenging your thoughts can often be awkward and even uncomfortable in the beginning, like working out a new and unfamiliar set of muscles. Luckily it gets easier the more you do it. Here are some classic examples of the kind of thoughts or ways of perceiving yourself, your life and the world around you that you might want to challenge:

○ There's no point in trying anything new because I'll probably fail.

○ Why does this kind of thing always happen to me? It's not fair!

○ You can't win. Life is hard.

○ I'll never be able to do/achieve that.

○ That's just the way I am.

○ Failing is the end of the world.

Try identifying your own negative thoughts (and your journal is a great way to capture these as they happen, so you can reflect on them later) and then:

ASK YOURSELF: *What's the evidence for this thought? Is it really true? Is it the whole story? What more rational, balanced thought could I put in its place?*

NEXT ASK YOURSELF: *What is my mindset – fixed, growth or somewhere in between? Which areas in the above table do I need to work on? What can I do to adopt more of a growth mindset?*

Here's one last tip for redefining failure and reframing any skills you haven't yet mastered. Instead of seeing it as a fixed state of affairs, simply tell yourself 'this hasn't happened ... yet.'

What's your style?

The learning style debate is a hot one in psychology with various competing models and not a little controversy. Undoubtedly, the idea was overegged for a while and to some extent educationalists have now moved away from it. Nonetheless, there is no need to throw the baby out with the bathwater. There is little doubt in my mind that people do prefer to learn in different ways. That's not to say they can't learn in other ways, just that they would prefer to learn in certain ways – and are therefore more motivated to do so.

One of my business partners, Paul, hates it when I send him stuff to read. He much prefers talking things through (there is an echo here of the 'reflecting styles' I mentioned in the last chapter). My own simple version of the various styles is as follows:

Reader	Prefers to consume information in books, articles or via transcripts
Watcher	Prefers watching presentations, videos or looking at diagrams or flowcharts
Listener	Prefers to have ideas explained verbally and then discuss them
Sketcher	Prefers to sketch out ideas as they learn them, using images and shapes (the person who will most get infuriated if all the lids have been left off the whiteboard pens)
Doer	Prefers actually practising in real life situations rather than learning abstractly

Common sense tells us that most of us can learn by all these means and do so. The 70:20:10 model of learning says that most (70 per cent) of learning should be by doing (i.e. 'on the job'); 20 per cent from being exposed to others (e.g. learning communities, coaches, mentors etc., what psychologists call social learning); and just 10 per cent from formal learning (workshops, webinars, seminars and so on).

When I raise this issue with clients, they will have some idea of what their preference is, but it is usually ill-thought through and hazy. Amazingly, few people have accepted the consequences of their preference, and even less have acted upon it. So this is less about providing an insight that you were hitherto blind to, and more about helping you take something you know, deepen your insight around it, and then equip and support you to actually *do* something with the thing you already knew but weren't putting into practice. For example, if you're primarily a 'watcher', don't buy books that will simply pile up on your bedside table; instead spend time googling for TED talks, author presentations and the like. If you're a mainly a listener, start exploring the fascinating world of podcasts. There's one to accompany this book called 'Create Space', and our company does another one featuring interviews with top leaders called 'Leadership Lessons'. By mastering your learning style you use your time and energy in the most efficient way and so create the greatest space possible for your actual learning.

ASK YOURSELF: *What is my learning style preference? Have I sought out information that corresponds to the way I learn?*

One last point about learning styles: social media is a fantastic way of finding learning material that suits your style. You can use Twitter, Facebook and LinkedIn to follow, like, or join with different people, organisations and groups. You will then be served endless links to articles, videos, blogs etc. that should match the interests you have chosen to connect with. I then use an app called Pocket as a way of storing these for later consumption, with just one click on my browser or iPhone. It's like having your own personal library with you at all times. There are also some fantastic magazines and books out there. I personally devour at least one business book a month (as well as a novel or two), and get the FT delivered to my door early every morning.

One cautionary note, though: it is easy to get overwhelmed by all the information out there. Signing up to just a few good feeds will still result in more stuff than you can consume, even if you set aside time and are disciplined about it. But what's to get anxious about? You wouldn't even know this information existed if you hadn't gone and found it, so let it go. Better to spend ten minutes in the coffee shop reading five good articles and letting fifty pass you by than feel a failure for not reading more, and then probably avoid reading them altogether. To quote the Tesco slogan, 'every little helps' – but you don't have to empty the supermarket shelves.

ASK YOURSELF: *Am I actively trying to increase my knowledge? Where will such knowledge come from?*

Knowing your personal potential profile

As mentioned earlier, the DEEP model of potential can help to identify the qualities that you need to spend time developing. You can use the model to self-reflect or as a stimulus for a feedback or mentoring discussion. It's not just about, for example, *how* innovative you are, it's also about the detail and texture of this: in what ways are you innovative? What brings out your innovative side and what stifles it? How could you be even more innovative?

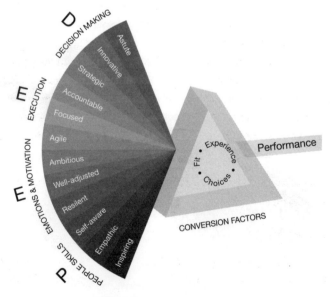

DEEP model of potential

In the diagram above, potential is indicated by how much of each of the attributes listed on the left-hand side you possess. These twelve factors look at who you are. They are 'converted' into performance through your Experience – what you've done; your Choices – what you want; and Fit – the interplay between you and your environment.

I use various measures to help determine an individual's personal potential profile but you can do a basic job yourself, looking at each of the factors and reflecting on how strong and weak you think you are in relation to it. Maybe ask a few colleagues what they think? Discuss your thoughts with your manager, or a mentor.

ASK YOURSELF: *How do I think I fare against each of the twelve attributes? Where am I strongest? Where am I weakest? What can I do to develop myself across the spectrum?*

In addition, setting goals and building in motivation are crucial. Set yourself a concrete goal, write it down, have a plan and set a timeline. What do you want to learn, how and by when? Don't be overly ambitious. Aim for 'one-degree shifts' rather than trying to make sweeping changes overnight. If you imagine a boat travelling 100 miles in a straight line across the ocean, and then altering its course by just one degree, the boat will eventually arrive at a completely different destination.

Build in motivation and reward, like my client who had sojourns in the library. For example: 'Once I feel I really understand all this talk of the "fourth industrial revolution" I will treat myself to that new bag/trip/slap-up dinner I've been wanting.' This is what psychologists call 'operant conditioning' and it can include punishments as well as rewards. As always, go with whatever works for you.

ASK YOURSELF: *Do I have a clear goal, how am I motivating myself to achieve this?*

Try a teacher

There is one last tip that you might consider if you want to create the space to learn more. Few people do it, even though it is blindingly obvious. If you want to learn, find a teacher. Whatever your learning style, being with someone who has the knowledge, skills and experience you want to acquire – and who is willing to spend time passing these on – is a fantastic resource.

Again, my experience shows that almost everyone knows this but hardly anyone acts on it. This is particularly hard to believe, as most people love to teach. Especially successful, accomplished people, who may be less driven by material rewards, and be highly motivated by the recognition and respect that comes with teaching and mentoring. Yet so few of us ask them to help us – what a wasted opportunity.

One of the most impressive executives I ever worked with was the Finance Director for a well-known retailer. He was a working-class guy who had surmounted a difficult early life by virtue of his intelligence, charm but above all, determination. When I asked him about his ambition he stated it simply: 'I want to be CFO of a FTSE 10 company.' It turned out that a couple of years earlier, he had done something that I had never heard of anyone doing before (though it is completely obvious, and, as we shall see, effective). He had emailed the CFOs of the FTSE 10 at the time, told them of his goal and asked for their help. Two didn't reply, five were supportive but essentially fobbed him off, and three offered to meet him. From those meetings he gained a couple of people he's still in contact with and a mentor who has devoted dozens of hours to teach, encourage and support him. Impressive though this client was, there wasn't anything that special about him. Apart from the fact that he knew what he wanted and asked for help in getting there. As he put it to me, 'I couldn't have bought what I've learned in the last year. I hesitate to say this as a finance guy but it was literally priceless.'

ASK YOURSELF: *Could I find myself a teacher? Who might that be? How can I approach them? Make best use of them? How can I 'pay it back' and teach someone else what I know?*

CHAPTER 3

Space to Decide

Hans and His Family of Tyrants

LESSON: *If you want to be a creative, visionary, strategic leader you have to create the space to be clear about what you think, make bold decisions, and communicate these with confidence.*

HANS IS THE FINANCE DIRECTOR for a key market in the Asia-Pacific region of a huge multinational. He has always had ambitions to become the global CFO, and even, one day, CEO. But his career has stalled, and from what he has picked up, he has been labelled as someone who doesn't quite have what it takes to reach the top. He has asked his HR Director if he can have some coaching to get to the bottom of this. Hence, here he was sitting across from me.

It was interesting to meet Hans and I was glad I'd insisted we met face to face, at least for our initial session. I always schedule these to last for three hours. That allows me to really hear the coachee's story and get a real sense of what they want to achieve. If they have flown in to see me, or if, as in this case, I'd flown halfway around the world to see them, I would follow this first, deep-dive session with a follow-up, goal-setting session the day after. That way, the bother and expense will at least result in a kick-start to the coaching that we can carry on, if necessary, virtually.

In person Hans was a strange mixture. I carry a rough scale of executives in my head that runs between two points:

Understated > > > > > > > > > > > > > > > > > Charismatic

Hans was certainly on the left of that continuum. Not that this is necessarily bad. One of the best known business books, *Good to Great* by Jim Collins, identifies – and lauds – what he calls a Level 5 leader who is quieter, more reflective and less showy than the Alpha Male stereotype we invariably associate with the so-called 'natural leader'.

Nonetheless, Hans may have taken this a bit far. He seemed subdued, even bland, and rather than create energy in the room, he seemed to drain it. Weirdly, though, there were moments when he would suddenly come alive and be really clear, assertive and almost mesmerising.

I suspected that the wider issues that brought Hans to see me would be explained if we could understand this contradictory dynamic. As he told me his story I began to see its genesis.

Hans had grown up as the youngest child in a fundamentalist religious family where humility was the family watchword. If he ever behaved in a bold or loud way, his parents and even his elder siblings would admonish him. His successes were to be enjoyed without fuss; pride in any achievements a cardinal sin. Only one 'person' could decide anything definitive, and that was God, as expressed through the Bible.

His father and mother would preside over the family dinner table, orchestrating debates in which the children were expected to contribute in a quiet, humble way, but only if they had something really insightful to say. If they got carried away, or said something that the forbidding patriarch and matriarch felt was glib or foolish, one of them would smack their hand down on the table, shaking the crockery and cowing them into silence. Even worse than this parental chastisement was how Hans felt when his elder brother and sister took his parents' side against him, being even more critical and belittling than mother and father.

I said I would leave Hans alone in the room on his own for five minutes and asked him to think about what this might have caused him to be like. When I returned he looked blank. Sometimes, as in

Rachel's case, the coachee gets there on their own, other times I have to offer an interpretation.

'Let me make a suggestion, Hans. I think many people would have ended up feeling cowed, that their contributions are not valuable, and maybe they would err on keeping their mouth closed, or not really committing to what they think.' Hans was silent, looking down and picking at his nails.

'It is exactly what I feel like in board meetings,' he eventually said in a low voice, 'unless I am talking about finance, of course.'

Those last few words were crucial. Hans's pathogenic belief was that he was only able to contribute effectively, even passionately, when he felt he was the expert – but even a degree out of that comfort zone would mean he hadn't very much to say. This made him an OK country finance director, but really strong FDs need to be able to actively contribute to general commercial debate, as well as be subject matter experts. As for being a CEO, forget it. There was none of the confident broad mastery, curiosity, agility, ability to connect and synthesise, qualities that people need from the man or woman at the top. Hans was unable to contribute to wider strategic discussions with views that were cut-through and decisive, and this failure kept him firmly in his finance function box. Yet I had a gut instinct that there was more to Hans than this. We went to work.

As well as processing some of the fear and shame he'd felt growing up, which hung around him like a cloak even now forty years later, we also looked at what thinking – and communicating strategically – is all about. I got him to complete a short survey on Strategic Intelligence (SQ), which I have developed (based on Michael Maccoby's book *Strategic Intelligence*). The survey asks around twenty questions that explore your strengths and weaknesses around foresight, visioning, and inspiring. I often find that this helps identify where people are weak in terms of the different elements of thinking and acting strategically. We also looked at how he could tap more into his intuition, and I suggested he read Malcolm Gladwell's book *Blink*. Finally, we worked on his executive presence and charisma; he would certainly gain from exuding a bit more passion and enthusiasm, even if he was never going to give people the old razzle-dazzle.

In terms of changing his problem behaviour, we decided that he would start slowly, with him committing to giving a firm view, just once, about something not in his area of expertise in a forthcoming meeting, and seeing how that landed – and how it made him feel. We agreed to speak before that meeting to tee him up for it, and afterwards to debrief on how it had been.

When the day of his meeting came along, I found myself slightly nervous on his behalf, but it turned out that the Skype call he made immediately afterwards was one of the most fulfilling calls I have ever had. Hans was beaming with pride. He told me about how he had spoken up about a marketing decision (as we'd discussed he would), initially fearfully, but that as he felt the room slowly paying attention he'd lost his nerves. Eventually the Chief Marketing Officer had asked bluntly, 'Well, what would you do Hans?' This had forced him to take a small gulp and give his view, which had ended up carrying the day. After the meeting the CEO had come up to him and thanked him for raising his point. As he told me this I could see him holding back his pleasure. I told him not to. Separated though we were by 3,000 miles, we had a mini-celebration, high-fiving our screens. Hans looked younger, more vibrant, more like Superman than his drab alter ego.

We'd had what some psychoanalysts would call a 'corrective emotional experience'. I thought of how grim things must have been for him growing up in such a crushing environment. 'Fuck the lot of you,' I thought as, through the virtual ether, Hans visibly glowed.

Taking risks and Creating Space to Decide

'You can't make decisions based on fear and the possibility of what might go wrong.'

Michelle Obama

Hans's story may not seem at first reading to be about making decisions, but it illustrates the essential first step to deciding anything – knowing what you think, and having the confidence to express it. Having the inner confidence to nail your colours to the mast and be held accountable for what you've decided – whether you prove to be right or wrong – is one of the true tests of leadership. Yet the art and science of decision-making is fraught with difficulty.

First, consider the sheer scale of things. We live in a world where we are bombarded with the need to make countless decisions. It is claimed that we make around 35,000 decisions a day as adults – if this seems like a high estimate, researchers at Cornell University claim that we make over 200 choices every day on food alone. Even if our childhood experiences don't cast a shadow over our decision-making faculties, as Hans's did, the here-and-now is so chaotic that it can wear out even the most resilient and decisive of us. In a world where a 'half-soy skinny decaf organic chocolate iced vanilla double-shot frappuccino' is a genuine order for a cup of coffee, it is no wonder that decisions can feel overwhelming. Working in a knowledge economy requires us to make a multitude of decisions daily within a complex environment full of intersecting, fluid factors. This almost universal nature of such working lives has an unavoidable psychological component as we are forced to navigate seemingly endless considerations, possible outcomes and power dynamics. It's enough to make anyone want to escape for a coffee!

In addition to having to deal with the stressful here-and-now, many of us are carrying a hidden world of memories and deeply held assumptions from the 'there-and-then' – our pasts. Perhaps even more than the outer world, it is our inner world that causes us a multitude of problems when it comes to making decisions. What often looks like a reasonable, rational approach to decision-making – weighing up the pros and cons, googling multiple perspectives, asking mentors, friends and the family cat for their opinion – can mask deeper psychological dynamics that may be playing out. Often, it masks fear: fear of getting it wrong, fear of emotional discomfort, fear of looking stupid, fear of losing our safety, security or reputation. We are often not cognisant of much of this psychological material – it lurks beneath the surface, ever so slightly beyond our awareness.

In Hans's case, it was not simply a lack of skill that inhibited him from making more of an impact; he was haunted by decades-old fear and shame, driven by an out-of-date need to protect himself by not voicing his own views. His formative relationships with his parents and siblings had heavily shaped his conception of authority and power; it was in these early experiences that he learned what he needed to do and who he needed to be in order to avoid punishment, rejection and criticism. Hans isn't alone in having learned his most foundational lessons about authority in relationship to his caregivers and siblings; since humans are wired to be social animals, we are all impacted by those primary relationships, and it is in those early experiences that many of our deepest fears are rooted. If this early learning goes well, we develop confidence in our own decision-making abilities. If it doesn't, we learn to hedge our bets and rely on our elders (or 'superiors') to take our decisions for us. That way we can never be wrong, but we also never get a chance to be right.

The problems Hans encountered in his role as an FD were fundamentally connected to his beliefs and experiences of power, authority and leadership. Committing to an opinion in his childhood risked exposing him to the undoubtedly frightening experience of one of his parents smacking their hand down on the table or being ostracised by his siblings, experiences which at that time in his life were painful, even traumatic. Alas, for Hans, as is invariably the case, the coping strategy that had served him so well in childhood had begun to limit him in adulthood. His fears were running the show. He needed to grow into being able to make decisions from an emotionally and psychologically adult space. Having these fears didn't make Hans weak or a failure; they simply made him human.

In previous roles, Hans had been able to get away with not contributing his broader, more strategic thoughts or opinions, but once promoted, he discovered that a lack of bold views and clear decisions is one of the least desirable qualities in a leader and one of the fastest ways to lose your colleagues' respect. Marie Beynon Ray, who edited

Vogue and *Harper's Bazaar* magazines, put it well: 'Indecision is fatal. It is better to make a wrong decision than build up a habit of indecision. If you're wallowing in indecision, you certainly can't act – and action is the basis of success.'

During a focus group I attended with a major UK retailer, a senior member of staff commented that although the business was supposed to be operating in a fast, ultra-responsive environment, in reality there were often so many decisions that needed to be referred up to more senior managers – decisions that would often be late in coming – that the entire buying process often virtually ground to a halt. This was resulting in stock arriving in stores on the tail end of trends rather than at their peak. The impact of this drag on decision-making was proving potentially devastating for the business. Getting people to make better, faster decisions was, in this case, worth millions.

Long before I became a psychologist I worked in politics and saw how different political leaders would handle decision-making. Along with having a lot of self-confidence, a vision they could communicate, and the ability to build relationships with all sorts of people, what differentiated the real leaders from the mediocre was the ability to make decisions speedily, and without angst. The best example of the former was Tony Blair.

In the 1990s, as Chief Aide to the politician Peter Mandelson (a future Secretary of State for Business and European Commissioner for Trade), I had a ringside seat as the UK Labour Party transformed itself into the more modern electable New Labour. I saw how Tony Blair ruthlessly focused on what mattered, yet also made the space to build relationships across the political spectrum and beyond. Even more impressively, he also got home most evenings to have tea with his kids. In 1996, before he became Prime Minister, I was setting up Progress, a think tank. This was an attempt to create a 'cadre' of moderates, and was seen as important to the success of the government he was planning. I had convinced David Sainsbury, the supermarket billionaire, to donate a substantial amount to make the idea happen. I went to Blair's house to discuss the idea. He made me a cup of tea and we went outside and sat in his garden. After hearing me outline my proposal for a couple of minutes (the PPT slides I had slaved over left untouched on his lap), he said he'd heard enough, fired off a few questions, drained his mug, stretched and said, 'OK, let's go for it, but for God sakes keep JP [his deputy] on board.' He then nodded over to the park beyond the back wall of his garden and shouted for his kids: 'Euan, Nicky, let's play some football. Wanna join us?' he asked. Other politicians would have discussed the idea ad infinitum, brought in all sorts of people to comment on and review it, and, ultimately, not have been bold enough to do it. Not Blair.

Peter Mandelson himself displayed many of the characteristics of a natural leader, but along with his powerful intellect, his greatest strengths were focus and determination. I remember once driving with him to his constituency in Hartlepool. It had been a long hard week and, understandably exhausted, he closed his eyes and napped in the car. After twenty minutes or so, his eyes snapped open and, from somewhere, he found the energy to pick up his laptop and dash off a series of emails: suggesting ideas, challenging people, making judgement calls, pushing things forward. Blair called it Peter's 'laser-like' focus, and he was right.

*

Creating the space to make good, speedy decisions requires the acceptance of three psychological realities. First, decisions will often cause you anxiety; second, you will never have all the information you need; and third, you will sometimes get things wrong. But that's all OK.

Decisions – or the change associated with them – can generate anxiety due to what psychologists call 'status quo bias', in which we subconsciously prefer not to make decisions so as to keep things familiar and, so say our brains, 'safe'. The human brain evolved to associate uncertainty with danger, and will go to any lengths to evade this danger. Unless we consciously acknowledge that we are susceptible to our evolutionary impulse to 'stay safe' by maintaining the status quo, we run the risk of buying into the lie that we just need a little bit more information or time to make the decision.

This takes us to the second reality we must face. You can't expect to have all the facts at your disposal before you make a decision. The world is too complex and messy for that. A good decision maker tries to assemble all the data, but a great decision maker knows she can't, and that at a certain point she has enough to go on.

As well as embracing the inevitable anxiety of decision-making and the need to act without perfect information, we must also accept the final reality: that we might get it wrong. I was in Silicon Valley a couple of years ago where I discussed this with a senior tech executive who told me of the popular phrase that informs much of the decision making in the big companies out there: 'Done is better than perfect.' In any given situation, there are so many unknowns, variables, ambiguities and constantly changing factors that it is literally impossible to arrive at a 'right' answer. Weighing and balancing perspectives can easily become an endless process; at some point, you have to decide to sacrifice an imaginary perfect decision with one that is good enough, and you have to risk getting it wrong.

Similarly, it can be helpful to remind yourself that a bad decision is better than no decision (within reason), and the experience of countless explorers, entrepreneurs and leaders bears this out. Arianna Huffington, the author of *Thrive* and founder of the *Huffington Post*, says, 'We need to accept that we won't always make the right decisions, that we'll screw up royally sometimes – understanding that failure is not the opposite of success, it's part of success.' Then there is Richard Branson, whose entrepreneurial journey has been full of ups and downs. Many of his 400+ businesses have been hugely successful, but he has also endured quite a number of public failures, such as Virgin Cola or Virgin Cars, as well as at least one brush with death. When flying a hot air balloon across the Atlantic in 1987, he and his co-pilot lost their fuel and calculated that they had a 5 per cent chance of surviving, eventually crash landing in Northern Ireland. His many unsuccessful business ventures do his words justice: 'Even if things do fall short and the decision turns out to be not so great, you stand to learn so much more from making a bad decision than you do from not making a decision at all. After all, failure is life's greatest teacher.' Embracing or at least being willing to accept the possibility of failure is a hallmark of a leadership mindset.

There are, however, certain particular circumstances when deferring a decision makes sense. Decision fatigue describes perfectly the exhaustion we can all experience from being bombarded by choices and decisions we need to make on a daily basis. The more we are required to decide, the worse the quality of those decisions. A research study published by the National Academy of Sciences found more concrete evidence of decision fatigue. The study of judges' judicial rulings demonstrated that the biggest factor influencing them was not the crime, gender or ethnicity of the offender, or anything else related to the crime itself; the biggest predictor of whether the judge would award parole or not was the time of day, and therefore how cognitively overloaded (aka tired) they were. The researchers found that of the 1,112 rulings they reviewed over a ten-month period, the most favourable decisions were made early in the morning or immediately after a break, when 65 per cent of parole requests would be approved. As the morning wore on, the likelihood of a criminal getting a favourable ruling steadily dropped until it reached zero, even if the case was almost identical to an early morning case. The same pattern repeated after lunch; immediately after food and a break, the judges' parole approval levels spiked once again, returning to 65 per cent, but as the afternoon wore on, decision fatigue returned. As decision fatigue sets in, people become what researchers call 'cognitive misers', hoarding their energy and ignoring complex and contradictory considerations. They become highly susceptible to making an impulsive decision. The lesson? Prioritise your most important, cognitively complex decisions for early in the morning or immediately after a break, take frequent breaks (every 90 minutes is a good rule of thumb, even if it's just a quick stretch or breath of fresh air) and make sure you eat and drink regularly. Especially when people's freedom is at stake!

Avoiding decision fatigue has led some leaders to try and minimise the number of decisions they face. Steve Jobs famously wore the same outfit every day – the iconic black polo neck and jeans – so that he never had to think about what to wear. Tim Ferriss, entrepreneur, investor and author, eats the same breakfast each morning, and the former US President Barack Obama used one-word replies to answer his low-priority emails, simply choosing either Agree, Disagree or Discuss. He, like Steve Jobs, also minimised decision fatigue over what to wear, explaining: 'You'll see I wear only grey or blue suits. I'm trying to pare down decisions. I don't want to make decisions about what I'm eating or wearing. Because I have too many other decisions to make.'

Luckily, most of us have fewer – and less world-changing – decisions to make than the President of the United States. Yet the forbidding atmosphere around Hans's dinner table when he was growing up meant that having a view and articulating it decisively felt like it was 'life or death' even when it wasn't. To break free of that bind, Hans had to accept the great irony in all this – that in order to offer an answer, you have to accept you may not necessarily have the answer. But, hey, maybe I'm wrong.

Watching your biases, listening to your body and other practical ideas to help you create space to decide

As we have observed, one of the barriers to good decisions is 'too much information'. So let's begin by stripping things down to their essentials using another model, the Deciding Cycle. This has clear parallels with the Reflecting Cycle (see p. 32), the main difference being that whereas the Reflecting Cycle has no end, the Deciding Cycle has – as indicated by the break in the circle at the top left-hand side. Reflection never ends; decisions are – at least for a moment – a clear and unambiguous end.

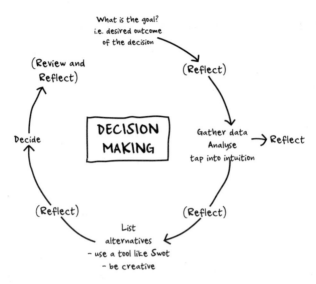

The Deciding Cycle

It is useful to compare and contrast the three elements of thinking we have looked at in Part 1:

Type of thinking	Focus	Dynamic
Reflection	Primarily yourself but also the world	Open up, close somewhat but stay open for more
Learning	Primarily the world but also yourself	Open up and keep opening up
Decision	A particular issue or question	Open up and then close

Give every important decision you have to make the attention it deserves and ruthlessly carve out the time to think deeply about it. Review the four types of space and see how your preferences around each will improve your ability to make decisions:

The temporal space – how do you make time to decide?

As with all thinking it's important to find the space to make your decisions in a considered way. As well as carving out the time itself, if possible try and think in stages. Have an initial deliberation to scope out the problem – what my dad calls 'seeing the rabbit' – and then come back to it, ideally a few days later. There is a reason for the phrase 'let me sleep on it'. If you can, create the space around decisions that allow your unconscious mind and your intuition a chance to do their thing.

The physical space – where should you decide?

Again, give some thought to the best environment for you to take decisions. Try to take them in as stress-free, relaxed a setting as possible. Try and avoid being bounced into making calls when you are not in the right frame of mind or emotional mood. One executive I worked with refused to make any decisions of consequence in his office and would slip out for a breath of fresh air and a stroll, mulling things over and only coming back to the office when he'd made up his mind.

The language around decision-making is bodily based: Are you using your head or your heart? Are you listening to your gut? There is a reason for this. Our 'thinking' doesn't always take place in the brain. We are not 'psyche' separate from 'soma' – that mind and body split so often evoked. We are, in fact, as psychoanalyst D. W. Winnicott expressed it, 'psyche-soma'.

A practical and very physical way to experience this is through an exercise I call 'Decision Jumps'. It is designed to make space, to give pause during your thinking, and allow you to listen, literally, to the wisdom of your body.

First think of a decision you have to, or want to, make. It doesn't have to be a life-changing one but something with a little more jeopardy than what to have for lunch.

OK, now slim down the options to just two. For ease let's call these options A and B.

Sit down comfortably in an empty room and assign a random place to option A and another place, as far from place A as possible, to option B. For example option A may be near the window, option B near the radiator. When I do this in coaching I ask the person to draw a big circle on paper and write down the choice in the circle, and then lay these, far apart, on the floor. For example:

A

Resign and take that job offer

B

Stay and wait for the promise of promotion

Next go and stand in one of the spaces. Move about a bit, jiggle, get settled in that space.

Then close your eyes and bring to mind that choice. Pay attention to any thoughts or feelings that come up for you, and any bodily sensations.

Next take a jump (or a run and jump depending how big your room is) and end up in the place that represents the other option.

Again, settle in and close your eyes. What thoughts, feelings and sensations do you have in this space? How do they contrast with what you felt in the other place?

Now jump from one space to another, what happens to you? What comes to the fore, what recedes, what does your body tell you about each possibility?

In the dozens of times I have done this exercise I have never known one place not be clearly more attractive or comfortable to my coachee. Some emotion like 'excitement' say, or a sense such as 'safety' will become manifest in the person's actual body.

Astonishingly, one of the two places will feel right – will be the place you want to be. Your body will tell you what your mind alone cannot.

The relational space – who can help you decide?

The points already explored in previous chapters apply here. Think about the right balance between making decisions on your own and consulting others. But don't let doing the latter delay you or waylay you. Have a clear sense of who you are asking and why, and retain accountability for having the final say.

Incidentally, if you're engaged in decision making as a group it can be useful to switch people around so that the proponents of one solution have to argue their opponents' case and vice versa. Not only does this tend to increase empathy for the different views on offer (for as someone once quipped, 'We think therefore we differ'), it simultaneously depersonalises and deepens debate.

The final way of using other people to help you create space to focus on the decisions that really matter is to use others to reduce the number of decisions you have to make. I come across many executives who hoard decision-making, as if somehow their status or worth depends on how many decisions they take – even when the decisions are 'below their paygrade'. We will look at delegating more comprehensively in Chapter 9, but for now it's worth considering that if you have people to delegate to, don't just delegate tasks, delegate decision making too. Only intervene when it really matters and don't second-guess your team's decisions. I know of one highly paid consultant who would stand over his PA's shoulder tinkering with how she laid out his PPT slides. I kid you not, there was one day when I knew his client had been desperate for the deck since that morning and yet he was still in the office at 7.00 pm, exasperated PA in tow, fiddling around with what exact shade of blue to use. Hours of highly valuable time wasted on what Sue Macmillan, who helps run UK website Mumsnet, scornfully calls 'faffing'. He could have left such second-order decisions to his PA and had the presentation with the client on time. The Australian political strategist Lynton Crosby has a great phrase that can be applied here – 'scraping the barnacles off the boat'.

ASK YOURSELF: *Have I passed on all decisions that I don't have to take? Am I concentrating on the things that only I can decide and that are of critical importance?*

The psychic space – what internal resources do you need?

In order to be in the best mental state to make decisions, we need to ensure that we are aware of our biases and have done as much as we can to eliminate them. We also need to make sure that we are tapping into both sides of our brain – the right-hand or intuitive, creative side, and the left-hand, more analytical side (there isn't much scientific justification for this notion of brain duality by the way, so just treat it as a useful metaphor).

Recognising our biases

Most human beings live under a great delusion – that we are rational, logical creatures who seek out the best for ourselves. Well, psychology and behavioural economics would indicate otherwise. First, as the stories of Raku, Rachel and Hans show, we can be prisoners of our core pathogenic beliefs, which cloud our judgement and perception. But even when these aren't present, there are a huge range of cognitive and personal biases at play that undermine our ability to make the best decisions objectively. These all crowd out the mental space we need for making clear, unbiased, optimal decisions. During my work with clients I have identified the ten that seem to crop up again and again:

1. **Confirmation bias** – we tend to see facts that match our existing views or prejudices and not those that challenge them, however 'open minded' we think we are.

2. **Illusion of control** – we like to believe we are more in control of things than we actually are, so assume things will go our way.

3. **Optimism bias** – we overestimate the likelihood of good things happening and underestimate the chance of bad things happening.

4. **Source credibility** – we tend to accept things from people who

are similar to us, or who we like more, rather than those who differ from us, or we don't like.

5. **Repetition effect** – we pay disproportionate attention to things that we have heard before, or heard several times.

6. **Prospect theory** – we are biased towards outcomes that minimise losses rather than maximise gains.

7. **Recency** – we tend to take more account of things that happened recently and less account of things that happened a while ago.

8. **Anchoring** – in contradiction to 'recency', at other times we are overly influenced by the first thing that we discovered or experienced.

9. **Groupthink** – we will tend – unknowingly – to conform to the consensus (or what we perceive to be the consensus) in a group we are part of.

10. **Sunk cost fallacy** – we persevere with things even when we have realised they won't work, just because we've already put time and effort into them.

ASK YOURSELF: *How many of these biases might I be susceptible to when I think I am acting rationally? What can I do to minimise these biases?*

Using your head and your heart

As we saw in Raku's story, there are two methods we all draw on when deciding things – analysis and intuition. In his book *The Fifth Discipline*, Peter M. Senge says, 'People ... cannot afford to choose between reason and intuition, or head and heart, any more than they would choose to walk on one leg or see with one eye.'

Nonetheless, it is worth attempting to tease out these methodologies when taking important decisions. Spend time consciously and deliberately gathering and interrogating data, using all your analytical rigour to surface patterns and conclusions that illuminate the matter in hand. Then make the space to step back from all that and check in with your 'gut'.

I tend to find that even in those disciplines where you would expect analysis to be at a premium (for example finance), the best people, and those that rise to the top as leaders, draw heavily on their intuition. One CFO I worked with said that he hadn't used his forensic analytical powers for years. 'These days,' he said, 'it's about my gut – how do these figures *feel* to me. If I had to stop and analyse everything, I would literally drown in numbers. Sometimes I think it's more art than science – even magic at times.' And he laughed.

Incidentally, as I noted earlier, the language around intuition is interesting. We tend to either say 'gut' or 'heart'. I think that 'gut' carries the echo of a second meaning – not just our 'non-brain' instincts but also something to do with courage – having the guts to believe in yourself and your view, which, outside of his technical specialism, Hans didn't have. Heart is interesting too because it raises an important point about intuition: it's not just the sum total of your absorbed experience but also relates to your values. What your instinct 'tells you' will depend a great deal on the importance you attach to different things, and the way you see the world. Hence two people with similar life experiences will have a very different gut feeling about whether something is right or wrong.

ASK YOURSELF: *What do I tend to draw on most when making decisions – analysis or intuition? How could I develop my less used decision-making 'muscle'? How could I better combine the two? Do I know what part my values play in my decision-making?*

SWOT away

I often suggest one last tool to help people, especially groups, create the space to make good decisions. It involves breaking down the decisions and looking at them through four different lenses, Most business people are familiar with the SWOT model (Strengths, Weaknesses, Opportunities, Threats), which is usually used to address possible new business opportunities or the strategic choices of an organisation. Slightly adapted, it can also be used to interrogate potential choices around decisions, which is especially important in a VUCA world. Does your decision allow for review and an agile

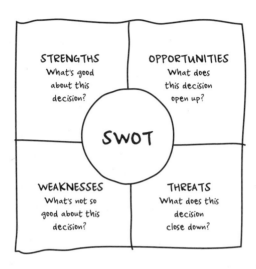

Adapted SWOT model

response if it turns out to have been wrong, or if circumstances change? Sometimes an inferior decision that can be changed might be better than a superior decision that can't be.

Done rigorously such an adapted SWOT analysis can be a very effective tool for systematically evaluating different possible decisions. I know of one CEO of a FTSE 100 company who uses it all the time during discussions, to the point where his top team groan when he brings it up. They also, though, acknowledge its effectiveness. He says why stop using something just because we're overfamiliar with it?

ASK YOURSELF: *What methods, tools and tips do you use to enrich and deepen your decision-making. Do I always think through the consequences of my decisions? What happens if I have to change my decision?*

Conclusion

In Part I we have looked at three elements of thinking: reflection, learning and deciding. While, in practice, these overlap and intermingle, we have teased them out as separate activities in order to explore them in detail and offer some insights – and practical suggestions – that should help you create space to think in a clearer, richer, deeper way.

There are three key lessons. First, you need to make the commitment, backed up with self-discipline, that better quality thinking is a priority for you – whether it involves reflection, learning or decision-making. Second, you need to examine whether there are any core pathogenic beliefs distorting how you approach the task of thinking, in its various forms. Once you have identified these you can challenge them and replace them with healthier, more realistic beliefs. Last, you have to set clear goals and clearly articulate the changes you intend to make to your behaviour around thinking – and hold yourself accountable for these.

High quality thinking is one of the two foundations of successful execution. The other is how we relate to, work with and get the best out of other people. So before we move to looking at Space to Do, let's first examine how we can Create Space to Connect.

PART 2

Create Space to Connect

S PACE TO THINK and to do are not lone endeavours, underpinning both is the ability to connect with other people and create
rich, deep, trusting relationships. In the modern business world,
where old hierarchies are breaking down and collaboration, partner-
ship and the matrixed organisation are the norm, your relationships
with other people are your main tool to get things done. Getting
these right requires three things.

First, we need to **Create Space to Check In**. This is about your
relationship with the most important person of all – yourself. In
order to relate to and empathise with others, you first have to know
what is going on for you. What are you feeling and why? We will
see, in the example of Nick, that if we're not careful our emotional
responses can be out of kilter with what's actually going on around
us, and that to set things right we need to exorcise our demons.

Second, we need to **Create Space to Share**. Once we know what
we're feeling and why, we have to be able to share this with others.
This goes beyond sharing 'intellectual' things like ideas and plans,
and is about sharing your emotional reality. This can make us feel
vulnerable and even scared, but it is the precursor to building the
strong relationships we need. We will see how hard the Spirits Team
has to work to recognise this and move beyond niceties and plati-
tudes to bring to the surface what was really going on.

Finally, we need **Create Space to Relate**. Once we are able to connect with our own inner emotional life and the emotional life of those around us, we need to create space to really get to know other people; nourish and nurture those relationships that we need to do our jobs well. Amir, like Nick, has demons to conquer, and needs to fundamentally alter his basic assumptions about himself and other people.

In all three stories, we will see that there can be deep, troubling and longstanding issues getting in the way of our ability to connect to others. If we don't make the space to identify and process these, we will end up sabotaging our own success.

CHAPTER 4

Space to Check In

Nick and His Three Deadbeat Dads

LESSON: *Being aware of what you're feeling – and why – will stop you being driven by buried emotions from the past and allow you to create the space to live fully in the here and now.*

N ICK IS THE NEWLY PROMOTED MD of a division of a big UK manufacturing company. He has hitherto been a high-flyer but people are now experiencing him as abrasive, moody and over-demanding. His boss is beginning to question whether he's been over-promoted and whether he has the maturity for this bigger job.

In our first session Nick was surly and dismissive. Whatever he may have been feeling, he looked pretty miserable and, I am afraid, that rubbed off on the people he was with, including me. He sat forward on his chair and seemed tense, as if he was containing a lot of repressed energy, his shirt straining across his biceps. I felt ever so slightly intimidated. Straight away I suspected that he had a problem both with 'authority figures' and also with asking for help. I felt he didn't trust me and wanted me to know it.

Nick had a pretty deprived upbringing. Brought up on a rough council estate, he'd been picked on as a 'swat'. His dad had been a drunk and had left home when Nick was very young. His mum had brought him and his younger brother up on her own until she remarried when he was about ten. His stepdad was a decent bloke but never really bonded with Nick (who admitted he hadn't made it easy) and was the sort of guy never to show emotion. He'd also been super critical of Nick, and seemed more jealous than proud of his academic and sporting achievements. Nick's cocky guardedness began to crack when he'd told me that he'd never had a hug from his stepdad but that was OK, he hadn't minded.

'So you don't hug your kids?' I asked with mock naiveté.

'Of course I do,' he shot back.

'Why bother, when they wouldn't mind if you didn't?' I retorted. This exchange triggered a real change in our relationship. He began to open up.

When he began to get a fix on what he was feeling and, crucially, felt safe enough to express it, he could admit to me that he felt scared and unappreciated. It was this that made him appear defensive and brittle. It became clear that underneath his tough-guy bravado he yearned for someone to tell him he was doing well, and this was where the problem lay. For Nick's boss was an ex-consultant whose sky-high IQ sadly wasn't matched by his EQ (emotional intelligence). He was distant, uncommunicative and unempathic. He would withdraw from Nick and let him fend for himself, and even when he did pay him attention there was never any praise, just criticism and a push for more.

In a not untypical twist, these unhelpful dynamics played out between Nick and his team too, where he, unconsciously, treated them as he had been treated. There was another breakthrough moment when I read to him some of the feedback I'd gleaned from his team in a series of phone calls. As I read their anonymous responses he stared at me. 'Fucking hell,' he said, 'that's Ron, my stepdad, isn't it? Word for word.'

Nick's core pathogenic belief was that he was unworthy and unlovable. When his colleagues experienced him as a truculent eight-year-old, that is because, at that moment, that was exactly who he psychically was. Breaking these toxic patterns required Nick to work on his self-esteem. He had to accept the aching need he had for praise and affirmation and stop pretending these things were beneath him. He also had to face the sadness and anger that resulted. Most critically, he had to accept that the love he needed (for that is what it really was) was clearly not going to come from either of his two 'dads' and certainly not from his rather cold boss. It could only come from himself.

We worked through a programme I call 'Break Free from the Past' (available at www.derekdraper.net). It helps people identify their core pathogenic belief and then to work on replacing the harsh voice of their internal critic with the supportive voice of their internal ally. We looked at how Nick could allow himself to feel more vulnerable, watching the Brené Brown TED Talk as I had with Rachel.

We spent some time exploring how he could change his relationships with his team, using the idea of 'Professional Intimacy' that I developed and often use with clients.

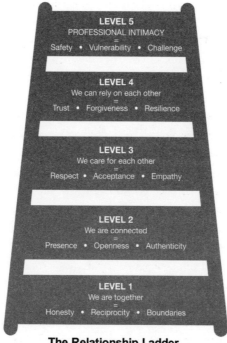

The Relationship Ladder

The first step on the ladder is to be together, which involves honesty, reciprocity and boundaries. The next level ('connected') adds in presence, openness and authenticity. The next ('caring') adds in respect, acceptance and empathy. The next ('rely') adds in trust, forgiveness and resilience. To reach the top of the ladder, Level 5 – Professional Intimacy – there needs to be a real sense of psychological safety (a concept we explore in the next chapter), alongside a willingness to be vulnerable and a comfort with real challenge. It is worth noting that Nick and his manager had never even achieved Level 1! This is not unusual. When I run this diagnostic with coachees and teams, even those who think they have got really good relationships at work realise that they are stuck at one of the first three levels. They often stumble around the trust and forgiveness required to reach level 4 and/or the vulnerability and challenge needed to reach true Professional Intimacy at Level 5 (as we will see was the case with Beata's team in the next story).

Achieving Level 5 isn't always possible, the model is meant to be descriptive not prescriptive, opening out the idea of what a relationship is so that we can approach the ones we have with more awareness and challenge.

In Nick's case, he was able to do some stakeholder mapping (see Chapter 6) using the Relationship Ladder to help analyse how strong his relationships were. Like many people, he found that they were not as strong as he might have assumed, and he was able to work out which needed work.

It takes two to tango, and it was pretty obvious that Nick's boss was unlikely to leap up the ladder with Nick. Nonetheless, the next step in his coaching was to sit down with his boss and share what he had learnt. How open would he be able to be? How vulnerable? How well would he cope if his boss failed to respond empathically?

In the event, he did brilliantly and I felt very proud of him, as I told him afterwards. He was able to tell his manager how he had got into a vicious spiral through projecting his issues with fathers on to both him and his team, and show how he was going to change that.

The most poignant moment came when he told his boss how upset he had been by the way he'd been treated, but that he knew that he wasn't going to get what he needed from him.

His boss found all this excruciating, avoiding eye contact, wriggling in his chair and bringing the meeting to an early close. Now there's a guy who needs some coaching, I thought as we left. Funny thing is, he has never asked for it and, indeed, has never asked me to coach any of his people since.

Once more with feeling: Creating space to Check In

'People will forget what you said, and they will forget what you did, but they will never forget how you made them feel.'

attributed to Maya Angelou

Our professional lives are relentlessly personal and intensely emotional – even if we consciously resist or deny this. In any given week we might be forced to deal with issues of greed, success, failure, resources, security, accomplishment, praise, authority, power, belonging, conforming, individuality, identity, competition, secrecy, pressure, expectation and status. Because our base survival needs depend to a large extent on work, our most primitive emotions and fears can easily be provoked and that doesn't always feel good.

We cannot, however, divorce ourselves from our feelings, even though at times we might really wish we could. We humans have an incredible ability for rational, intelligent, logical thought processes, but we are first and foremost emotional beings. At best we can numb out, act out or avoid them, but the fact is that we were emotional beings long before we were rational and logical – the limbic brain, often called the emotional brain by scientists, is the first part of an infant's brain to get 'wired', and the quality of that wiring varies based on our genetics, and our environment. It is also the second oldest part of the brain (after the reptilian, primitive region) predating, in evolutionary terms, the more 'advanced' pre-frontal cortex by a few million years, hence its other name – the 'old mammalian' brain.

Human beings have just a few basic emotions: fear, anger, disgust, shame, loneliness, sadness, surprise/startle, excitement/joy, trust/love. This idea is adapted from Paul Brown, Joan Kingsley and Sue Paterson, authors of *The Fear-Free Organisation*, in which they suggest that emotions are '...real, physiological events and they exist *whether we recognise them or not in conscious awareness.* Emotions happen whether we like them or not.' So we can either choose to pay attention to our emotions, or we can ignore them and live our lives at the mercy of their undeniable, unavoidable influence on us.

The study of the impact of emotions on business was popularised by the work of Daniel Goleman on EQ (Emotional Quotient). Your EQ is the level of your ability to understand other people, what motivates them and how to work cooperatively with them. It is made up of five areas, which Goleman describes in his book *Emotional Intelligence* as knowing one's emotions (emotional awareness); managing emotions (your ability to respond rather than react – what you do with emotions when they arise); motivating oneself; recognising emotion in others (empathy); and handling relationships (such as conflict management, collaboration, the ability to influence and inspire, and bonding). The great news is that our EQ can be developed. Your level of emotional intelligence is not fixed and immovable, even though some people are more predisposed to higher emotional intelligence than others. According to John Cooper, co-founder of consultants JCA Global, people who work diligently on improving their EQ will typically have their levels improved by around 20 per cent. Echoing the ideas on Reflection in Chapter 1, EQ involves knowing what we are feeling and thinking, and also knowing what we feel and what we think about those thoughts and feelings.

By far the biggest factor influencing our interpretation of events is our inner world (which I discuss more in Part 5): our internal, psychological landscape made up of conscious, semi-conscious and decidedly *un*conscious associations, memories, beliefs, relationships and stories that we've collected over our lifetimes. Our brains store all of these up in our long-term memory, and when 'something happens' in our daily lives, the brain filters the present moment through the lens of the past, quickly flipping through its thousands of reference files until it finds a match. This is why a child who got barked at once by a dog can easily turn into an adult who feels nervous, and even afraid, of dogs. They are not actually fully present to the dog in front of them, or to the reality that they are adult and that the scary moment from their childhood is long gone and forgotten. In that moment, the adult has left the building and the memory – the childlike sense of smallness, powerlessness and fear – takes over.

Many psychologists refer to this as projection: our past psychological and emotional experience is played out not as belonging to the past but as if it applies only to the present moment. Very often this is a result of interacting with other people, as Nick found with his boss, who unconsciously fitted the mould of his dad(s). In the moments when he was making himself and others feel bad, Nick wasn't a psychological grown-up. Emotionally and psychologically he was the little boy being neglected by his dad or stepdad. His mind automatically overlooked the reality – that he was a kind, generous, imperfect human being – and the old script played itself out over and over like a broken record. Such is the power of projection.

Nick and all of us who are affected by projection are not weak; projection is a universal process. I've yet to meet anyone who is immune to it. The simple truth is that we are often unable to fully metabolise and understand significant parts of our early life experience, and so we carry it with us into adulthood where it can wreak its havoc, as we saw with Nick. The present becomes the landscape where our unfinished business from the past expresses itself. If we are brave enough this offers us a profound opportunity to increase our self-knowledge, self-compassion and sense of true authority, as we disentangle the 'there and then' from the 'here and now'.

A final note about projection: it is incredibly tempting, as we saw with Nick, to make the issue about 'them' – the boss, colleague or client. This dynamic is underpinned by a concept introduced by the psychoanalyst Melanie Klein – that of splitting. This involves an attempt to get rid of an unwanted, intolerable or otherwise undesirable characteristics or emotion by 'planting' it outside of oneself, not unlike the way a criminal might plant false evidence to implicate someone else. We may use other people to stand for different parts of ourselves – obstinate, rude, bossy and controlling parts, greedy and destructive parts, passive, acquiescent parts – those parts of the self that we fear and have disowned, which we then 'see' in other people at work. Rivalry with colleagues or other organisations might be a psychological re-enactment of our sibling or peer relationships; our boss(es) may represent one or more parents; clients may conjure psychological echoes of people who have been dependent on us, or on whom we are dependent. Millions of us convince ourselves, and anyone who will listen, that what is upsetting or annoying us involves that person or event 'out there', but this can often evade the real issue, which is inside us.

Nick's story proved that actually, the external circumstances do not need to change and the people who populate our lives do not need to behave differently. Nick's manager continued to relate poorly to people, but that didn't matter once Nick had fully accepted that he didn't actually need his boss to meet his needs. Now he was more of a true 'grown-up' he could acknowledge them, own them, and start to meet them himself.

Blue skies, being as young as you feel and other practical ideas to help you create space to check in

People vary in their ability to feel and connect to their feelings. Some people are highly sensitive and can easily become flooded by their emotions; others are very disconnected from them and may not have 'felt' any strong emotion for years, almost as if they were switched off. If you're more like the former, learn to step back, observe and notice your feelings rather than being completely caught up in them. For those of us who are less aware of our feelings, we often have to work backwards to get to this point, starting initially with noticing our reactive, automatic behaviours, then getting curious about what we might be feeling underneath it. Then we can begin to practise observing the emotions rather than being driven by them.

Here are three practices that you could consider adopting to help you create more space for greater self-awareness about what you are feeling and why:

○ The feeling and number check-in

○ The blue sky visualisation

○ Not being as young as you feel

We will then look at how you can vanquish your internal critic and strengthen your internal ally.

The Feeling and Number Check-In

A simple yet effective way of checking in with yourself is the 'feeling and number' method. Take a couple of breaths and ask yourself how you are feeling, and how intense that feeling is on a scale of one to ten. You can focus on emotions (such as sad or anxious) or physical sensations (such as tightness, tension, a burning tummy or fluttering chest). Sometimes, feelings are hard to identify because there is so much head noise; if this is the case, imagine dropping below the mind chatter and noticing what feelings might be present underneath the thoughts. If you notice multiple feelings at the same time, ask yourself which one is front and centre. The deceptively simple act of naming and numbering an emotion can be enormously effective in creating enough psychological space for you to experience feelings without being controlled by them.

I suggest using this technique at the beginning and end of your day, before or after a big meeting, or even in the middle of a task or meeting – if you start to notice yourself being overwhelmed on the one hand, or distracted, disengaged or not fully present on the other. If you struggle to identify a feeling (many of us are so practised at numbing or being disconnected from our feelings that it can be difficult to know what we are feeling), take a few seconds to breathe deeply and allow your attention to turn inward. Instead of focusing on the sights, sounds and smells around you, focus on your body. Ask yourself, 'how do I feel right now?' and see if any images come to mind. An image can convey a lot of information, and from there we can gain insight into how we are feeling. An image of a hurricane might indicate that you are feeling angry or perhaps even scared; an image of a brick wall could represent feeling stuck or frustrated; an image of a person crouched in a box could show you that you feel trapped or 'boxed in'. There are no right or wrong answers here; the point is to allow yourself to join the dots between any images that come to mind and the underlying feelings associated with those images.

This technique is an integral part of the training of consultants and leaders at the Tavistock Clinic, where I serve as a governor. The feeling and number check-in helps you take your own emotional temperature, and best of all, no one needs to know you're doing it.

Checking in need not be just an individual practice, you can also use this exercise with a check-in partner, or even at team meetings, as a very effective way to get a sense of where people are at. It gives you a sneak peek into at least a part of everyone's inner world. Many of the world's most innovative and forward thinking companies are already weaving it into their culture, including giants such as Google and LinkedIn – acknowledging and welcoming 'the whole person' to the table is becoming increasingly common. Bear in mind that if your workplace culture has not typically involved this, it might seem a bit strange at first.

Blue-sky visualisation

Another way of tuning into your feelings involves using the metaphor of 'being the sky'. A quick 'glance' at your 'inner sky' can give you a lot of information about what might be happening for you. Is the sky clear? Stormy? Cloudy, with patches of blue peeking through? Is it daytime or night? Another option is to envision your mind as a road and imagine that you're sitting at the side of it 'watching' the traffic – the thoughts and feelings – pass by. Many Zen practitioners imagine their mind as a lake. As thoughts come, they cause ripples on the water, but the ripples are just that, they're not tidal waves. Allow the ripples to happen – in other words accept your thoughts and feelings – and they should soon pass.

Not being as young as you feel

A favourite tool of mine for helping clients (and indeed myself) figure out whether projection is active or not is this simple question: *How old do I feel right now?* Taking a moment to 'tune in' and get a sense of how old we feel can be very illuminating because of the simple yet powerful realisation that we often don't feel our age. Instead of 24 or 60, we feel 6 or 17. This alone can be enormously enlightening. We might not know why we feel that age or what it means, but even if we go no further, getting a sense of our emotional age in the here-and-now can help bring us fully back to the present.

If you want to go a little deeper, you can ask a follow up question: *What happened back then at that age that I might be emotionally re-experiencing or even re-creating in the present?* In Nick's case, he was acting like an eight-year-old at work because, psychologically, the situation mirrored his life at that age, when his male authority figure left him to fend for himself without any praise, appreciation or support – just like his boss was doing in the here-and-now. Nick's boss provided a pretty solid match for Nick's memories of his dad and stepdad, and bingo! Nick's mind conveniently ignored anything that didn't quite correlate (such as the fact that he was now a grown man). Nick, like most of us, got so caught up in the drama that was unfolding (the mind does love a bit of drama) that he failed to see that what was happening was projection – he bought into the story as if it were fact.

So next time you are triggered (annoyed, angry or upset in any way) by another person or something that happens, try using this technique; ask yourself how old you feel in that moment. As uncomfortable as it is to admit to the truth that we don't always function as psychological adults, as soon as we own up to it, we take responsibility for ourselves, and that shifts us back into being the adult we are today. Anytime you *feel* younger than you actually *are,* it is worth questioning what unfinished business or dynamic you might be playing out from the past in the present.

ASK YOURSELF: *What am I feeling right now? How old am I feeling right now?*

Strengthening your internal ally

As well as checking in to find out more about what you are feeling and why, a key part of creating more space to better identify and manage your emotions involves identifying and strengthening your internal ally. Part of Nick's work involved this – getting to know his internal critic and internal ally, recognising when the shaming, self-destructive voice of his internal critic was present so that he could consciously employ the constructive voice of his internal ally instead.

Before any of us are leaders, executives, employees or entrepreneurs, we are first and foremost human beings – and *all* human beings have to wrestle from day one with primal emotions like envy, greed, fear, hatred, need and love. All human beings grapple with their own worthiness. Regardless of whether we were the apple of our mother's eye, or the bane of our father's life, or whatever, we were all born into relationships – the effects of which are lifelong. Consequently, we all have fears, shame and insecurities. As we grow up, perhaps experiencing moments of profound belonging and moments of terrifying abandonment, isolation or shame, we internalise and absorb the messages we hear from the world around us. These include societal messages about our gender, sexuality, class, ethnicity and so on, and intensely personal messages about our worthiness and lovability, given to us by our parents, grandparents, siblings and friends. Most children's sense of self is easily affected and influenced by the way they are spoken to and treated by the people that matter, and how we interpret and process the events of our lives – what we make them mean about us – shapes our internal dialogue. If our core needs are not met, or if we are spoken to like shit, told that we're ugly or that we'll never make the grade or – more positively but still invidiously – that we are extra special, this tends to be the narrative that we internalise. Our thoughts begin to replicate those of the people we grew up with – sometimes we'll even hear 'their' voice in our head saying the exact words that they said to us ten, twenty, thirty or more years ago. We supposedly think 60,000 thoughts a day, and unfortunately for many people, if left to its own devices that internal voice tends to default to criticism, shame, blame and attack, constantly on the lookout for external threats and turning on itself and becoming its own worst enemy. Also, as Nick found, the way we treat ourselves often unconsciously spills over into the way we treat others

Dr Kristin Neff, an associate professor of human development and culture at the University of Texas, conducted pioneering research into self-compassion, which is the hallmark of the inner ally. Her excellent quiz on self-compassion (which you can easily find online) highlights the contrast between the messages of the internal critic and those of our internal ally. Where the internal critic is disapproving and judgemental about our flaws and inadequacies, the internal ally reminds us that most people have feelings of inadequacy. When feeling emotional pain, the internal critic tends to blow things out of proportion, while our internal ally takes a balanced view of the situation and tries to be loving towards us. When feeling down or going through a rough patch the internal critic is cold-hearted, snide and even cruel; the internal ally, on the other hand, reminds us that we deserve support especially when times are tough. The internal critic is intolerant of vulnerability; the internal ally embraces it.

The seeds of the internal critic are planted in childhood and we spend many of our days watering them. For those of us who recognise this, the task in adulthood is to consciously develop a sense of our internal ally and to make its presence strong enough to combat the often relentless nagging of the internal critic. We often fail to realise that we actually have a huge amount of creative control over that voice.

Cultivating a conscious sense of connection to one's internal ally can bolster you from the inside out. Your internal ally is what it sounds like: an inner resource that will stand by you no matter what challenge you're facing or what mistake you've made, holding your feet to the fire, challenging you to embody your values and live, work and lead with integrity. Your internal ally helps you to create – and keep open – the space to operate in the world as the best you, not the one bedevilled by negative thinking and past trauma.

Developing an internal ally is often an awkward and uncomfortable process. Saying or thinking nice things about oneself can feel arrogant, silly or just plain wrong. It's not necessary to become ultra-perky cheerleaders patting ourselves on the back every time we send an email, or high-fiving our colleagues when we get anything done, but we could all afford to turn up the volume a bit on the voice of our internal ally. Doing this can bring up old messages from the past that we have internalised so deeply that we don't stop to question whether they are true or not. It shows us the ways in which we have agreed to undermine ourselves. You can have fun with this, perhaps giving your internal critic and ally names. One of my colleagues calls her internal critic 'Nasty Nina' and thinks of her internal ally as herself, twenty years from now.

In the book *Playing Big*, author Tara Mohr suggests a number of simple, practical techniques for how to bring your internal ally closer. 'Sometime today,' she writes, 'ask yourself, "What would my inner mentor [Mohr's name for the internal ally] do in this situation? What would she say?" Check in with her and see what the answer is. Do or say that.' Mohr invites you to relate to your internal ally as you might to an actual mentor. Imagine how they would act in the world, and emulate that. Before composing a difficult email or engaging in a challenging conversation, ask yourself how your internal ally would approach it. You could even practise writing the email in the voice of your internal ally or do some stream-of-consciousness writing, perhaps writing back and forth between you and the internal ally, or simply allowing 'their voice' to speak to any challenges or opportunities you might be facing.

If you are a visual learner, you could use a powerful technique used by top athletes and do a visualisation in which you 'meet' your internal ally, noticing how she holds herself, how she interacts with other people, how she dresses and what her environment – both professional and personal – looks like. These techniques might seem fluffy but they are not; they are 'right-brained' activities, which help us tap into our creativity and emotional intelligence, enabling us to respond in more creative, mature or constructive ways.

It's a bit like having a coach you can call on at any moment to help you figure out how to deal with the challenges that are part of daily life in the twenty-first century. Instead of calling or emailing this coach, all you need to do is tune into him or her, finding their presence within you. Your internal ally is the wisest version of yourself that you can conceive of: unflappable, principled and calm in the face of any crisis. Who would you rather have on your team during a challenging time – someone who believes in you, motivates you and gives you pep talks and reality checks when your motivation or confidence start to wane, or someone who is constantly criticising you and telling you what a piece of shit you are? There's only one sane answer to that question, and anyone who'd rather be talked to like shit probably needs to address where they learned that.

ASK YOURSELF: *What is my internal critic telling me? What about my internal ally? How can I strengthen the latter at the expense of the former?*

CHAPTER 5

Space to Share

The Spirits Team and Their Need to Get Nasty

LESSON: *You need to create the space to be in touch with – and share – what is really going on for you if you are to have real, rich relationships.*

BEATA IS THE LEADER of a team in a global drinks business. It is not a simple team, though it has a simple job: to sell more of the company's most successful and iconic spirit. Some of the members report directly to her in the traditional sense, others report officially to someone else but have a dotted line to her. Some members are there because they are attached to the brand itself, others to the wider business unit the brand sits in (spirits); some have regional roles, some global roles. Beata's job is to herd these cats – and she's not doing a very good job of it. There's nothing terrible going on, at least on the surface, but quarter after quarter the team just isn't hitting its targets. Something subterranean is hampering the performance of this apparently functional team. But what?

No one seems to know why, least of all Beata. A cool, funny, self-possessed woman, she reminded me, maybe because of her Nordic origins, of a member of Abba. From the first moment in coaching she is open and trusting ('Knowing me, knowing you, Aha!') and quickly tells me how upset she feels about what is happening. She says that for the first time she feels out of her depth and doomed to

fail. This tears at her sense of herself. It was her Waterloo. OK, I'll
stop now.

After our initial conversation, and after checking in with her boss,
we decide that as well as doing some coaching with Beata we would
also do an intervention with the whole team. The following week
we carried out a team diagnostic – a survey that asks members of
the team, and those outside it who rely on it, to rate how they are
doing against CDP's 3D team model. This looks at the three key
foundations of a high performing team: Direction, Dynamics and
Delivery. We also undertake various psychometrics with the team to
shed light on their relationship and decision-making styles and how
these interact.

Sitting late one night, poring over the results, I too am puzzled.
The objective analysis would indicate that this is a good team. It has
an inspiring purpose, clear ways of working, a high level of positivity
among its members and respect from the rest of the business. Most
impressive of all, people enjoy being in the team, and others enjoy
working with it. So why has it not been able to perform well? What is
holding it back? I go to bed confused – and feeling a little like Beata –
that I too may be out of my depth and about to be exposed as a failure.

The next morning I try to settle my mind and re-read the data. In
the team survey, people are able to put in comments as well as fill in
the ratings, and suddenly one comment leaps out at me. A relatively
junior member of the team had written, 'Sometimes I wonder if
we are all too nice?' This simple question opened up an interesting line of inquiry, and sure enough there were other clues about
the team's tendency to avoid conflict scattered through the data. I
got on the phone to some of the team members and, armed with
this insight, found a deeper layer of unease that hadn't surfaced first
time around. As one person said, 'I hadn't wanted to say this as it
seemed a bit mean.' The core pathogenic belief of the team had
emerged: they thought that being a team meant always being 'nice'
and accommodating to each other. The development phases of a
team are sometimes characterised as formin', stormin', normin' and
performin'. They'd missed out the stormy bit.

I redesigned the forthcoming team day so it focused on bringing conflict to the surface and embracing challenge. Halfway through it was like I'd opened less a can of worms than a can of snakes. There were huge issues and resentments that had been repressed. We slowly worked through these using the model of Professional Intimacy. We then used a tool I often use called Challenging Conversations, which I outline later in this chapter. Basically, this creates the space for people to go to a more vulnerable, challenging, but safe, space so they can confront repressed conflict.

By the end of day one it was clear to me – and the team – that they had been living in a bit of a parallel universe, one where conflict was avoided and feeling good was more important than doing what needed to be done. Thanks to my prompting, the real issues had started to emerge. By the time people went to bed that night the team seemed broken, fractious and a bit scared. Good, I thought. My own challenge, at this point, is not to get despondent but hold the idea that the team can and will heal, and be stronger as a result. Indeed by mid-morning the next day something almost miraculous began to happen.

In pairs, interacting in front of the whole group, we led people to a place where these hidden feelings emerged. As we did so a flowering of creativity began to emerge from the conflict. When we repress scary, uncomfortable parts of a relationship, we inevitably repress other things too – with no conflict, there is little real difference of opinion, a lack of creative friction, no spark. Big, scary questions about the brand's positioning and future emerged. Not only had people's genuine feelings been smothered in a bland niceness (which did, to a large extent, flow from Beata's own style), so had their views about the brand and what needed to happen to it.

By doing this intense and brave work they had found that they could face conflict and that it wouldn't shatter the team, or make things feel horrible. They had learned a new way of working, one that left them energised to get back to work and get really stuck in. They had ceased to be in a place where making people feel good was all that mattered; they had turned into a real team.

Psychological safety and Creating Space to Share

'Vulnerability is the birthplace of innovation, creativity and change.'

Dr Brené Brown

Beata's story highlights a number of key themes. First, teams, not just individuals, can have core pathogenic beliefs, psychological stories about the way the world works that influence how they behave. Second, because of their authority, a leader has the power to exert a high degree of influence over which core pathogenic beliefs a team adopts; any unaddressed or unresolved psychological 'stuff' the leader is carrying will at some point impact the people they lead or are in charge of. Third, to the extent that a team denies, prohibits or otherwise represses unpleasant relational content, such as conflict, this will limit the degree to which the team will be able to fulfil its potential. Fourth, high functioning teams are not characterised by niceness but by resilience, courage, transparency and the skills required to navigate interpersonal challenges. Finally, unless a team goes through the 'storming' phase in its development, a group or team will not be able to reach the 'norming' and 'performing' stages that lie beyond. Sooner or later, the cracks will begin to show, as they did with Beata's team.

Businesses often struggle to survive for the very same reason that other businesses thrive: because of the relationships between the people who work there. Nowadays, teams are the central unit of organisation, with research showing that colleagues spend three-quarters of their day in communication with each other. Figuring out team dynamics and becoming conscious of the impact we make on the people we lead are, therefore, two vital aspects of effective leadership – and the two are often inextricably intertwined.

The messages leaders send, whether explicitly or implicitly, are adopted and often copied by those who 'follow'. Leaders set the precedent for what is acceptable and unacceptable, and establish the tone for the culture, not only in what they say but in what they don't say, in what they do and what they don't do, and in the principles they embrace and those they reject. At least some of this takes place in the zone seen by others but not by us – our blind spots. Some-times, as in Beata's case, something might be unknown to us and to the people we work with – a sort of collective blind spot.

As the academic and organisational consultant William Halton writes, 'Like individuals, institutions develop defences against difficult emotions which are too threatening or too painful to acknowledge.' We might unconsciously agree to ignore, deny or repress things that we'd rather not face until those things silently return to undermine us. This is often the unspoken reason for calling a consultant in to work with an organisation: to shine a light on the organisational blind spots via a third party who can see and make sense of what people inside the organisation cannot.

Beata's unconscious commitment to being conflict-avoidant – and her unspoken imperative to her team to follow her lead – eventually reached a point where it became more counter-productive than pro-ductive. The team presented itself as high-functioning, but in truth they were quite far away from this as they had never ventured into more challenging, honest, vulnerable territory. Their 'nice' working atmosphere was devoid of depth, and although people enjoyed working there, they weren't passionate about working there. I came to realise that my initial impression of the team was fairly surface. The longer I spent talking to them, the more I realised that these people were going to work every day with a mask on. They had fallen into the classic trap of subduing their multi-dimensional per-sonalities and presenting only the 'best' and 'nicest' parts to each other, camouflaging the thoughts, perspectives, opinions and, cru-cially, the feelings they were having that didn't toe the party line. A failure to acknowledge what the psychoanalyst Carl Jung called our 'shadow', or, to use the phrase inspired by him that lies at the heart of the *Star Wars* films, our dark side.

In his book *The Five Dysfunctions of a Team* consultant Patrick Lencioni details the key dysfunctions that cause teams to unravel:

absence of trust; fear of conflict; lack of commitment; avoidance of accountability; and inattention to results. These build on each other, creating a domino effect. Despite Beata's unconscious reign of nice-ness, her team hadn't cultivated much trust. Trust cannot occur at a distance – you cannot really trust someone you don't really know – and Beata's team members had never bridged the gaps between them by expressing or getting to know all the different sides of each other. When trust is absent, people become guarded and subtly (if not overtly) defensive. Obviously, too much conflict can lead to a huge breakdown in trust, particularly if it is not handled well and if people are allowed to emotionally dump all over each other without being held accountable. In Beata's team's case, the defensiveness was much more low-key; everyone had simply agreed not to cause any trouble. Rather than creating a sense of trust, this actually eroded it. The lack of conflict reflected a fundamental lack of psychologi-cal safety, which Amy Edmonson, a professor at Harvard Business School, has found is the key factor in high performing teams.

This finding was confirmed by work done at Google. Over the last decade or so, their People Operations department spent a huge amount of time and money analysing, measuring and studying any and every aspect of their employees' lives. Google launched Project Aristotle in 2012, studying 180 teams from all over the company, with the goal being to understand what makes a high-performing team. However, they hit a snag: no matter what data they reviewed or how they looked at it, they simply could not find any patterns that shed light on what made a team of people work well together. It wasn't as simple as putting all the smart people together; sometimes, a group of more 'average' people outperformed a group with superior IQs. They eventually discovered that the 'secret ingredient' to a high per-forming team was psychological safety. When this was present, the team performance was high, not just once, but repeatedly in various exercises.

Psychological safety is a shared belief within a group or team that the team environment is a safe space in which to take interpersonal risks. When it is present, team members feel respected and accepted.

William Kahn, a professor at Boston University's Questrom School of Business, defined it as 'being able to show and employ one's self without fear of negative consequences of self-image, status or career.' When it is not present, people retreat, protecting themselves and guarding their ideas or opinions for fear that they will be harshly judged. There are two key differences between psychological safety and trust: trust occurs at the individual level, while psychological safety is a group phenomenon; trust is about how you perceive others, while psychological safety is about how you think others perceive you.

When psychological safety is present, the relational climate is characterised by transparency, engagement, resilience and the willingness to make mistakes and grow. Psychological safety shifts teams out of black-and-white thinking where mistakes are seen as wrong; risk-taking goes up, and with it, creativity and innovation. Conversely, when psychological safety is absent, there is an underlying sense that people will be ostracised or somehow rejected if they challenge the status quo.

If it doesn't feel safe to bring one's whole self to the table, people are not fully committed, however amenable they may appear. How could they be? This is why such safety is the last thing needed before true professional intimacy can occur.

*

Although it wasn't initially apparent, it became undeniably clear that Beata's fears and defence mechanisms were running the show, and even though people couldn't necessarily express that that was the case, they could somehow feel it. Beata had unwittingly taken the right to experience or engage in conflict off the table for everyone who worked with her. She had dictated the tone: *we are here to be nice to each other above all else*. While she hadn't been able to admit it, Beata told me that she was aware – at times painfully so – that her team was lacking the spark of aliveness that accompanies outstanding teams.

Sometimes, we aren't in touch with what's going on for us under the surface. There can be lots of reasons for this: perhaps it would be too painful to admit, or perhaps it's simply a blind spot. However, in leadership, perhaps more than anywhere else, once we are aware of what's going on for us – of what, emotionally and psychologically, is driving the bus – we have a responsibility to share this (or at least to share the learning) in an appropriate way. Many leaders might baulk at this notion; in leadership there's historically been a 'behind closed doors' culture in which we don't share vulnerable, personal information with those we work with. Times are changing. We have to be brave enough to share. Vulnerable leadership is, I believe, necessary in the VUCA world. Without transparency, without the room to acknowledge our shared humanity, we jeopardise the very organisations that we work so hard to make succeed. Why? Because it is under the illusion of invulnerability that mistakes become 'sins', insurmountable and unacceptable. Without transparency, we do not give others the stories and data to allow them to learn from our mistakes. Secrecy begets secrecy, and even if nobody takes advantage of a secretive culture to act unethically (sadly, all too often a temptation for human beings), a lack of transparency creates the perfect breeding ground for misunderstandings, misinterpretations and conflicts of interest.

We have to be brave enough to share and to listen, not just to what we want to hear, but to the whole person. Listening well is about more than simply hearing the words the person in front of you is saying.

When Beata really listened, she discovered that her team could in fact endure conflict and the accompanying discomfort without falling to pieces. This was revelatory for her. 'I realised that it was time to grow up' she told me in a follow up conversation over a cup of coffee. She recounted the last few weeks, saying that people had begun to share with each other when they disagreed or held a different perspective. They had started to do what Patrick Lencioni writes about: admitting their mistakes, weaknesses and concerns without fear of reprisal. Two of the team had been able to admit that they had been working from entirely different assumptions about what needed to be done, and that neither had wanted to confront the other. Another pair admitted various things they had found intensely irritating about the other, and acknowledged that they were on such a different wavelength that they could never be friends – but that that was OK.

As the team built up its levels of psychological safety, the level of creative risk and innovation in the team spiked for the first time since Beata began to lead it. 'We have been so much more vibrant as a team since embracing conflict,' Beata said. 'It's been hard and anxiety-provoking for me, and I feel like my whole body is having to learn a new way of being, but what I keep experiencing is that conflict isn't as devastating or disastrous as I had made it in my mind. In fact, I've seen the team come alive because of it.'

Elephants, dead fish and other practical ideas to help you create space to share

Doing development work on ourselves is vital, but it is only half the deal. How do we expand this so it encompasses the teams we are part of? What does 'sharing' look like and how should we go about it? Well, first it's worth acknowledging that there is no perfect or right way. There is no exact science to this, and any attempt to create formulas is, I think, a defence against the vulnerability inherent in sharing and opening up difficult topics. Each team is unique and what suits them will be different from what another group needs. Consider the difference between a team of paramedics and a team of teachers; a team of accountants in a huge firm compared to a team in an early stage start-up; introverts compared to extraverts, not to mention any cultural differences that may exist. Building awareness, cultivating emotional intelligence and taking space to reflect, checking in with yourself and risking failure are all important here.

Below I outline four specific suggestions – team dynamics, group check-ins, connecting as humans, and challenging conversations – for how you can create the space to share and really connect in your workplace. This is followed by two exercises that I use a lot with clients: Co-active listening and creating 'Your Lifeline'.

Team Dynamics

If you work as part of a team, it may be valuable to take some space to quietly reflect on your team's dynamics. Perhaps conflict isn't an issue for you, but something else is? You may wish to ask a trusted colleague for their perspective – particularly if they are not part of the team, as it is often hard to see what's happening when we're too close to the action. Or you might want to invite your team to do a team survey (even talking about doing a survey can bring up some interesting material). It could also be productive to reflect on the pivotal moments in the team in the last few years. Use the 3D Teams model to help you think this through:

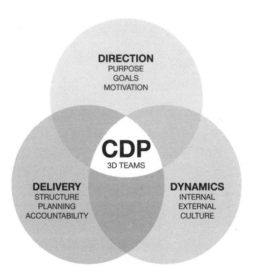

3D Teams model

Think and discuss your team through each of the nine lenses. For example, do you have a clear, agreed sense of purpose? Is it clear who is accountable for delivering what and why? What is the culture you are trying to create?

Exploring team dynamics and looking at what's happening

beneath the surface – what we at CDP refer to as 'working deep' – necessitates venturing into uncomfortable waters at different times. Find a suitable time to acknowledge out loud to your team that conflict is welcome and is part of what makes a team productive, and that many teams try to avoid this. Co-create some ground rules for healthy conflict, such as not making personal attacks; a commitment to accountability alongside freedom of speech; and the clearing up of any misunderstandings as and when they arise.

Depending on your role, consider the rules in your team or organisation; write them down on your own and as part of a team-wide exercise. What emerges will be fascinating. Give yourself and everyone on your team permission to say previously unacknowledged things and remind people – especially yourself – that daring to hear and voice what feels uncomfortable will ultimately benefit everyone. If left unsaid, these things are quietly in control, dictating what is and is not allowed; only by doing what one of my former clients calls 'saying the thing' can its grip on us lessen. Publicly saying that you welcome conflict, challenging conversations and controversy can be extremely powerful for the people who work under you, allowing everyone to breathe a sigh of relief. Teams that permit healthy conflict tend to solve problems quickly and with fewer issues; they have lively, stimulating meetings; they speak directly to the critical issues rather than tiptoe around them and, as Google discovered, have higher commitment and engagement, and perform better.

ASK YOURSELF: *What is allowed or permitted in my team? What is prohibited, either overtly or implicitly? Who set these rules, when and why? What are they trying to protect from happening? Are they really necessary now?*

Group check-ins

Creating space to share takes time. It is an investment, but one that will pay off in increased safety, trust and therefore performance. Because of the nature of what it addresses – the emotions and psychological inner world – it isn't neat and tidy like an Excel spreadsheet or a company policy or procedure. Sometimes it is messy, and it can be tempting to think it is more efficient to repress any uncomfortable material and just keep going. And sometimes, it *is* more efficient to do this. But only ever temporarily, and at a real cost

We don't all have the time or resources for group awaydays to build rapport and deepen the level of psychological safety in our teams, so what can we do on a more day-to-day basis to share more and build safety and trust? We start each team meeting at our company CDP with a quick 'check-in' and finish with a 'check-out'. Since none of us are mind readers, and since things happening in our personal lives can have a huge impact on our productivity, taking a few minutes to hear everyone is enormously beneficial. While it takes a bit more time in the short-term, ultimately it saves time as relationships deepen and collaboration improves.

Decurion, one of the world's leading organisations when it comes to developing its people, also puts the inner lives of its employees in bounds rather than out of bounds as a way of acknowledging that one's full humanity is welcome, and indeed required, if we are to do the best work we're capable of. As such, they too conduct regular check-ins and check-outs at the beginning and end of meetings. The chairs get arranged in a large circle, enabling everyone to see everyone else's faces. As the meeting begins, whoever wants to speak starts by saying their name – not because their colleagues don't know it, but as a tangible reminder that people are human first and employees second. They then check in, sharing whatever they need to in order to be able to be fully present. They might voice a physical state, an emotion, something that's happening in their life which they want, or need, to voice in order to bring themselves fully to the room, or they may say how they intend to make use of the meeting to help them achieve one of their development goals – e.g. contribute more in areas outside their expertise. COO Bryan Ungard emphasises that the point of the check-in is not to follow a script, but to engage people fully and authentically. Check-outs are briefer than check-ins but are seen as just as non-negotiable. They offer people a chance to create closure, ask for support, or share anything else to allow them to end well – to an extent, the artificial boundary between the work self and the real self is dissolved through this practice.

We are complex beings and our behaviour and interpersonal dynamics often defy compartmentalisation. Practices like check-ins give us a chance of surfacing some of that complexity before things get as bad as they were for Beata's team, when remedial action became necessary. As her story demonstrates, even when a team appears to be doing all the right things, there might be some cracks present, and those cracks – such as Beata's feelings of being out of her depth, the underperforming, and the comment by the most junior member of her team – can indicate to us what might be going on.

Once all this became overt, things shifted. Though a good leader in some respects, Beata was forced to face her anxieties about conflict and to come to terms with the fact that not knowing how to tolerate or navigate conflict had begun to suck the life out of her team.

Connecting as humans

If you lead a team, you should also try to get people together in both formal and informal ways. I've known leaders who take their team for pizza once a month, fund team lunches once a week, celebrate big wins and get together to learn from mistakes. Make work human. You won't be alone in doing this; many innovative, creative and wildly successful businesses are now doing this. The technology start-up Unbounce gives every employee $500 annually to spend with colleagues outside the office, while Warby Parker's famous 'lunch roulette' randomly selects colleagues to eat lunch together.

You can also build space to relate into the working day, for example by implementing a Daily Huddle, a quick but mandatory, absolutely non-negotiable fifteen minute meeting that takes place early in the morning. Each day a different chairperson is selected to direct the meeting, and in turn each person shares 'one good thing' (something fun, uplifting, positive or just plain good that's happened in the past twenty-four hours), what they're working on that day, anything they're stuck on and anyone they need to meet with later in the day. This deceptively simple format has been tried and tested by many companies and teams, including virtual ones, and it has multiple benefits: it is obligatory to attend, which establishes it as a team ritual, cementing it in people's minds; it demands clarity from people about what they are working on and where they are stuck; and it invites everyone to get to know each other a little bit more each day in the sharing of one good thing.

Creating space to share and truly connect can feel awkward at first. Many 'Culture First' companies, including global leaders such as Airbnb and Zappos.com, acknowledge that putting the organisation's culture front and centre requires dedicating time during and outside working hours to nurture and strengthen the relationships at the heart of the organisation. Airbnb's communication philosophy aims to engage everyone in the company in honest, two-way dialogue. After a company survey suggested that things weren't as open or honest as the company would like, one of the founders, Joe Gebbia, introduced the idea of 'elephants, dead fish and vomit'. Elephants were the unacknowledged 'elephants in the room', dead fish the things in the past that people still held onto, while vomit represented people's occasional need to just get stuff off their chest once in a while. Airbnb also enlivens its company culture with pop-up celebrations for birthdays, anniversaries, or baby showers, as well as themed events.

ASK YOURSELF: *What can I do in collaboration with my team that will help us all feel more connected, fully committed and deeply engaged?*

Challenging Conversations

You will recall that I used this exercise with Beata's team. It allows teams and groups, or even pairs, to try and surface buried conflict. It is a process that stops our normal rushed, defensive interactions and creates the space for us to go deeper into how we feel and what we need from others. It is the exercise I do that is always the most moving and cathartic. I literally have never used it without someone, at some point, crying or getting very close to crying (but in a good way). It's deceptively simple and you could use it today – with a colleague, your partner or even one of your children.

One person starts by going through the list of questions below, coming up with their ten answers. Then the other does the same. Then both people answer the final question through discussion. You can ask questions once they've finished, but don't interrupt until each person has answered all ten questions:

1. What do I think we are really talking about? (The real, uncomfortable truth not the surface version)

2. Why do I think we haven't talked about this properly before?

3. What am I feeling about this?

4. What am I thinking about this?

5. Why do I care about this?

6. What will happen if I do nothing?

7. What's my contribution to the way things are?

8. What do I want to happen now?

9. What will I do?

10. What am I asking you to do?

(Together) What do we commit to doing?

ASK YOURSELF: *With whom could I have a challenging conversation today. And if I don't have one, why not?*

Co-Active Listening

The Co-Active Coaching model of listening addresses three different levels at which it is possible to listen. These are not only helpful for managers, but for anyone working with other people. Level I listening is internal listening, paying most attention to your own thoughts, feelings and agendas, rather than the other person. In a business context, this might mean only paying attention to the parts of what someone is saying that help you tick the necessary boxes you are trying to tick. Sadly, this is all too common in my experience, but it will not create a psychologically safe environment because people know when you're not paying full attention. Level II listening is called focused attention, and involves shutting everything else that's going on out of your mind and giving the person you're listening to your undivided attention – even if it's just for a minute or two. To get a sense of Level II listening, imagine a mother's attention on her newborn or someone listening to their best friend telling them some really serious news. At Level II the listening is one-way: you are completely focused on the other person. Level III listening (called global listening in Co-Active Coaching) involves listening to the other person's words while being aware of tone, body language, subtext, emotion and energy, plus your own thoughts and feelings, plus the space between you. You 'soften the focus' and pay attention to what isn't said, as well as what is.

Creating your Lifeline

The full assessments I specialise in take four hours (longer in the case of some senior executive assessments), and a large part of that is the telling of the person's own personal and professional story, their 'lifeline'. Even when I'm coaching rather than assessing, I always want to start by hearing this. Sometimes, if the coaching programme or practicalities don't allow for a four-hour session, I will try and speed things up by asking the client to do some preparatory work beforehand, filling in their lifeline on a piece of flip-chart paper. This is designed to capture the important points in someone's life. People who complete one invariably say that they have found it surprising and useful.

I also use the lifeline when I am doing team awaydays. I gather the participants the night before for an informal dinner. Rather than just let them chat, I use this exercise to create a deeper understanding and empathy between people. I ask everyone to bring their lifeline to dinner and people then take turns sharing these. It is incredibly moving and usually results in a few tears and some hugs. I did it once with a very hard-bitten team from the subsidiary of a FTSE 10 company in a private dining room in Gleneagles, and when one of the participants revealed he'd been adopted and then bullied by his adopted father the whole room fell silent, and everyone had to dab at their eyes. They'd all worked with this guy for years and no one knew this part of his history. He had been hesitant to share it but emailed me the following week saying it was one of the best things he'd ever done. He'd gone home and told the full story to his wife and children, something he'd never done before.

But you don't need to share your lifeline for it to be valuable, just doing it can create a deeper understanding of your own journey. Here's how.

This exercise encourages you to think about your personal and professional life journey in a deeper way. First, draw a long, horizontal axis across the middle of a suitable piece of paper e.g. flip chart paper (A4 is fine if that's all you have). The right end of the axis is the present, the other end of the line is your earlier life. Divide the line up into five-year chunks. The top of the vertical axis represents positives and the bottom negatives. Your axes should look roughly like this:

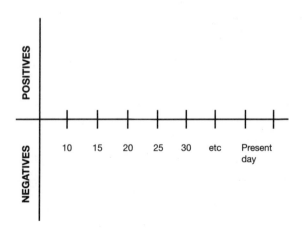

Now draw three lines relating to the following three areas:

○ Your success in your work life.
○ Your happiness in your work life.
○ Your happiness in your personal life.

Label the highs, lows and plateaus with what was happening at the time. I have deliberately asked you to draw two lines about your work life. While achievement often brings happiness, try also to think about the type of work or environment that you enjoy the most or least. What I want you to tap into is what you find intrinsically motivating as well as what you are good at. To bring your line to life you might want to annotate it with photos, quotes, drawings, memories or any important triggers to help you remember and focus in on the key events that have shaped the person you are. Feel free to share the process with those important to you.

When drawing your lines, think about the following questions:

○ What are the chapters in my life?
○ What are the major turning points? How did I change? Are there times where I have appeared to change but haven't really?
○ What are the dominant patterns or themes in my life? What is the story running through my life?
○ Who has been important to me in my life? In what way have they been important?
○ What are the principle reasons that explain why I am the way I am?
○ When have I performed at my peak? What contributed to this performance? (Divide factors in aspects of yourself and environmental aspects.)
○ When have I performed least effectively? What contributed to this performance?
○ When was the best time for me professionally?
○ When has been the toughest time professionally?

○ When was the best time for me personally?

○ When has been the toughest time personally?

I would suggest that you take a little time out now to complete one of your own. Better still, see if you can get your team to set aside some time, a working lunch, say, for you all to bring your lifelines and share them.

CHAPTER 6

Space to Relate

Amir and His Time in the Doghouse

LESSON: *However many strengths you have, you must create the space to build rich relationships to be truly successful.*

I WAS ASKED TO COACH Amir because, despite his massive potential, he had an Achilles heel that was preventing him realising his lifelong ambition – to be the Managing Partner of his prestigious City law firm.

Amir had several strengths. He worked incredibly hard, could process huge amounts of information quickly, and had unerring judgement about how hard to push and when to settle, and a presence that combined silky charm with a hint of menace. He had been a key rainmaker in his prestigious City law firm since joining it after law school, and had a fearsome reputation in the international legal world. If you were a beleaguered corporation – or ultra-high net worth individual – you could turn to Amir and feel you were in the safest of hands. Everyone respected him. Many feared him. Very few, it seemed, liked him.

When he was just a regular partner that didn't really matter. The occasional complaint about rudeness was a small price to pay for all the fees he brought in. Besides, the junior associates who found him too much to take steered clear and he built a tight group, 'Amir's Army', who felt challenged and stretched by him, and offered him unswerving loyalty.

His bulldozing methods raised more eyebrows once he won a coveted place on the firm's management committee, but even there his ability to cut through bullshit was valued, and the outgoing managing partner, Alison, had been equally tough when she had to be. It was she who had been forced to explain to him that what he saw as his anointment as her successor had hit some obstacles. While no one doubted his abilities, enough people had voiced reservations about him to suggest that he wasn't going be the shoo-in for a position he'd assumed would be his. He had managed to join several exclusive clubs as he climbed the ladder, some old-school gentleman's clubs and some newer, flashier establishments. He had never been refused entry. Now, here he was, in danger of being blackballed by his own firm.

He was furious. He was even angrier when Alison suggested that some coaching might help, which might at least show that he was willing to listen to what people were saying. After he refused, she showed some of her own, more hidden steel to make it clear that if he wanted her job, he had no option. Which is how he came to be sitting, glowering, across from me. I started by asking him to tell me his story. He kicked off with talk of law school, but I gently insisted we start earlier.

'If I am to understand Amir the top lawyer, I need to understand Amir the man, and part of that is about how you were shaped – your earliest influences.'

'You mean Mum and Dad?' he asked, grimacing. 'You can count out Dad before we start.'

'How come?'

His tale was tragic but not, alas, that unusual in its psychological fundamentals. His father had been an immigrant who had never quite been the success he wanted – and pretended – to be. Various failed businesses and financial scrapes with relatives had made him flee to the other side of the country, and as Amir turned from high-achieving schoolboy to growing teen, his dad faded out of his life. He had seen him once, in the last ten years, for a drink, which had lasted ten minutes and, as Amir put it, started with the usual bullshit and then the usual running away. He paused in his story.

'Mum was OK, though. A bit of a doormat, if I'm honest. You know, weak, and a worrier. Did her best, though, to hold it together for us, me and my sister.'

'Do you see her much?'

For the first time, the angry scowl he'd shown since I gathered him in reception, slipped a little.

'Not as much as I should,' he mumbled.

The rest of his story was as you might guess. Scholarship to a boys' private school, incredible academic results, some sporting prowess and then his rise through the ranks of his firm. A rocket shooting to the stars, now suddenly stalled, drifting in orbit.

'So, why are you here?'

'I don't have a choice.'

I waited.

'Look, I have to do this. I don't want to.'

'You're perfectly happy with how you are?'

'I didn't say that.'

'In what ways aren't you then?'

He looked at me, properly, for the first time.

'I could make a good lawyer out of you. Well, an OK one,' he deadpanned.

We both smiled. Again, I waited.

'Oh for fuck's sake, I know what they say. Amir the bastard. Amir the cut-throat. They don't mind it when I'm cutting our competitor's throats, do they?'

'You feel what they say is unfair?'

'Yes and no.'

'No?'

He became animated.

'I'm not bloody interested in them, OK? It's work. I have got my clients, my family, my friends. I don't need to be schmoozing people who work for me, right? I save that for people I need to win over.'

'You don't need to win over people at work?'

'Hah! Well, I clearly do or I wouldn't be sitting here would I?'

As our time was coming to an end, I said I wanted him to do

some psychometric tests before our next session. I also said that I thought we'd made good progress and thanked him for being so open. He didn't really respond, just shook my hand and hurried off.

When the results of the psychometrics came back I wasn't surprised. I had used them more as a check on what I was thinking, and also because I find that interpreting test results back to people can open their eyes somewhat. As we will see with Amir, it turned out that they helped him to make a breakthrough.

I had used the Hogan test, which measures many aspects of personality including sociability. As I suspected, Amir's score was low – 17 on a scale of 1 to 100. Incidentally, when I met Dr Robert Hogan, the creator of these tests, we discussed how businesses could best instil high performance. After decades working with some of the most senior leaders in the world, he was blunt: 'Trust. That's the thing. Determines everything. Trust in one's boss predicts the whole range of desirable organisational outcomes: productivity, job satisfaction, and organisational commitment.' It would have been interesting to survey Amir's colleagues about whether they trusted him. I suspect very few would have said yes.

The other test I used, the Firo B, measures inclusion (how much people want to be with other people); affection (how warm they are with others); and control (how much they need to be in charge). Amir's scores were very high on the latter and very low on the first two – 1 out of a possible 9 for both measures. These scores confirmed that Amir was a very self-sufficient person. He didn't need a lot of social interactions. He didn't enjoy being warm towards people beyond a small group, and he didn't want most people getting close to him. Relationally, he largely operated as a lone wolf. When we next met I explained all this to him and he had the grace to accept the results.

'I'm happy with it, though.'

'Well,' I replied, 'I am not so sure. But this isn't therapy, it's coaching, so let's think about the effect of this on your work life. How might such a person be perceived?'

He smiled: 'A bastard.'

'Maybe,' I replied. 'Does that bother you?'

'Not really.'

'It's enough compensation for missing out on being managing partner?'

He looked at me quizzically.

'Look, Amir, no one has told me this but here's what I suspect, you think this coaching is a formality, something to be ticked off, so that your promotion can happen. I suspect you're half right. It is a formality, so that they can refuse you it.'

He stared at me, his eyes hooded and cold. I felt how his adversaries must feel. It didn't feel good.

'But I can help you. I can help you have a real shot at what you want. But only if you want to be helped.'

I waited. He said something, in a whisper. I waited more.

'I do. I will.'

'You mean it?'

'Yes. I do.'

Again the moment of vulnerability was snatched back. He leant forward, his expression becoming aggressive, almost taunting.

'But how?'

I explained how. Coaching isn't always about fundamental underlying change. Maybe it's better if it is. I don't know. That's a philosophical debate we can have one day. To me, it's about helping people be better at work. If that comes about because of some Damascene conversion, some deep personality shift, that's great. If it comes about more tactically, more transactionally, that's fine too. I explained all this to Amir.

He grinned, 'So you're going to help me fake it.'

I smiled back.

'I'd prefer to say I am going to help you compensate.'

Now I have to admit, I wasn't being entirely honest with Amir. I have seen, many times, and hoped it would be true for him, that once someone has opened themselves up to a change of being, even if done cynically, they actually do experience a deeper shift, one that becomes more authentic. They may fake it. But with luck, they fake it until they make it.

When we next met I asked Amir if we could do a stakeholder map.

Stakeholder mapping

This is a great tool that almost anyone can benefit from using. Again, like most of the best tools, it's simple. On a piece of paper you draw a small circle in the middle with your name in it. You then draw other circles around it, which are linked by a line to you at the centre. In each of these circles is the name of a stakeholder. Stakeholder is just jargon for someone you should be connected with. After people have done their initial map, I ask them to create an outer periphery with people they are less in contact with but who they should still have good relationships with. An example would be the woman in Accounts. She may not matter day to day, but she will matter come the year's end, so lay the relationship groundwork now.

After you have drawn the map, rate (on a scale of 1 to 10) how good your relationship with each person is right now (using the 'Professional Intimacy' model in Chapter 4 as a guide) – then rate how good (again out of 10) it should be. Do some soul-searching and be brutally honest. I have done this exercise hundreds of times with people and, almost always, the disparity between what you know is needed and where you are now is sobering.

The ideal score will vary. For example, you should have at least an 8 or 9/10 relationship with your boss, despite any difficulties, whereas your relationship with the person in Accounts who oversees financial control for your business unit may only need to be a 6. The late-night security guard shouldn't be forgotten, but a 2 or 3 will probably suffice. You can then go on to devise strategies for each person, having prioritised the person you should work on most.

One thing that I always stress to people, especially those who feel very busy or are introverts, is that it's actually a lot easier to create a rich connection than people often think. A dinner, lunch or even an hour's chat over coffee can create relatively deep bonds that can sustain a working relationship for a long time. The key is to spend some personal, professionally intimate time with the other person, so you cease to be a name on one of hundreds of emails, or someone they said hello to at a meeting, and become an actual person.

*

My motivation for doing stakeholder mapping with Amir was about opening up the whole idea of relationships in his mind and moving him into a different space. Doing the exercise split him into two. His rational side knew that the people he'd sketched out were important, and that having good relationships with them made sense; after all, his lack of these was precisely – despite his hard work – what was looking to cost him the top job he so desired. His more emotional side, though, couldn't resist being contemptuous of that idea. So as he rated people he would deliver crisp one-liners about what he thought of each of them.

'Utterly useless ... Wanker ... Couldn't argue his way out of a paper bag ... Stupid tart ... Empty suit ... Arse-licker.'

'Wow,' I said, 'Joe in research must have really done something to upset you.'

He looked at me, surprised. 'No ... Why?'

'Well, you seem so angry and scathing about him.'

He paused for thought. 'Oh, give me a break, it's just how I talk.'

He had particularly singled out Norma, one of the junior secretaries in his team. Nearing retirement and lowest in the pecking order, she sat below his PA and the team's senior secretary. His wishes would mostly reach her via them, but occasionally he had to speak to her direct.

'She's such a wet blanket, even her name annoys me. You should see her desk. Little knitted bits of crap everywhere, and about a hundred pictures of her bloody dogs. Two ugly little terriers. You'd think they were her kids, the silly cow. Plus she's useless. Always slow, never takes initiative. I'd sack her but for some reason they won't let me.'

After he'd finished his rant, I said, 'I think, Amir, it is possible, that this level of anger and contempt is not actually about these people at all, least of all some lonely elderly lady and her dogs.'

His arrogant look faltered slightly.

I took my chance.

'Now Amir, I know you a bit by now and I know that what I am about to ask you to do is a bit weird, but will you have a go?'

He looked sceptical.

'It's just an experiment.'

He sighed, 'OK.'

'What I want to do is lead you through a visualisation …'

Visualisations

These are a way of tapping into our unconscious minds and bringing things to our attention that our rational 'watchful' minds may not want us to know. The technique is very simple and anyone can do it. It's not 'hypnotism', although, done properly, you do enter a light trance, and feel deeply relaxed. Here's how I make people ready.

Sit comfortably in a chair, with both feet flat on the floor and your arms supported in your lap or on the armrests. Close your eyes. Begin to breathe slowly, consciously and deeply, in through the nose and out through the mouth. As you do so, let yourself relax. Allow your shoulders to drop and then soften your stomach, bottom and legs, letting go of any tension. After ten or so breaths, let your breathing return to normal. Notice if any thoughts creep in, and just allow them to pass by as if they were clouds in a breezy sky. You are now ready to address a particular question you'd like to shed light on.

There's nothing stopping you from trying this yourself and simply thinking about some issue or dilemma you have and seeing what comes up.

★

When Amir was ready I asked him to tell me what he saw.

'Nothing. A blank. Greyness.'

'OK. Now, look out into that space and tell me what reaction you have to the idea I am about to mention. It could be a thought, a feeling, a bodily sensation. Whatever you experience, tell me. Try and describe it. Now take a few more deep breaths.' I paused. 'OK, now imagine that another person appears. What happens to you?'

'Who is it,' he asked, his voice sounding a bit dreamy.

'Anyone, no one in particular. Just a generic person. Someone else, other than you.'

He took a deep sigh, and leant back.

'What happened?'

'I ummm ... I felt invaded, he, it's a he, he's too close.'

'Try and stay with it. What's happening now?'

'I feel bothered, messed with ...' He waved his hand in front of him, as if pushing something away.

When leading visualisations, I often find that the first reaction, while meaningful, covers up a deeper, more fundamental reaction.

'What might you be feeling, underneath that "bother"?' I asked.

He flinched. Then grimaced.

'What, what is it Amir?'

'It ... It doesn't make sense ...'

'What doesn't?'

'I umm ... I feel ...' His voice dropped to a whisper. 'I feel frightened.'

'OK, do you feel safe?'

'Yes, yes, I'm OK. It's just not pleasant. Really not pleasant.'

'OK. Well, let that figure back off or fade away. Has that happened?'

'Yeah, yeah, it's happening ...'

'Have they now gone completely?'

'Yes, yes, it's all OK now.'

'Now feel the sensations of you sitting in the chair here, and the sounds of the room, and take some deep breaths.'

I waited.

'Then, when you are ready, open your eyes.'

After a few moments he opened his eyes. He looked puzzled, and still a bit scared. It was time for an interpretation: a statement that explains what is happening, or has happened. A key insight, if you like. Some coaches prefer to couch these as questions, but if I feel I am on to something, both intellectually and also in my gut, I will just say what I am feeling. Other times, I might ask the person what they think something means. You'd be amazed how often they get it bang on the money, as Amir did.

'So, what do you make of that?'

'Well,' he said, looking at me and sounding a bit vulnerable for the first time since I had met him. 'I guess that's what I think of other people. All other people. No wonder I keep my bloody distance.'

I paused while his words sunk in, for both of us.

'I think that's right,' I eventually said. 'What your dad did, and your mum to a lesser extent, was teach you that other people were trouble, burdens, unreliable. If you come to believe that, it's no wonder you'd decide to keep away. That was a perfectly sensible coping mechanism to deal with those people, but not ...' I paused again and we finished the thought together, '... not everyone.'

'I fucking hated him, but there's a period before that which I never think about. It's weird, I know it's there but it almost isn't. I will it away. There was a period when I didn't hate him, I loved him, and I wanted him to love me. But he was such a pain, so angry, so moody, that I couldn't get close to him, in fact, a lot of the time I was scared of him ...'

He was beginning to tear up.

'You took that idea, that people had to be fended off, otherwise they would scare you, and let you down, with you through life. But it isn't what everyone is like.'

'It isn't what Sandy's like,' he said, referring to his wife.

'No, you let Sandy in, somehow she proved herself.'

He smiled at that. 'You should ask her! She'd say it took a while. I finished with her three times. She said I was a nightmare.'

I paused.

'Yes, you were a nightmare. You *are* a nightmare.'

He took a really deep breath.

'Look, our time's up, but reflect on all that, and let's talk about it again when we next meet. If something comes up that upsets you, you can call and we can talk before then, OK?'

He didn't call (I hadn't expected him to). After all he was a tough, resilient guy, but at our next session, for the first time ever he wasn't late, in fact he was sitting in reception twenty minutes early.

As soon as the door closed on our room he started talking excitedly.

'Last time was really interesting, right, I talked to Sandy about it and she said it's spot on, that's what I'm like.'

He went on to give some examples from earlier in his life, and from his marriage. Then his energy subsided and he looked directly at me.

'I guess I am wondering what we do about it, though?'

'Well, here's the idea. What we discovered last time was what in my jargon I call a core pathogenic belief, or CPB.'

I went through all that with Amir. We then spent some time reviewing what had happened in our last session, and what he had thought and felt. I then said I was going to leave the room for five minutes and see if he could come up with an articulation of his CPB. I handed him a marker, pointed to the flip chart, and left. The phrase has to come from the heart. It can't be my language, it has to be theirs.

'Be bold, be true. Don't pull your punches. Tell it like it is.'

Five minutes later I came back in and he was sitting quite still in his chair. On the flip chart were various sentences with words crossed out and added. After the jumble, he'd written, confidently and clearly (I apologise for the language):

I think other people are cunts, so I get being a cunt in first.

He looked up at me and smiled a shy smile. It was as if a different Amir was emerging. I smiled back. He held up his hand. We high-fived.

'Wow,' I said.

'Indeed.'

He smiled again, this time sadly. 'And who'd want a cunt as Managing Partner?'

We sat in silence for a while.

'OK,' I eventually said. 'I'm going to leave you for another five minutes. See if you can come up with the antidote. The belief you want to have, even if it's not fully there yet.'

When I returned, the flip chart paper was blank. He was standing looking perturbed and pensive. I wondered what had gone wrong. Then, with a smile and a flourish, he pulled the paper up and revealed this:

People are OK, I'm OK, stop being such a dick.

I laughed out loud, and again, we high-fived.

We talked about what he might do to remind himself of this new, more realistic, helpful mantra. In a typically ballsy move he said he was going to have it as his smartphone screensaver.

Though it would take time to be fully digested and acted upon, now that we had dealt with this enormous semi-conscious blocker to Amir behaving differently, we could start the detailed work of building his relationships.

Over the next few sessions we talked about what he might do. He bravely decided he was going to open up to people. Explain what he'd learned in coaching, ask forgiveness, and ask if they would give him a second chance. Many people were sceptical, thinking he was just playing them to get his promotion. Others were more receptive. Over time he worked through the people on his stakeholder map. As we neared his final session I noticed that there was one person he hadn't tried to interact with. Norma, one of his secretaries, the one with the dogs he found so annoying.

'Well, she's like third down in my support staff,' he began justifying himself. 'I mean is it even …'

As he was about to say 'worth it' he caught my expression, and laughed.

'All right, all right, lay off, I'll do it.' He looked reflective. 'You know if I'm being really honest, I've been avoiding doing it with her. No idea why.'

I decided to hazard a guess. 'Does she remind you of anyone?'

'Umm, no. I don't know many people like poor old Norma. I can honestly ...'

He stopped abruptly and slammed his fist down on the arm of his chair.

'Jesus. You're right. Jesus. My bloody Mum.'

We let it sink in.

He shook his head, 'Fuck me.'

'You know what to do.'

A couple of days later, for the first time, in what had been a rather intense coaching assignment, Amir called my mobile and left a voicemail:

'It's me, Amir. Look I did it. I went up to Norma and sat on the edge of her desk. She nearly had a heart attack. I smiled and picked up a particularly garishly framed photo of the dogs, and said, "Who are these fellas then?" She looked startled but then reeled off their names, ages, favourite food. I thought she wasn't going to shut up. But then she said, "Oh, listen to me going on, you've got work to do, off you go." My assistant was looking over, couldn't believe her eyes. Anyway, you'll never bloody guess what happened. I'm just forwarding you an email. You won't fucking believe it, have a read and call me back.'

I checked my inbox and clicked on his email. It was a forwarded one from Alison, the current Managing Partner, who had sent him for the coaching.

FROM: Alison B—, Managing Partner
TO: Amir K—, Litigation Partner
SUBJECT: Change?

Hi Amir,

I just wanted to ask you to come and see me to talk about the future. It seems to me that there is now a chance to progress things. I have been watching you for the last few months and have to admit I've seen someone who has changed quite a bit. There are far fewer outbursts, far less noise (informal and formal) getting back to me about your behaviour. It's a black joke, but one of the other partners asked if maybe you'd had some terrible health scare. I've also heard the words, 'considerate' and 'collaborative' used in connection with you, both a first as far as I can remember. Of course some people are suspicious but yesterday something happened that made me think that whatever is happening has to be real. You won't know this but Norma Blackwell works here because she is an old school friend of my mum. Well, our visits to her in the Hospice overlapped last night and we had a little chat. She mentioned you'd been asking her about her dogs, and even said she could bring them in to the office one Friday (which incidentally I think is against our health and safety policy). Nonetheless, I thought as she bustled away, if Amir is chatting with Norma about her dogs then something really has changed. Pop by later and let's talk.

Best,

Al

Making love not war: Creating Space to Relate

'When dealing with people, remember you are not dealing with creatures of logic, but creatures of emotion.'

Dale Carnegie

If Amir could have chosen which chapter his story would have featured in, a chapter on connecting and relationships would probably have been bottom of his list. Yet it was around relationships where his work lay. First, he had to get to grips with understanding his behaviour and the underlying feelings he had about relationships. After this, he had to set about building his relationships in a new way. While Amir would probably have preferred to be featured in the 'Do' part of this book, presented as someone who was crushing it, it's no accident that he appears here. His story demonstrates that however we feel about other people, we cannot *not* be in relationship with them. If we believe, as Amir did, that people are four-letter words, then that is what we will experience as we interact with them. As he found, it's also often what we end up becoming. This applies whether we believe people are by and large kind, or pathetic, or cold, or annoying. Our perceptions are the baseline for how we interact with the world, and as Amir's story demonstrates, how we view our relationships makes a huge difference to how fulfilling or irritating those relationships are. In the previous two chapters we looked at how we can get in touch with our own emotional reality – and share that with others. This chapter takes those ideas to a deeper level and looks at how we can create the richest relationships possible at our work.

When an organisation starts to struggle, something is usually happening relationally. In their book *Real: The Power of Authentic Relationships*, the clinical counsellors Duane and Catherine O'Kane share their belief that *all* issues are actually relational: we might think we have productivity problems or a problem with morale, but the real issues are relational. For example, mental health issues cost the UK £70bn per year, with 15.8 million work days lost due to stress, anxiety and depression. While many people see this as an intrapersonal issue taking place within the individual alone, the O'Kanes suggest – and I agree – that much of this is actually to do with what's happening between people. Some work issues patently involve relationships: your boss might not pay you as much attention as you'd like, your team may not have gelled, a new colleague may have joined who you're threatened by, you may feel your peers exclude you or you might be weary of office politics. But many other issues are actually relational ones in disguise. They might look like lethargy, lack of motivation, low engagement, underperforming, being close to burnout, overworking, high turnover, high absenteeism and so on, but underlying those symptoms the root cause is often problems with one or another relationship. Maybe right now at work you feel yourself holding back and not giving your best? Maybe your direct reports are holding back, and you are not getting the best out of them? What relationship issues could be playing a part in these problems?

I once worked with an MD who ran the biggest of several UK regions for a FTSE 100 household name. As we discussed his development areas, he wrote down on a flip chart that he wanted to move from a leader who 'gets on OK with most people' to a leader who 'as well as doing the day job builds deeper relationships.' I had to gently rebuke him. For someone at his level, building deep relationships *was* the day job. There was nothing more important. Everything else stemmed from that. Once he thought about it he ruefully agreed. This isn't just true for senior executives, your relationships at work – whatever your role – are the bedrock of what you can achieve. I used to work in a consultancy where there was always competition for the best rooms to work in and see clients. My colleagues were always a bit mystified (and annoyed) that I always seemed to get allocated one of the large, airy corner offices. What they didn't know is that every time I went on an assignment abroad I would bring back a little present – a keyring from Moscow, a fancy glass perfume bottle from Saudi Arabia, a small carved tortoise from Africa – for the receptionist, who was the person who allocated the rooms. There was a tale told of Robert Maxwell, the overbearing media tycoon. At a fancy dinner he asked the waiter for an extra bread roll, the waiter apologised and said that he'd see if there was one left over once he had served everybody. Maxwell grew angry and boomed the inevitable rebuke, 'Don't you know who I am?' Prompting the waiter to respond with a whispered, 'Don't you know who I am sir? The man in charge of the bread rolls.'

While every relationship is unique, healthy relationships share a number of characteristics that can be 'tested for' and developed if they're found to be lacking. These are identified in the Professional Intimacy model I have referenced before (see p. 95). They include empathy, openness, authenticity, trust and boundaries. Let's look at each of these in turn.

Empathy is quite simply the ability to put yourself in someone else's shoes, to get a sense of what they might be thinking, feeling and experiencing – to see things from a different perspective. This sounds simple but takes quite a lot of emotional maturity to be able to do well, since it often requires that we suspend our preconceptions and judgements towards another person and make understanding this other person and their experience as important if not more important than our own.

At Ray Dalio's hedge fund, Bridgewater, the culture is characterised by its **openness**, built around the principle of total transparency. If you consider yourself to be a fairly open person, consider this: at Bridgewater, there is no such thing as a 'private' meeting since anyone can see who is in any meeting at any time, and every single meeting, whether internal or with clients, is recorded and the files are made available to anyone in the company who wants them (excluding proprietary client information). Openness might seem antithetical to how many businesses have traditionally operated, but it's actually a secret weapon for businesses – and leaders – wanting to get ahead. In a world characterised by KPIs, targets, baselines and other often mind-numbing statistics, taking a brief moment to acknowledge another human being in your daily business can really, *really* make a difference. Openness can mean many things: sharing your ideas in a meeting rather than hiding and protecting them; looking a colleague or client in the eye and smiling; sharing aspects of yourself that feel slightly vulnerable, such as your sense of humour. Openness can also just take the form of asking your colleagues questions about themselves. I quoted Dale Carnegie at the beginning of this section. He also said, 'You can make more friends in two months by becoming interested in other people than you can in two years by trying to get other people interested in you.'

Authenticity has become a buzzword in recent years, and for good reason; we crave authenticity in all our relationships, and work is no exception. Authenticity, as Amir found, can feel frightening. It requires us to let go of our safe, impenetrable business personas and to bring our whole selves to the table – quirks, imperfections, emotions and all. Doing this might bring up old feelings, or it might throw us into uncertain waters in which we experience new feelings. Either way, it can feel a bit risky leaving the metaphorical masks and armour behind. Understandably, many businesses get a bit nervous about this, but there is a fast growing movement of people and business leaders who recognise that welcoming authenticity has many tangible benefits. Authenticity has the potential to make loyalty and engagement skyrocket. For example, a Gallup study found that 87 per cent of workers worldwide feel emotionally disengaged, and yet it's clear in my mind that even one moment of authenticity can really brighten someone's day. Authenticity doesn't mean blatantly ignoring or disrespecting agreed business codes or ethics, and neither does it mean sharing every personal and private detail of our lives at work; it simply means that we do our best not to deliberately hide parts of ourselves that could actually add something brilliant and enriching to our experience of being at work. Authenticity sometimes means mustering the courage to be ourselves in a world that tells us to be anything but, and choosing to practise authenticity will sometimes feel challenging as we push back against the strong urge to fit in at any cost. Authenticity allows us to bond with others at certain moments, while other times it leaves us feeling more alone. Either way, people know that they are dealing with someone real. As the philosopher Alain de Botton once wrote, 'Intimacy is the capacity to be rather weird with someone – and finding that that's OK with them.'

Trust is an interesting one, particularly because in many business settings, people are decidedly wary of and guarded around each other. I like this simple trust test, which I came across a number of years ago. See if you can answer yes to the following two questions. First, would you buy a used car from this person? Second, if something happened to you, would you leave your kids with this person? These questions cut to the heart of what trust is about – your belief that another person's intention is to deal fairly with you and does not intend to rip you off, and your belief that they care enough about what (or who) you care about to take care of it (or them).

Strong relationships are also characterised by clear **boundaries**. These set the 'rules' – what's in and what's out. Clearly an aspect of this would be inappropriate behaviour, but it could also be subtler than that. For example, if someone is going through a difficult divorce, they may or may not want to talk about it, however close to you they feel. Rather than hazard a guess, or taking the safe option of saying nothing, you can set the boundaries using the kind of clear communication we have been discussing. For example, saying something like: 'Hey John, I know things are tough at home at the moment, if you want to talk about it let me know' might elicit the response, 'I'd love to actually, it's weird never to mention it when we get on so well.' Or it might be met with, 'Actually Michelle, I'd really rather not talk about that at all, but thanks for asking.'

Boundaries also relate to self-esteem. Whatever someone says about you shouldn't easily penetrate your boundaries – you don't need to take on board other people's negativity. Try seeing yourself as someone in control of what you allow to get to you. If too much gets through, imagine yourself having a tougher boundary – a suit of armour, say, that repels bad stuff from other people.

Finally, boundaries link to accountability and help us clarify what is our responsibility and what isn't. They help us build strong relationships through being honest, straightforward and direct with the people we're dealing with. When *I can get that to you by Friday morning* means *I can get that to you by Friday morning*, trust and rapport strengthen; when however we try to please people by never saying no, or do not accurately assess what's on our plate, or are disorganised and scatty, and *I can get that to you by Friday morning* means *by Wednesday next week*, or *I meant <u>next</u> Friday morning*, it can really knock the quality of our relationships, as Tamsin finds in Chapter 8.

How we **communicate** with others is also crucial – both verbally and non-verbally – and determines the quality and depth of our relationships to a large degree. Our communication styles tend to reflect how we perceive and feel about people deep down; consider the example of someone who is constantly apologising to other people, or the person who never makes eye contact, or the person who talks incessantly and doesn't ask other people questions, or the person who uses humour so much that you never really get to know them. Communication can make or break a relationship.

The tricky thing with relationships is that the characteristics described in the Professional Intimacy model can be as elusive as the snitch in a game of Quidditch at Hogwarts. They certainly need as much effort to find and keep.

We are thrown into relationships at birth, and regardless of how loving or well intended our upbringing, we have all been 'fucked up' to some extent, to quote the wonderful poet Philip Larkin in his ode to parenting, 'This Be the Verse'. When it comes to relationship issues, there are literally thousands of strange and wacky human behaviours. No doubt you've witnessed (and exhibited) a few in your lifetime. Triggers for relational anxiety are everywhere: anytime we encounter leadership or followership, our brains kick into gear, connecting the dots between the present situation and all the times in the past when we've encountered this kind of situation. The same goes for making mistakes, taking risks, facing change, uncertainty or the unknown, or embarking on beginnings or approaching endings.

No two people are alike, but many of our worst work behaviours can be summed up by the following quote from the book *An Everyone Culture* by Robert Keegan and Lisa Laskow Lahey. At work, they write, 'Most people are doing a second job that no one is paying for … covering up their weaknesses, managing other people's impressions of them, showing themselves to their best advantage, playing politics, hiding their inadequacies, hiding their uncertainties, hiding their limitations. Hiding.' When we hide, we present only certain aspects of who we are, often shutting the personal away, making it private and inaccessible while we're at work, perhaps only letting our defences down (a bit) when we are at the pub. We live double lives. The skills, qualities and assets that make up these more 'personal' parts of our identity get shelved. At our absolute worst we hide, we lie and we fake our way through the working day. A point echoed by the O'Kanes, mentioned earlier, who have worked with individuals, couples and groups for well over fifty years between them, and who describe three categories into which almost all of our limiting behaviour fits: hiding, pretending and defending.

I have known three of the last four British Prime Ministers and was once lucky enough to be invited for Sunday lunch at Chequers, the Prime Minister's country residence. Over the roast beef the conversation was free flowing, fun and quite personal. After lunch, during more of a working session, the mood shifted, as the then Prime Minister moved back into his 'professional mode'. There was no more joking or emotional connecting, just a cold, intellectual focus on the question in hand. While this shift was understandable up to a point, so defensive was the atmosphere that you could almost feel the life draining out of the room. I certainly don't think it brought out the best in people, however serious the subject.

Amir, too, was a skilful defender. Nobody ever got the chance to get close to him. His brash, rude way with people often offended, and was extremely effective in keeping people at arm's length. We all have mechanisms and strategies for dealing with people, formed in response to the core pathogenic beliefs we make up at different times in our lives. Some of us present very differently to Amir. We might have learned that the world responds well to us when we are sweet, or intellectual, or bold, or funny or seductive. Much of this will depend on the unique circumstances we found ourselves in when we were younger. For many of us, the person we become often mirrors – or contrasts sharply – with an important person in our life who let us down. Amir's relentless achieving stood in stark contrast to his dad's underachieving, and his aggressive manner was formed with his mum's weakness as a backdrop. While many of our personality traits are what make us uniquely ourselves, it's also worth considering the contexts that shaped us – the whens, wheres, whos and whys that influenced the people we became. As Amir found, the behavioural patterns that served us brilliantly in childhood eventually become obsolete or even outright damaging to us as adults, creating the very thing that we initially tried to defend ourselves against. Amir was shocked to realise that, deep down, he was frightened of other people; I'm sure Amir's colleagues would also have been shocked to learn this, since he did 99 per cent of the frightening! Our defences are clever like that. They often cover up the truth so effectively that we're gobsmacked when we discover it.

Some of the forms defending takes include criticism (cleverly putting the focus on someone else's weakness and keeping one's own out of the limelight); stonewalling (in which we go cold on one or more colleagues, quite literally shutting them out); contempt, working in silos; or being outright hostile. Whatever form it takes, the same principle applies: any time people position themselves defensively instead of relating openly and with candour and trust, things start to become difficult. Underneath all defences is the fundamental defence against vulnerability.

There is one further way we can stop ourselves from building richer relationships. It is by thinking that we don't have enough space to talk to people properly, because we are all so busy, something I raised with Amir when we were doing his stakeholder mapping. I find that people who are less naturally relational assume that if they start talking to people it'll never end, and consume all their time, but generally, people will know what's appropriate (just as Norma did). They just like some sort of connection, on a more personal and 'real' level. That will still leave us with our own particular mix of extraversion and introversion, and varying levels of inclusion needs and sociability – which is all fine. The purpose of Amir's story is not to prescribe a certain way of being, but to help you think about how you relate and why, and what you might do differently, given your unique make-up, in your own chosen way. How might you create space to connect with people on a deeper, more real level? As the stakeholder map shows, the pace and depth of these relationships will vary. Making this space is not about being nice – or even available – to everyone. It is about making sure that the relationships that matter are healthy and nurtured.

With the influx of an entirely new generation – a generation who have grown up in a culture deeply immersed in sharing and social media – I think we're going to see a further shift towards employing people not simply for their skills and experience, but for personality, values and cultural fit. Consider again that Gallup finding that up to 87 per cent of workers feel emotionally disengaged from work. It's crystal clear that relationships have the power to be the gateway to a transformed, more engaged, more resilient workforce where people are encouraged to work and play together, to be entrepreneurial and intrapreneurial, to study and learn and fail and try again, not in isolation, but in an engaged, creative, thriving community. Rich, real relationships have the power to transform our levels of satisfaction, fulfilment and creativity. But they can only do this if we open our minds and hearts, risking hurt, risking loss and risking being fully alive. The choice is always the same – to greet and interact with the world from a place of defence, or to show up from a place of love. It's as simple and as difficult as that.

Taking inventory, stepping out of the office and other practical ideas to help you make space to relate

Whether you love being around people or at best merely tolerate them, the one thing you cannot do is divorce yourself from other people – even if you take a break, leave or 'end' a relationship. Very often, a relationship that is 'over' still continues in our mind; have you never found yourself thinking about someone years – even decades – after you've lost touch with them? The other thing to bear in mind is that relationships are like living organisms: they need ongoing attention, time, energy and care. Mastering relationships is a practice, not an event.

Taking inventory

Use the stakeholder mapping exercise and the 'Professional Intimacy' model to audit the quality of the key relationships in your working life. Work out a plan to take you from where each relationship is now to where you want it to be.

To go even deeper you can do what in twelve-step fellowships, such as Alcoholics Anonymous, is described as 'taking inventory'. We can learn a lot about relationships by looking at what's not working, focusing our attention on our contribution rather than the other person's. Take some quiet time to mentally run through all your main day-to-day relationships and notice how you feel as you reflect briefly on each one. If there is any judgement, resistance, discomfort or unease, it might be a sign that you have some work to do – even if it appears to be the other person's behaviour that's 'making' you feel a certain way. The foundation of real emotional accountability is recognising that nobody has the power to *make* you feel anything. If we feel something – hurt, offended, violated, talked down to – it is because on some level we agreed with the other person's assessment of us. That doesn't give anyone the right to do or say what they want; words can sting and actions can wound. But it does emphasise personal responsibility, which – especially when it comes to relationships – our world could do with more of.

Making space to reflect on your relationships can be powerful, as Amir found. You might realise, like he did, that someone you dislike or have a problem with at work subconsciously reminds you of someone from your past (remember how Norma reminded Amir of his mother?). Or you might acknowledge that you're caught up in – and possibly perpetuating – unhelpful relationship dynamics, such as power games, office politics, infighting, gossip, teasing, bullying or people pleasing. You might be hiding, lying, faking, pretending or defending. Acknowledging this doesn't make you a bad person, it simply makes you a person, and a responsible one at that. We rarely want to admit that we have been mean, or lazy, or calculated, or petty. It's much less embarrassing to point out how Sandra in Finance or Tom in Marketing messed up. It's hard and uncomfortable to acknowledge our mistakes and it requires guts, maturity and humility. In short, it requires vulnerable leadership. It might comfort or inspire you to know that at Bridgewater, the following equation is deeply embedded in the minds of every employee, associate and partner: Pain + Reflection = Progress. Take any pain or emotional discomfort stirred up in your work relationships, add a dose of reflection and you will inevitably learn, grow and make progress. If you're in a leadership position of any kind, it's worth acknowledging that your action and inaction may have more of an impact on those around you and the wider relationship system than someone more junior to you.

Once a month, you might want to take some space to reflect

on any key relational issues that you encountered in the previous thirty days. As I said earlier, wherever you find people, you also find unspoken yet powerful psychological content concerning authority, leadership, gender, intimacy, power, control, individuality and togetherness. If something nags at you, or you realise that something happened which isn't resolved, focus on *your* contribution to the upset only – much more easily said than done! Aim to take from it only what's going to help you develop, and clean it up, communicating with the intention of being accountable and kind.

ASK YOURSELF: *What's not working in my work/personal relationships? What am I contributing to the problem? Where am I hiding, lying or faking? What's one step I can take to change this? When will I take it?*

A curveball for leaders – step away from the office

It is incredibly easy in our fast-paced, metrics obsessed world to go for months or years without pausing or making enough space to reflect on what we're doing it all for. This chapter has encouraged you to make space to relate, and part of that, for me, necessitates remembering that there is sacredness in the everyday mundanity that we can all too easily take for granted – and that much of that occurs not in the office or on the road, but at home.

Bronnie Ware worked in palliative care for many years, with patients who had between three and twelve weeks left to live. She found that over and over again, people shared a few key regrets as they looked back on their lives. Sometimes it takes something as final and confronting as coming face to face with our mortality to look at what really matters. In a 2012 article for the *Huffington Post*, Ware reported that the second most common regret was, I wish I hadn't worked so hard. She writes: 'This came from every male patient that I nursed. They missed their children's youth and their partner's companionship. Women also spoke of this regret. But as most were from an older generation, many of the female patients had not been breadwinners. All of the men I nursed deeply regretted spending so much of their lives on the treadmill of a work existence.' There are many caveats and nuances to all of this, and each of us has to decide for ourselves whether we are living to work at the expense of other aspects of our lives. We'll return to the idea of Balance in Chapter 11.

But for now, with regards to the topic of Relate, I'd like you to consider whether this applies to you – not only from your perspective, but from your family's, too. It can often be tricky to challenge what is expected of us by our employer, but any uncomfortable conversation has to be better than looking back and really wishing that you'd been home for family supper at least a few nights a week. So the final 'tool' I offer you in this section is simple: *step away from the office*. You might even use the Professional Intimacy model to throw some light on how your personal relationships are faring. It may not be a pretty sight! Go and connect and create space for the most important people in your life. You will not regret it, and your to-do list will be waiting for you in the morning.

Conclusion

In Part 2 we have looked at three aspects of connecting: checking in (with yourself and others), sharing what is going on for you emotionally, and relating on a deeper level. We have looked at some ideas and models that might stimulate and support you in making your relationships even richer.

There are a multitude of lessons – tuning into yourself; sharing your emotional reality with others; and creating the space to audit and then build the relationships that matter. Above all, though, you must be willing to be vulnerable and take risks, and show up as the 'real' you, albeit with the right professional boundaries.

I named our relationship model 'Professional Intimacy' on purpose so it would raise eyebrows and make people think. There's no doubt in my mind, though, that the right sort of intimacy is both appropriate and necessary between colleagues at work.

Now that we have explored the two foundations to execution, thinking and connecting, we can move on to look at the action that flows from these – Creating Space to Do.

PART 3

Create Space to Do

I T'S NO USE HAVING the best ideas if you can't make them happen. An ability to get things done – to execute consistently and well – is essential to success. While high-quality thinking and connecting with others are necessary prerequisites to doing, there are three further elements required in order to create real impact:

First we have to **Create Space to Plan**. This builds on the decision-making and strategising we discussed in Part 1. If we don't adopt clear goals, and have a well worked out plan to realise them, we will limit what we can achieve no matter how good our ideas or how hard we work. The brothers running Red Technologies are finding that a failure to plan is causing real damage to their business.

Second, we need to **Create Space to Deliver**. This is about making our vision – and plans – a reality and actually getting things over the line. Tamsin doesn't seem able to make the transition from being a 'Jill of all trades' to having the discipline to get on with delivering the few things that really matter.

Finally, for those of us whose job involves leading people, we must **Create Space to Lead**. It is vital that we learn how to deliver through others rather than tending to deliver ourselves. As Yulia discovers, that is about making a fundamental change in who you are and how you behave at work – becoming someone who motivates and empowers those around you, rather than just yourself.

In all three stories in Part 3 we will see how an ability to step back and really master the art (and science) of getting things done is the foundation of real and sustained success.

CHAPTER 7

Space to Plan

The Brothers and Their Failing Magic Show

LESSON: *Having a clear goal (what you want to do) and a clear plan (how you are going to get there) are the prerequisites of executing successfully.*

RED TECHNOLOGIES was a successful company supplying specialist financial software to the City. It had been built up by two brothers: Tom, the archetypal geek, and Darren, a natural born salesman. The company had done very well and grown quickly.

About a year ago, after their 200th employee had joined, the brothers decided they needed a proper HR director. They appointed Philip who, on his arrival, was pretty appalled by the situation. There'd been a culture of, if not outright sexual harassment, then certainly inappropriate banter. This atmosphere hadn't been helped when Darren began dating his PA, only for the relationship to end in tears and her leaving – 'Bloody inevitable,' Tom had commented to Philip. A similar thing had happened a couple of years before, with a new Head of Marketing. The pay scales were a mess, reflecting Tom and Darren's tendency to fix problems by throwing a bit of cash at them, and also their pattern of rewarding their favourites. The engagement scores (how happy and fulfilled the staff were) were very poor. Furthermore there were murmurings among the staff about how the company didn't seem to know where it was going. People didn't have clear goals to work to, and this meant it was hard to prioritise where they put their effort. This had all been reflected in the company's performance. The 20 per cent+ historic annual growth had been dropping for a few years, and this year the company had barely grown at all.

Philip had been a more junior HR guy at a client I'd worked with and we'd kept in touch. Having asked me out to dinner, he was explaining the situation with the air of a man who regretted his decision to take on the job. 'I don't suppose you'd come in for a couple of days to try and help me figure out what to do?' he eventually asked over the dessert.

Two weeks later I was sitting at the back of Red's weekly management team meeting. It was pretty chaotic. There was no agenda, decisions seemed to be taken on a whim and people drifted in and out. Darren dominated, with a mixture of charm and humour that was very seductive. He seemed to pull ideas and solutions out of thin air. The fuel the company ran on was testosterone.

That afternoon I carried out some interviews with key people, as usual reaching across all levels of the company. What became clear was that Red was run like a fiefdom. There were few formal structures, everything was referred to Darren, or, if it was a technical matter, Tom.

This style had worked well when the company was smaller. The brothers could get their arms around the whole thing and people felt connected to them. Today, as one engineer put it to me, 'You wait around for Darren or Tom to notice you and then bask in their attention for a while, then it's like the sun's gone behind a cloud.' Another said, 'I feel rudderless. In my last company we had a clear strategy so we knew where we were going. Here, we're all over the place.'

What the company needed was a more grown-up structure and set of processes, and a more grown-up way for its leaders to run them. I presented these conclusions to the Board, which consisted of Darren, Tom and a few people who'd invested some money in the early days. Darren was polite but dismissive. His angle was that while I understood 'big corporates', I didn't appreciate smaller companies that had to be more agile. I argued back a bit, but at the end of the day, as the Labour politician Gerald Kaufman wrote in his memoirs, 'Advisers advise, Ministers decide.' As I packed up my stuff Philip was apologetic. I waved him off. We had tried.

As I was outside their offices waiting for my taxi I heard a quiet, 'All right mate?' and turned to see Tom. 'Got time for a coffee?'

I cancelled my car. After we settled down in a café around the corner, he said that he'd thought I'd been right, but that Darren doesn't like to admit when he gets things wrong. We had a long chat and as he spoke about Darren and the troubles they'd had setting up the firm, the situation began to make more sense. He also shared his worries about Darren's womanising and inability to settle down. Tom asked whether I'd have another go at talking to Darren.

What became clear when we met a few weeks later was that several things were going on. Over the years Darren had built up both a rational and emotional resistance to the idea of planning. He'd seen how too much planning and deliberation slowed every-thing down in the corporate job he'd left to set up Red. And he'd seen how the plans that he and Tom had originally made had also needed to be ripped up as they built the company in its earliest days. They'd brought in someone to help them do some strategic planning a couple of years before, which hadn't worked out, as they had both felt the person concerned had turned out to be useless.

This is sometimes how pathogenic beliefs are formed. They aren't always a result of formative childhood experiences. They can be the result of an accumulation of experiences, which slowly form into an attitude that, while understandable, isn't the true or whole picture.

In Darren's case, his rational resistance to having clear goals and a strategy to realise them was reinforced by his emotional sense of what being a leader meant, and how he personally provided leader-ship. As he put it, 'Tom's the brains, all I do is sell what he does. I make things happen, solve problems. Make myself useful. My job is pulling rabbits out of hats.' Darren, for all his bombast and bluster, felt inferior to his shy, quieter younger brother. Put at its simplest,

Darren's core pathogenic belief was that if he were to make a clear plan and run things in an ordered, more traditional way, he would lose power. He'd be less important within the company and less needed by Tom.

Darren vastly underestimated what Tom thought of him. We had a three-way session in which I asked each brother to talk about what the other meant to them. It was very moving. In Tom's eyes he'd be nothing without Darren: a nerd sitting at home, tapping on a keyboard in his underpants, eating Pot Noodles. When I mentioned that Darren felt he needed to ensure there was a bit of chaos around so he could keep producing rabbits out of hats, Tom playfully punched his shoulder. 'We're not running a magic show, you berk, we're running a business.' Darren laughed, and I felt a great big wave of relief run over him.

We then moved on to surface some of the things that frustrated each of them about the other. We did this using 'Challenging Conversations' (outlined in Chapter 5), a tool that I often use when I am working with teams. This work left Darren and Phil feeling they'd cleared the air and got a good understanding of what each needed to do going forward.

Sometimes, when an assignment comes to an end, I feel I have said all I have to say. Other times, as in this case, there are other thoughts I have, or interpretations that I could have made. I had a strong feeling that Darren's way of working was tied up psychologically to how he was in his personal life. As well as being a serial seducer of women he was, at heart, a serial start-up founder: happiest in the exciting early stages but less suited to the different pace and long-term commitment of a mature company (or relationship). I also felt that Tom was quietly impressive, and that if he were ever to escape from Darren's shadow, he might actually prove to be the leader the company needed. It might be better either to let Darren go off and start something new, or for him to set up an innovation lab within Red to create and trial new ideas and products. But as I say, I hadn't been brought in to do business consultancy, or psychotherapy, so I kept these thoughts to myself.

In any event, over the next six months, with Philip's help, the brothers revamped their company's culture and ways of working. They started to plan more carefully what they wanted to achieve, adopted some clearer goals and held a company-wide 'strategy day' for the first time ever. All this helped get Red Technologies back on a growth trajectory.

A while afterwards I bumped into Darren at a party.

'Hey, how's it going?' I asked.

He smiled, 'Well, good. I suppose I'd better thank you.' He sounded unconvinced.

'What's the matter?' I asked.

'Honestly?' he replied. I waited.

'Well. Tom's happy. Philip's happy. The staff are happy. But I preferred it before, to be honest. *I* was happier then, you know, pulling those rabbits out of my hat.'

I didn't know what to say.

'Well,' he paused, eyes darting round, looking, I assumed, for a woman to work his charms on, 'Abracadabra, eh?' and whoosh! He was gone.

Can't live with 'em, can't live without 'em: creating the space to plan

'Give me six hours to chop down a tree and I will spend the first four sharpening the axe.'

attributed to Abraham Lincoln

Whether you run a company or not, there are a number of lessons to be learnt from Red Technologies. As strange as it might sound, core pathogenic beliefs can get in the way even when it comes to something as seemingly unemotional as planning. For Darren at Red Technologies, planning equalled powerlessness, so it's hardly surprising he avoided it like the plague. But neglecting planning at Red Technologies had a detrimental impact not only on Darren, Tom and Philip as individuals but also negatively impacted the company as a whole. Tom and Darren had fallen into the common trap of fixing problems in a reactive way, typically by throwing a bit of money at them, but failing to address the underlying factors that had created the issues in the first place. In failing to plan they had fulfilled Benjamin Franklin's famous quote, and had inadvertently 'planned to fail.' They had both fallen into the trap of reacting to whatever immediate situation presented itself, but without an eye on the bigger picture or the overall strategy or the culture they were trying to create.

Their team meetings reflected this. Aimless and with no clear expectations or boundaries around who was expected to attend or what the purpose of the meeting was, it felt like the whole organisation – especially Tom – had made an unconscious decision to defer to Darren's charismatic but structure-less leadership style. Decisions were random, lacking in any kind of overall strategy, and the whole organisation had a feeling of being run by the seat of its pants (at least to the extent that Darren could keep his on).

This can and does happen to many an individual as well as in organisations, and in fact Darren and Tom's story demonstrates how permeable the boundary is between an individual's working style and the culture of the organisation, especially if that individual is in a leadership position.

When working with organisations, I use a very simple model (opposite) that encapsulates all of this. It identifies the three interlocking elements of any high performing organisation.

At one point in my work with Red I had showed this slide to Tom. He laughed ruefully, pointing at the Purpose circle and saying: 'well we had that but I'm not so sure now.' The Culture circle prompted the comment, 'That's all pretty dysfunctional', the Design circle caused him to sigh and say 'and that is just a bloody dog's dinner'. He looked at me and admitted, 'we've never stopped and thought about any of this stuff. It's time we did.'

Choosing between various goals, strategising around these, and drawing up a plan that flows from that requires time and space, and these often feel too scarce to spare. Our frantic, multi-tasking minds

The High-Performing Organisation model

and double-booked schedules suggest that time used to plan will be wasted time. As well as believing that we're too busy to plan properly, we also look at a world where change is the new homeostasis and wonder 'what's the point?' If we are all at the mercy of endless disruption, surely planning is futile? Reflecting this, a Harvard Business Review report found that just 11 per cent of CEOs believed that strategic planning is worth the effort. For sure, five and ten year plans are dead – for individuals and organisations – with many entrepreneurs advocating 12–36 month plans at most. None of this means, though, that planning *per se* should be abandoned. While we may need to plan over shorter horizons, or in less detail, we still need some roadmap so that we can anticipate what is ahead of us. We may need to rip up that map and draw up a new one more frequently than before but that is still preferable to driving blind.

When I met them, Darren, Tom and their company had reached a point where they had outgrown their childlike way of working; they had to let go of running Red Technologies the old way, or risk letting the old way squeeze the life out of what it had the potential to become. They had to grow up as leaders, and planning (like the other eleven practices outlined in this book) is central to that process. Creating space to plan requires discipline. It means overriding the primal 'lizard brain' – the amygdala – which is responsible for fear, self-protective rage and the urge to reproduce, and which doesn't want to slow down, review or really think. Darren and Tom had to deal with the discomfort of implementing more formalised structures and processes as part of their inevitable evolution.

The real difficulty with planning isn't in figuring out which system or tool to use, it is that you might have to face up to some really tough decisions and choices that you've been avoiding. You might realise that hitherto you have been working in a state of semi-permanent vagueness about how you spend your time and the company's money.

The real challenge, though, is as much psychological as operational. You run the risk of disappointment if plans go wrong, like the brothers had experienced during the early days of Red Technologies. Planning also forces you to face unpleasant aspects of your personality, unhelpful habits or outright immature ways of working. You might discover in the process of planning, that much of what you think you 'have to do' is actually fairly unimportant, leaving you feeling a bit lost at sea or embarrassed at all the meaningless work you've put in. You might come face to face with your lack of discipline or your laziness. You might feel the pain of facing your past mistakes. You might have to acknowledge some uncomfortable truths about yourself, like Darren did when I met him at the party – perhaps that there are certain types of work that you are more suited to than others. In short, planning forces us to face ourselves.

The more tangible benefits are legion. Planning allows us to allocate our limited resources in a meaningful way. It allows us to have a sense of progress – where are we on the plan? It also allows us, by dint of the intellectual process behind it, to have considered alternative scenarios and options. As we face external pressures, anticipatory thinking may better prepare us to react well. It also allows us to harness the widest canvas of people's views. Planning should be a process where everyone, at whatever level, can contribute. This will make our plans better but also creates a shared sense of ownership of the plan we eventually arrive at.

There's another phenomenon that points to the benefits of planning. Psychologists have long studied something called the Zeigarnik Effect, which describes the tendency of the human mind to fixate on unfinished tasks and forget those we've completed. In a 2011 study, psychologists Roy F. Baumeister and E.J. Masicampo found that people were less competent at a brainstorming task if a simple, unimportant warm-up task was left incomplete; the warm-up task got stuck in their active memory, distracting them and interfering with their attempts to complete the main brainstorming task. What the psychologists learned was fascinating: it was not the task itself that needed completion in order to free the participants from being preoccupied with the warm-up task; they simply needed to be able to make a *plan* to complete the task. The simple act of making a plan freed up the participants' cognitive resources, making them fully able to concentrate on the task at hand.

So there's no doubt that planning is essential if we are to utilise our time, energy and resources optimally. The more complex the organisation and difficult the task the truer this is. That is why a lack of planning became more detrimental to Red Technologies as they grew in size. Darren, as well as having various psychological hang-ups about planning also failed to see that planning is not the enemy of agility but its partner. An idea best summed up by the man who planned some of the key battles that led to Allied victory in the Second World War and later became US President, General Dwight D. Eisenhower: 'In preparing for battle, I have always found that plans are useless but planning is indispensable.'

Your personal strategy, BHAG and other suggestions for creating the space to devise – and deliver on – your plan

The setting of your goal, the devising of the plan to make it happen and the execution of that plan combine to form what we might grandly, but correctly, call your strategy. The *sine qua non* of setting your strategy is choosing your goal. The great 1960s adman David Ogilvy hit the nail on the head when he remarked, 'The essence of strategy is sacrifice.' Nowhere is this more true than when it comes to choosing what it is you want to achieve. You need to create the space to really think through what you want to achieve – and how – before rushing on to try and do it. If you don't, you will be building your house on the proverbial sand.

Setting your goals

You are very familiar with the last big goal I set myself – you're reading it. After a couple of years' preliminary work on this book, and a few false starts I finally committed to making it happen. I typed out this little card and then put it in a small frame on my desk. It kept my commitment very front of mind!

As you can see I set myself a twelve-month goal, though I broke it down to what I needed to do daily. Quite a few people I've worked with like the idea of quarterly goals (possibly because it reflects the way big corporates tend to plan and review their financials). In his 2002 bestseller *Mastering the Rockefeller Habits,* Verne Harnish suggests that

> **A BOOK IN A YEAR**
>
> **To publisher by the end of 2017**
>
> 100,000 words in 12 months
>
> 20,000-word draft to people before Easter
>
> Rewritten 20,000-word draft to possible agents etc. post-Easter
>
> Then:
> An average of –
> 10,000 words a month
> = 2,500 words a week
> = 500 words a day
>
> **PUBLISHED SUMMER 2018**

working in ninety day blocks will provide enough time to make tangible progress on one or more important projects, but is short enough for you to see the finish line.

Ultimately, how long you set for your goal depends on what it is and what resources you can commit to it. I would offer a word of caution, though. We tend to get carried away with excitement when we set ourselves a goal, and this can lead us to underestimate how long it might take. We also forget how much we will likely be blown off course or hit obstacles. We will also have work (and maybe personal) emergencies and inevitable fallow periods when our mojo gets a bit depleted. So it's a bit like when you get the builders in to do work on your house: always add a third on to the time they say it'll take and the same onto the cost they quote.

Audit your goals

One useful exercise is to take a moment to list the goals you are currently pursuing and see if they need pruning back, or, potentially (but less likely), adding to. It always amazes me that when I ask people to do this very few have actually articulated what their goals are. They usually have a vague idea of what they are and can talk around them, but usually they have never taken the obvious and essential step of being crystal clear about them, and writing them down so they can monitor their progress. Another, surprisingly large, set of people don't have any sense at all about what their personal goals are. Talk about shooting in the dark.

However many goals you may have, one of them should stand out as a fundamental, more ambitious goal. Your ancillary goals can be met with some hard work in the 'business as usual' mode, but this other 'big goal' is the one that could be transformative and which you really need to make space for. It's the one that might seem too big or ambitious, or – if not thought out properly – too ill defined or nebulous. Take your inspiration from the military strategist, Carl von Clausewitz who, at the beginning of the 19th century, wrote: 'Pursue one great decisive aim with force and determination.'

Often, this goal will be developmental, about you, part of what I call your *personal* strategy, which I will explore later on. It could, on the other hand, be an intrinsic business goal, tied up with the strategy of your workplace. It might not even be about work at all. Or it could be a precursor to a professional goal, like the work Almantas has to achieve in Chapter 12.

One client I worked with felt that unless she spent considerable time improving and renovating the beautiful but ramshackle house she lived in, she wouldn't be relaxed enough to really pour herself into work. She prioritised getting it all done within a year, achieved that and then turned her focus onto work where she eventually led a management buy-out.

I suspect that any big goal (what Jim Collins and Jerry I. Porras in their book *Built to Last* call your BHAG or Big Hairy Audacious Goal) should have a year horizon. If you do want to commit to a three-month goal or a six-month one, fine, but if I were coaching you I'd be asking if that timescale was realistic and, if it was, whether it was actually a big enough goal. If we do assume a twelve-month rhythm, your goal template should be something like this:

My Goal: In one year's time I will …	?
To achieve that every month I need to …	?
To achieve that every week I need to …	?
To achieve that every day I need to …	?

Did I write 500 words every day? Of course not. Did I think I would when I set out my plan? No. But it was a good rule of thumb. Sometimes the demands of the 'day job' overwhelmed me. One day, I remember, I wanted to meet the kids straight from school and take them to the park for the first sunny day of spring instead of ploughing on with the writing, so I did. But overall I pretty much stuck to the plan. Which is the only reason I reached my goal and you're reading these words now.

Opposite is what my own mindmap for my goals looked like at the point I decided to prioritise writing this book.

So many people stagnate or flop around because they 'can't

Prioritised Goals Mindmap

decide' between various possibilities. But you only get one life, so stop dithering, choose a path, and set off down it. You can always adjust your route later. Don't wait for the perfect decision that can't go wrong. Have faith in yourself and set off.

Other people decide to do 'too much'. They have a whole list of things that they want to do, and, unsurprisingly, they spread themselves too thinly and they fail to make an impact. This can sometimes be due to undisciplined thinking and lack of willpower, but it can also be indicative (as I think it was with Darren) of an inability to commit. This in turn can stem from worrying that you haven't got enough knowledge to make an informed choice. But no one ever has perfect knowledge. Again, it's about forcing yourself to make a choice and then committing. If you can't or won't do that you will never get off the starting blocks.

Create the space to document and share your goal

One last point about your goal. Research tells us that writing down a goal increases our chances of achieving it. Even better than writing it down is to share the goal with someone else and ask them to help you hold yourself accountable. I'm a huge fan of mentors but this is a bit different. Find someone who you trust, that you feel achieves the things they set out to do, and make them your 'goal mentor'. Have a coffee with them and explicitly ask them to be your witness on this journey. Share why the goal is important and put it in your diaries to meet or at least speak every month with the express purpose of talking about how things are going. Use them as an external, ancillary source of willpower.

ASK YOURSELF: *Do I have a clear set of goals? Do I have a 'big' goal? Is it stretching enough? Do I measure my progress towards it? Do I have allies to support and encourage me?*

Setting your strategy and sticking to it

Once you have set your goal, you need to devise the strategy for achieving it. Strategy is a word that is thrown around and is sometimes used to intimidate people. But you don't need an MBA to understand it (though if you want to understand it better, there is a reading list on my website). Strategy is simply the way in which you seek to achieve your goal. It describes how your ends (goals) will be achieved with your means (resources) and how. It should play to what Michael Porter, the great strategy theorist, calls your 'competitive advantage' – what can you do differently or better than others.

You may be in a position where you are responsible for building the process and culture that drives execution across all or part of an organisation. Or you may not have that level of management responsibility. The next section applies in all cases. I tell clients that in practice, they should always be guided by a dual strategy. You should have a strategy for achieving your *business* goals, as you are obviously beholden to your organisation's strategy and objectives, and your success will be bound up with delivering on these. But you should also be following a strategy for *you* for achieving your *personal* goals, which is just as clearly thought through. I am endlessly struck by how almost everyone I work with, and especially senior executives, will have a clear sense of the first but not the second. But as soon as you raise the question of why you would have a strategy for your *role* but not for *you*, they instantly get it and want to get on with creating one. Here's how that would look. You will see that your goals should be broken down into SMART objectives, the business acronym popularised by management guru Peter Drucker, which stands for Specific, Measurable, Attainable, Relevant and Timebound. These are the core of your plan:

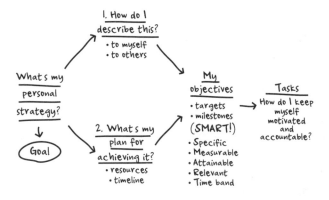

Personal Strategy Execution Roadmap

This effectively becomes your personal plan. It should be as clear and detailed, and as ruthlessly executed as the plan you have for your 'day job'. Indeed you will notice how closely it mirrors a standard strategy roadmap that you might have for your business, and this is the one I use with clients if that is what we are looking at:

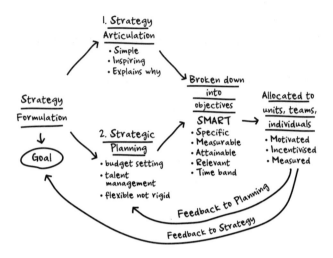

ASK YOURSELF: *Do I have a clear strategy for what I want to achieve? Is it written down? How much of my time and effort do I devote to it? Am I on track?*

Finalising your plan

Once you have set your goal and your strategy to achieve it you can begin the more detailed process of planning. At the heart of any good plan are three things, and each flows from your personal strategy:

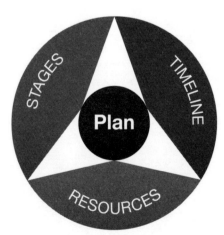

ASK YOURSELF:

1. *Stages – what are the specific steps that will lead to my goal being achieved?*

2. *Timeline – which of these steps will I do when?*

3. *Resources – How am I going to do these things? Using what time, energy etc?*

Good luck!

CHAPTER 8

Space to Deliver

Tamsin and Her Missing Delivery

LESSON: *Only by ruthlessly focusing and prioritising will you be able to create the space to think about – and deliver – what really matters.*

TAMSIN IS THE CEO of a healthcare company. She has built her reputation on being able to juggle a hundred things, with the ability to fix any problem and always deliver. But as the business has matured, she seems to have lost her touch. The private equity firm that had originally backed her energy and passion early on are now raising doubts about whether she is the right person to lead the business going forward. They see an inability to focus on what really matters and to deliver the things that will make a real difference to the company. While they still appreciate her enthusiasm, they feel that the discipline to follow through on a plan, and get things over the line is missing. There is too much time being wasted. Too many missed deadlines. Ruthlessly, the board has recently parachuted in a new Chair who Tamsin feels is super-critical and dismissive of her efforts. I'd worked with the Chair before at another company, and she asked me to see Tamsin and talk about what was going on.

Easier said than done. Getting an appointment took all my guile. When we finally did have a time, she cancelled on the morning citing an emergency that came up at work. I'm always sceptical about people who use this as an excuse to break a commitment. If they are in charge of a Police Terrorist Unit, maybe, but otherwise what's so urgent?

Anyway, I persevered and two weeks later I was sitting in Reception. When she arrived, twenty minutes after we were due to start, she was talking simultaneously to a colleague, who was trailing along in her wake, and on her mobile. You get the picture.

Once we had finally settled down in a meeting room (she'd had to kick people out because she hadn't booked one), she spilled her phone, iPad, notebook and numerous folders all over the desk. 'Busy?' I asked. Not one for irony, she launched into a breathless, detailed list of all the things she had to do, and how brilliant everything was.

'Well, luckily I don't give a shit about any of that.' I smiled.

That stopped her.

'What's *not* going well?'

She looked genuinely confused, as if I had asked her to explain the theory of relativity. Her phone rang. Saved by the bell. She at least had the awareness to look at me as she reached for it. I grimaced and shook my head. Her hand froze. A second later she answered it, mouthing apologies to me. She ended the call quickly and put the phone back down, glanced at me, and then with a look of genuine pain on her face reached forward and put it on silent.

She began to talk about what she felt about the investors' and the Chair's criticism. How unfair it was.

'What bit *is* fair?' I asked.

This question seemed to slow her down. You could almost see her embrace – or at least begin to tolerate – something she had tried to shut out.

I smiled at her. 'It's so hard, this,' I said, 'because it really strikes at your own image of yourself. What has made you strong for so long.'

'Mmm…' she said ruefully. 'It is hard, you are right.'

She started to tear up.

'I know people have started to lose faith in me, not just the investors, but my team … I know I'm letting people down …'

As she started this more real conversation and focused on being in the room and in the moment with me, she gradually relaxed. She was able to own some of the criticisms that were being made of her. But I could see, even when she let down some of her defences, that she was in denial about how bad things had become. I suggested that I get some feedback from her colleagues and that we look at all this again next time we met. As time was of the essence, that was going to have to be in the next couple of weeks. She reluctantly accepted this. When I told her we'd be meeting for three hours, in my office not hers, she looked like she was going to be sick.

Hats off to her, though, the next week she turned up. The feedback was, alas, absolutely awful, the worst I'd have to relay in over a decade. When faced with reporting such negativity I have learned that it is OK to deliver it straight. It serves no one to pull punches and deep down the person almost always knows all this anyway. Which doesn't make hearing it any less a slap in the face. Nonetheless, a slap is sometimes exactly what is required to wake someone up. So I took a deep breath and read out what people really felt about Tamsin:

> *She doesn't listen*
> *She is all talk*
> *I've basically caught her out in bare-faced lies*
> *You can't trust her*
> *I now just avoid her and let her live in her fantasy world*
> *She never does what she says she will do*
> *You can't rely on her to deliver*

As I related all this, her expression was blank. Then she slowly turned red and began to sob.

'I know. I know. I know,' she sniffed. 'They're right.'

I gave her some space to get her emotions out and slowly pull herself together. I then asked her to tell me about herself. It was a sad story.

She'd never known her dad, and her mum had died when she was very young. She'd been in a series of foster homes, and ended up as a slightly unruly teenager in a children's home. There, she had faced chaos, but had eventually found some happiness by making herself useful. Helping out the adults, dealing with the other kids, doing the cooking, babysitting, DIY. She felt she had a purpose, and she got praise for all she did.

When she left the home, she got a job as an admin assistant in a care home and the pattern repeated. She took on everything, never said no to anyone, and worked all the hours God sent. She eventually became the owners' right-hand woman and when they retired, she took over, growing the company almost by sheer force of will. Keen to expand even further, she had taken outside investment a couple of years ago. She explained how taking over and then growing the company in its early days had been the best few years of her life.

'Now they're spoiling it,' she concluded.

'They?' I challenged.

'OK, maybe I am too, I don't know. I don't know what the hell's going on.'

Tamsin's core pathogenic belief was that her purpose, her value, came from fixing everything herself. This fierce independence had driven her through the first part of her working life, but was ill-suited to the demands of a bigger, more formal business like the one that she had, ironically, built for herself. She overcommitted, let people down and couldn't seem to see the wood for the trees, as someone put it to me in the feedback. When it was all about Tamsin, she and the business had thrived. Now it was about her planning and orchestrating a much bigger operation, she was like the proverbial fish out of water. As we discussed this, she recognised its truth.

Over the next few sessions we visualised her saying no to people (which she found excruciating, almost physically painful), and we explored the art of delegating. We worked on prioritisation and goal-setting, and discussed the notions of 'perfectionism' vs 'good enough' (which I explore on p. 271).

In the midst of all this, there was one 'Eureka' moment when we met one Monday morning. She mentioned that she was tired, as she had spent all weekend rewriting a PowerPoint proposal that had to be sent to a potential partner. She had felt she hadn't done a good enough job, and had asked him to delete the original version and read her new one instead. Luckily, as he'd received the first version at 9.10pm on the Friday and the second at 7.45am on Monday morning, he hadn't looked at it and so was able to do as she asked. Anyway, with Tamsin's permission I conducted an experiment. I called the guy she'd sent the PPT to and asked him to do me a favour. I then re-sent him the original version that Tamsin had judged inadequate and asked for his sense of how they were different. I received an unfriendly email a day later implying I had wasted his time – 'they are effectively the same' was his terse conclusion.

Slowly, all of this, plus the other work we were doing, and the feedback from her team – which was now more open and frequent – began to make a difference. Tamsin seemed to realise that she had developed a way of working that left her in the midst of stress and chaos. She wasn't prioritising what she needed to do, wasn't planning her day, wasn't creating the space to react thoughtfully as circumstances changed around her. Gradually, with my help, she began to change her approach to these things and started to develop a new Personal Operating System (or pOS, as I like to call it) – the set of very personal habits, rhythms and discipline that we bring to bear as we each try to get things done in the most productive way. We each have our hardware – intelligence, stamina etc. – but we need to integrate that with our own software – when and how we prefer to work – so that we can function optimally, just as Apple do with iPhones and iOS.

I introduced the idea of developing more discipline. Tamsin knew that she didn't just need to stop doing certain things, she needed to start doing things differently. We spent about an hour discussing her current approach to working, dissecting each behaviour in turn, turning it around and imagining in vivid detail what she could do instead.

One practice in particular made a huge impact on her – time blocking. This involves organising your day in a more structured way, allocating time slots for particular activities and diarising these as you would a meeting or call. She immediately experienced a shift in her productivity levels and told me that it totally revolutionised how she plans and executes her day.

I was feeling good about the coaching and so was pretty surprised when my friend, the company's Chair, rang me up with the news that Tamsin had resigned. She didn't know much about why.

Later that day Tamsin called me herself and asked if we could meet for coffee.

'I'm not ungrateful,' she insisted, 'and I have learnt some stuff that will stay with me, but the bottom line is, I'm not happy. I don't want to be all "process" and structured. I don't want to hem in my diary, delivering according to someone else's plan not mine. I like being spontaneous, doing my firefighting and fixing. It's what I do best.' Her words had an uncanny echo of Darren's in the last chapter. But then people are who they are – unless they decide they want to change, and put in the work to do so.

Her eyes searched mine.

'I suppose you think that means I will fail.'

I took a breath. 'I don't know, Tamsin. I guess it depends on what you want to do.'

'I know what I want to do,' she said, sounding excited. 'I want to start up a new business. I've got this idea ...' and she was away, not dissimilar in tone to how she had been when we'd first met that morning four months before.

As she held forth I felt we were about to see a classic example of what Freud called the 'repetition compulsion'. Having failed to fix the great fixer, it was my turn to feel like a failure.

Deciding what really matters as a way to Create Space to Deliver

'Einstein didn't invent the theory of relativity while he was multitasking at the Swiss patent office.'

David E. Meyer, Professor of Psychology, University of Michigan (quoted by Winifred Gallagher in her book *Rapt: Attention and the Focused Life*)

There is one aspect of work that is non-negotiable: delivering results. Unless you produce tangible results – however those results are measured – it is fair to say that you cannot be described as a truly effective professional. You can create space to reflect and learn and make wise decisions. You can focus on goals and develop great strategies, but without actually doing the work to deliver results, it will – in the commercial world and in many other contexts – all be for naught. As the popular business saying goes, execution is *everything*. The question everyone at work faces daily is how to be productive (not just busy) and deliver a task on time and to specification. Creating space to deliver means understanding how you work best; creating the conditions where your work can happen; then actually doing the work.

Executing, like all aspects of business life, has been the subject of many books and articles, and has been defined in numerous ways. In the seminal book on the subject, *Execution: The Discipline of Getting Things Done*, Larry Bossidy, former CEO of Honeywell, and author and consultant Ram Charan state that 'Execution is not just tactics – it is a discipline and a system. It has to be built into a company's strategy, its goals, and its culture.'

Excelling at execution is also the worry that regularly tops the list of CEOs' concerns in multiple surveys. Of all the skills required of a business leader, execution is the one which, in my opinion, depends most on the experience of having done things; of having done different things, in different circumstances, with differing degrees of success or failure. I would also suggest that, while people will have differing inherent executional capabilities, out of the key capabilities needed by executives it is the most developable. People's ability to think strategically requires a particular way of thinking, and intellectual self-confidence; their purpose springs from deep within; their people skills are linked closely to genetic disposition and early upbringing; as is their sense of self-awareness. Executing, though, to an extent, is more of a discipline (hence Bossidy and Charan's subtitle) than these others, so it should be more able to be learnt, practised and mastered.

When I reflect on my work with Tamsin, I see two issues. Here was a woman who had built her whole identity around being a fixer (what psychologists call 'overfunctioning') to such a degree that she couldn't take the next step she had carved out for herself. Instead, she was driven by a need to be needed that had its roots in unfinished business from her childhood and young adulthood. Secondly, Tamsin had developed a set of habits that were not only damaging her reputation and risking her role in the company, they were also affecting her brain and physiology.

The identity Tamsin had constructed for herself – an identity which helped her feel secure and important, feelings which she hadn't experienced in her early childhood – hinged on perpetual busyness. She had succumbed to the seductive idea that her worth as a human being correlated to hours spent on a never-ending treadmill of activity, but she had not learned how to attend to those activities in a focused way. Many of us are like Tamsin: we've got so much in our heads and on our plates that we stagger from one day to the next, almost everything on our to-do lists seeming urgent. We spread ourselves too thin, spin too many plates and juggle too many balls (and use too many metaphors), all the while quietly priding ourselves on how 'busy' we are – because, after all, busy must mean important. Busyness has become a badge of honour, and as Dr Brené Brown writes in *The Gifts of Imperfection*, anxiety has become a lifestyle and exhaustion a 'status symbol of hard work.' In a world where even children have schedules that are bursting at the seams with 'play dates' and extra-curricular activities, white space is often hard to come by.

What Tamsin didn't appreciate is that it's easy to be busy. Anyone can rush around like a blue-arsed fly, as my mum calls it. It takes enormous skill, discipline and leadership to be singularly focused – and it is increasingly rare. If, like Tamsin, you find yourself really, really busy, it might be uncomfortable yet revelatory to acknowledge that you may also be, counter-intuitively, really, really unproductive.

Overfunctioners like Tamsin are often driven by a need to prove how needed they are. Their behaviour is characterised by the busy work of taking care of everyone else: they are highly adaptable, dish out advice without being asked for it, 'know' what is best for others, rarely if ever say no to a request, feel responsible for every-one, put their hand up when volunteers are needed and commonly experience periodic, seemingly out-of-the-blue, burnout. A typical overfunctioner's response to any request is 'of course I can', with barely a pause to reflect whether it is a priority or how doable the request is. In coaching, they often need reminding that they are here on earth first and foremost as human *beings* not human *doings*, and that their worth remains intact whatever they do or achieve (though it might take a while for this kind of feedback to 'land' and observ-able changes to begin).

There is another group of people, whose essential dynamic is the opposite to Tamsin's. People who don't take on too much but too little, who are unambitious, have low expectations and poor produc-tivity. You might call them the world's underachievers. Getting to the root cause of these people's problems is hard as they can be many and varied. By definition I never come across them in my leadership consultancy work – they'd never get to that level. But I do occasion-ally see such people in my private psychotherapy practice, and even there, once we have looked at any deeper psychological and emo-tional issues, I will use the ideas contained in this part of the book – about prioritising, goal setting and planning – to try and lift people out of their rut. Sometimes the underlying issue is related to their sense of purpose, a subject we explore in Chapter 10.

For over- and underachievers, ironically, progress requires similar things: an exploration of what core beliefs underlie their behav-iours, and a commitment to change, abandoning ingrained habits and forming new ones. There is one very modern habit that, in my experience, bedevils both types of people, which was personified in Tamsin. Her whole approach to working – the task juggling, the simultaneous conversations, the phone calls during her session with me – can be summed up in one word, multitasking.

Our understanding of this once prized capability has evolved dramatically in the last few years, and what we now know is that multitasking leaves a lot to be desired. While we can technically *do* two things at once, what we cannot do is *concentrate* on two things at once, as a 2014 study in the *Journal of Experimental Psychology* found – interruptions of just 2.8 seconds resulted in double the errors by participants in an assigned task.

Yet most people whose jobs are primarily based in an office, even if they are not prone to Tamsin's bad habits, have incredibly fractured workdays. A stream of meetings, emails, calls, texts, social media to check, colleagues dropping by your desk etc. One study found that CEOs, who you would think had the best chance of planning and policing their own time, experience on average just twenty-eight minutes of uninterrupted time a day. Lee Iacocca, the legendary CEO of Chrysler, described the problem pithily, describing how CEOs spend most of their time 'fighting off time-wasting bullshit like a frantic fellow futilely waving his arms at a swarm of angry bees on the attack.'

The research is clear: we can't dip in and out of activities with ease (and women, incidentally, are no better than men at this, despite the myth). It takes us quite a while to get back on track, or back into our 'flow', as one leading psychologist calls it, that mental state in which a person performing an activity is fully immersed in a feeling of energised focus, full involvement, and enjoyment. Alas, according to Steven Kotler, author of *The Rise of Superman: Decoding the Science of Ultimate Human Performance,* the average worker spends just 5 per cent of their work day in flow; echoing an almost unbelievable 2015 Microsoft study that found that humans have a natural eight-second attention span – officially shorter than a goldfish. Furthermore, evidence shows that the average office worker switches tasks every three minutes on average, and it is estimated that it takes around ten times the length of the interruption to get back on track. So a two-minute chat with someone who stops by your desk can mean that the report you were writing just took twenty minutes longer. Even a sneaky glance at your inbox for thirty seconds can mean five minutes of lost time. This bombardment of information, the mania induced by trying to cope with it, and the sense that we never really can has been likened to a constant low level feeling of jet lag, or a constant GSA – Gnawing Sense of Anxiety.

Incidentally, as well as being victims of all this, we also have a deep-seated reason to play along. Those little snatches of information that we get in texts, emails and conversations – or even just the possibility of them – tantalise the ancient part of our brains that is primed to look out for them ('Will that email saying yes to my proposal have arrived?' 'Will that guy I fancy in accounts have texted about a coffee?'). Imagine that archetypal tribesman that I referred to in the Introduction, standing on a bluff overlooking the Serengeti. Archaeological and neurological science is certain that our brains are effectively the same as his 40,000-year-old Cro-Magnon one. He didn't develop to scan several screens, but he did adapt to do something remarkably similar: repeatedly scan the valley below looking for any change – the possibility of an animal to hunt, or a signal of danger, a predator or enemy moving in. Ping! There's a shadow that could be a lion. Ping! No, it's a gazelle. Ping! There's a movement in the trees. Ping! No, it's just the wind. To make sure we spent time, alert and searching for new information, evolution made sure that we got a little rush of dopamine every time we did spot something new (or even thought we might have). Flitting from activity to activity – what we delusionally and grandly call multitasking – literally gives us a buzz.

Scientists have repeatedly found in studies that multitasking creates a never-ending dopamine feedback loop, and dopamine is a powerful chemical indeed. In laboratory studies conducted by James Olds and Peter Milner in the 1950s, the lab rats got so fixated on getting their dopamine hit that given the choice, they would forego eating, sleeping, nursing their young or resting in favour of hitting a lever that would do nothing except trigger a dopamine release. They did this over and over (and over) again until eventually, they died of exhaustion and starvation. If this sounds too primitive to be relevant to us humans, bear in mind that people have also died, tragically, from playing computer games for too many hours without a break. Glenn Wilson, former Visiting Professor of Psychology at Gresham College in London, claims that multitasking is worse for your cognition than smoking cannabis.

What the evolutionary process certainly hasn't caught up with is that we now sit on our backsides seeing thousands of potentially titillating bits of new information ping by every day. Plus, of course, our ancient human didn't have as many other things he was supposed to be getting on with. So, if we are to create the space to concentrate on what we really want to achieve, multitasking is, literally, a drug we have to kick.

*

Tamsin's frazzled, haphazard working style badly damaged her rapport with her colleagues and the board, and she seemed to be barely coping, constantly dancing on the knife-edge of some sort of disaster. The other big thing Tamsin failed to do amidst all her scurrying around was to get clear on what really mattered. Driven by anxiety and the need to do it all, she failed to get a handle on her own or the company's goals and priorities.

This is about more than just not being very productive. It's actually about sleepwalking through life, living less consciously and with far less presence than we have the potential for. I really felt for Tamsin. She had unwittingly recreated the exact situation she was defending herself against; in trying to make herself invaluable by doing it all, she'd actually ended up delivering very little of substance, shot herself in the foot, and then – when crunch time arrived and she had the opportunity to evolve – sadly, she jumped ship. The good news is that life tends to force us to face the same lessons again and again until we learn them, so I have no doubt that sooner or later she will have another opportunity to confront herself – and hopefully choose to learn the deeper lessons.

Not that I blame her. What she was trying to do wasn't easy. The difficult – and demotivating – truth is that creating space for any of the things we have been discussing is very hard. There is a particular psychological aspect to the idea of focusing and prioritising that makes them extra hard. Without them we can enjoy the fantasy that we can do everything – that we don't have to choose. Think of the almost physical pain Tamsin went through when I first suggested she start saying no to people. The novelist Stephen King once remarked that writing is hard because you have to 'kill your darlings'. He didn't mean killing off a favourite character within the book, but cutting one of his favourite characters out of the book. However much he liked them, and however much he felt the reader might like them, if they weren't essential to the plot, out they would go. Activities inessential to the plot you've set for your life should go the same way. Only then have you got the best chance of authoring your own happy ending.

Blocking, batching, eating frogs and other suggestions for Creating the Space to Deliver

There is a profound truth in Nike's annoyingly simple aphorism: regardless of how many tips, tricks, tactics or strategies you employ, sooner or later you do have to just sit down and 'do it'. Or as Anna Wintour, Editor-in-Chief of *Vogue*, puts it: 'Leadership is coming up with an idea and executing it. Ideas are a dime a dozen.' Prioritising, planning and preparing can only take you so far. Whatever your position – even if you are in a role that primarily involves managing other people – in today's knowledge and ideas economy, we all have long, long lists of things to do. At some point, the report has to be written; those emails (as annoying, numerous and never-ending as they are) need to be sent; that proposal to be sent out; the agreement has to be reviewed.

Creating the space – physical, temporal, psychic and relational – to do our work is an essential prerequisite to actually doing it. Again, creating space must come first. Without some kind of deliberate intervention by us, many of us would find our days full of reactive 'busy' work such as answering one email after another, saying yes to every favour or request asked of us, being unable to concentrate and getting sucked into endlessly fascinating distractions. Reviewing and addressing the four kinds of space in order to set ourselves up to be productive is an essential part of self-leadership. Each of these will call to mind the exploration we undertook in Part One around

Creating Space to think, but this time our focus is not on thinking but doing.

What we are trying to discover is which approaches, rhythms and habits are the right ones for *you*. 'Taking Care of Business', as Elvis Presley called it (it's emblazoned on the tailfin of his plane at Graceland), is largely dependent on knowing ourselves, and creating daily and weekly plans that work with rather than push against our rhythms, energy levels, commitments and deadlines. Too often advice on getting things done assumes that people are similar. My experience of working with hundreds of executives is that people are incredibly diverse, as we noted when looking at how people like best to reflect and learn in Part 1. Rather than offer a 'one size fits all' solution, let's explore various aspects of getting things done and you can consider which one best fits your own preferences. Though, it's worth adding, it can be interesting – and productive – to experiment and try out a different *modus operandi* now and again, just to see what happens. For example, maybe you are not someone who takes regular breaks, but what would you find out if you did? Maybe you don't feel a need to plan out your day – but what would doing so feel like, if you tried it for a week?

Physical Space

Many people who work from home complain that they struggle to get work done there because of the blurred boundary between their work day and their home environment; there's always a wash load that needs doing, some personal paperwork to file or a cupboard that needs cleaning out. But working in an office often isn't much better; there are endless rabbit holes to fall down or conversations and projects to be pulled into. It's remarkably easy to fill a day with busy work, but fail to move the needle in any significant way on an important project. This challenge echoes the one we addressed in Part 1, when we looked at creating space to think. Most offices are pretty poorly designed when it comes to actually getting work done. Open-plan spaces and open-door policies allow anyone to interrupt you at any time and can make it very hard to get 'in the zone' – and the zone is where we want to be working. Being distracted by interruptions from colleagues or from overhearing office gossip rank very highly in any list of productivity killers in the workplace. You might not be able to redesign your workspace, but there are some things you can consider, such as working with noise-cancelling headphones on for a 'Power Hour' and listening to ambient background noise, or working a few hours a week in a different part of the office such as a designated quiet zone, meeting room or even in a café. Do what you can to set your environment up to support you in working well.

Also pay attention to the productivity sapping potential of meetings. These can give the illusion of productivity, but often become centred on discussions and debates about what *could* be being done rather than on what *is* being done – and by whom. We're all familiar with the soul-destroying potential of meetings to simply result in more meetings.

I once worked with a big infrastructure company who were trying to break out of a cycle of too many meetings. The first thing we did was work out how much the meetings were costing. If you added up both the salaries people were paid and how much they were supposed to be contributing to revenue, some regular yet rather listless meetings were actually costing thousands of pounds each, not to mention the cost in lost motivation. We then looked at what the meetings were for. The company, rightly, didn't want to lose the connection and relationship-building that occurred at meetings, so some meetings were kept, with that as an implicit if not explicit purpose. But lots of status meetings were moved onto zoom (similar to Skype), enabling people at their desks or on their mobiles to achieve in fifteen minutes what used to take an hour.

The CEO of Yahoo, Marissa Mayer, is known for her ability to conduct up to seventy micro-meetings per week. Mayer's approach trains people to value her time as well as their own, not to waste it, to plan ahead and be extremely clear about what they need from her. Other CEOs I know have ten-minute meetings scheduled one after the other in blocks of time on certain mornings, and some do these standing up. In just a few hours they can connect with twenty people, and each feels they have had real 'facetime'. You should also think consciously about the frequency and length of meetings you are involved in, as these have a real impact on the space you have to actually do things.

The same goes for our digital environment. The average worker receives over a hundred emails a day (and rising), and many of us work in cultures where those emails are expected to be answered within minutes or hours. There's a shared expectation nowadays that if someone asks us a question or needs something from us, we owe them a reply ASAP – regardless of any effect on us. Taking charge of this by setting clear expectations about your availability, perhaps via an email autoresponder or in conversation with relevant colleagues or stakeholders, will help free up much-needed space to get work done.

A discussion of creating space to work would not be complete without mentioning smart phones. It is hardly surprising that numerous studies have found that phones have a hugely detrimental effect on our ability to get work done. According to a survey by Open Market, 83 per cent of millennials open text messages within ninety seconds of receiving them. This isn't surprising given what we know about the pleasure-boosting effects of a dopamine hit, but it can create very real problems in terms of focusing on complex and/or creative work that requires 'deep' attention. The lure of a quick feel-good burst of dopamine can have us opening new emails, answering text messages or scrolling on our preferred social media channel of choice (again), all ultimately at the cost of doing something truly productive.

A study by Career Builders found that mobile phones and text messages surpassed even emails as the biggest productivity drain at work, with three out of four employers saying that two or more hours a day were lost in productivity because employees are distracted. Forty-three per cent reported at least three hours a day being lost. When asked to name the biggest productivity killers in the workplace (respondents could give more than one answer), 55 per cent said mobiles and texting, 41 per cent said the internet and 39 per cent said gossip. Social media came in fourth with 37 per cent, followed by co-workers dropping by at 27 per cent, with smoke breaks or snack breaks also at 27 per cent, email at 26 per cent and meetings at 24 per cent. These numbers give a powerful indication of the kind of things that are stopping work from getting done.

It isn't just the time spent on the phone that we lose. A study at Florida State University in 2013 found that the probability of making an error increased 28 per cent after getting a phone call and 23 per cent after receiving a text. That's fine, you might think. 'I don't answer my texts immediately, and I don't always pick up the phone.' That's all well and good, but as research in the *Journal of Experimental Psychology: Human Perception and Performance* reported, people who just received a notification about a call were found to be three times more likely to make an error in their task – even if they didn't answer it! I think the solution here is pretty simple: when you sit down to work, put your phone out of sight, on flight mode or do not disturb mode. The difference between the two is that flight mode disconnects your phone from being able to send or receive calls, so voicemails, texts and any app notifications will come through in a flurry once you turn flight mode off; in 'do not disturb' mode, however, texts and calls will still come in, but the phone will not alert you about these. The caveat to using do not disturb mode instead of flight mode is that you must have your phone face down or stashed away somewhere, otherwise you'll see any incoming communications flash up on the screen. If your phone is nearby, it's very tempting just to pick it up and check a few apps. A small act of self-discipline here can work wonders on your productivity levels. Put your phone away and see for yourself if you get more stuff done.

The same obviously goes for browsing on your laptop, desktop computer or tablet. I suspect there is a very high correlation between poor levels of productivity and a high number of open tabs on your browser. Not only does this slow your computer down, but every extra tab sends your brain the message that there's something else vying for your attention, something incomplete or more interesting than the thing you're working on. Indeed, work offline wherever possible. Similarly, if you habitually open a new tab and hit 'f' for Facebook, and you notice yourself doing this when you ought to be in the zone with work, you could play with using an internet restriction app to force your own hand. One of the best known of these apps is Freedom, created by Fred Stutzman while completing his PhD. Freedom takes you completely offline for up to eight hours. If that is a little too extreme, there are other options such as Anti Social, SelfControl, Cold Turkey and StayFocusd. Some of these apps force you to commit to a schedule, which, as we explore next, can be a profoundly simple way to reshape and transform your working day.

Temporal Space

This mirrors our discussion around creating space to think in Part 1. Creating temporal space to do can feel equally challenging, especially if your calendar is full of meetings and appointments. Even (in fact especially) if you face a lot of demands on your time that you *can't* control, you need to have an iron grip on the time you *can* control. Which makes planning your day essential. Here are seven ideas which you should consider as you create and refine your own pOS and find your unique, optimal way of creating space to do.

First up is **structuring your week**, which you should consider before you plan your day. Some people like to have broadly similar days; others like to separate out, as far as they can, different days for different tasks. This second approach is advocated by Dan Sullivan in his Entrepreneurial Time Management System. It involves planning three types of day into your week: buffer days, where you churn through the myriad smaller items that need doing; rest days, which some people suggest are best spent screen free; and focus days, where you move the needle on big projects. This is pretty much how I tend to work, attempting whenever I can to have a different rhythm to my Wednesdays, even being a little fallow if at all possible. This seems to punctuate the week for me and give me the energy and motivation to end the week with a bang rather than petering out, which I think is what most people tend to do – 'casual Friday', in many workplaces being not just about what you wear. I am aware of how lucky I am to have this level of control over my week.

Next is **reflecting on each day**. One helpful way to create temporal space is, ironically, to take some time – roughly ten minutes – at the end of each working day to review and reflect on what you achieved, what is incomplete, what you delayed or delegated, and what needs doing the following day. That way, when you arrive at your desk the following morning, you do not have to try to figure out the day ahead – it's already mapped out for you, and you can tweak and alter if necessary. I always think it's easier to work *with* something rather than face a blank canvas, especially first thing in the morning when our brains haven't fully kicked into gear! Of course some people prefer to write such a list at the start of the day; as with all of these things, what will suit you is something only you can determine.

Some time management advice insists that morning is the best time for creativity, and for getting 'bigger' pieces of work done. Productivity experts advocate **eating the frog** first thing in the morning, in other words getting the hardest, biggest or most important thing out of the way first. Don't ease into your day with a bit of social media or a bit of emailing; hit the ground running and tackle the thing that you really don't want to do. You'll feel great afterwards and it will free up a lot of headspace. Peter Drucker described these as big rocks, using the analogy of filling a glass jar with big rocks before you add in pebbles, sand and water. Put any of those other three things in first – smaller tasks, quick actions or emails – and the danger is that you will find that there is little space left for the big rocks, those more demanding and complex chunks of work that really require your peak energy and attention.

Research and my experience of clients suggest that this is true, but only for most people, not for everybody. I know of one very successful executive who feels they need a long, slow start to the day, so he does minor pieces of work first before 'revving up' to do the complex stuff in the late afternoon. As ever, each to their own.

The fourth idea is the one I introduced to Tamsin – **blocking out**

time. This is a way of organising your day and your work by splitting them into a series of themed time blocks. It's the daily version of the approach to the week outlined above. Multiple studies have proven that we are able to do focused work with good levels of creativity, attention and accuracy for anything from 20–90 minutes. Working in twenty minute blocks is known as the Pomodoro Technique, a very popular time management strategy wherein you set a timer for twenty minutes, work on one thing during that time, and then take a five-minute break, before rinsing and repeating. This means for every hour worked, you take a ten-minute break (sort of like a therapist's 50-minute hour). For some people, twenty minutes isn't long enough to really get into their groove; they prefer to work for half an hour, forty-five minutes or even longer before taking a break. The longest time recommended for working without a pause is an hour and a half, but I have known people get their head down and only emerge after a whole day has gone by. As always, find out what works for *you*, but don't be afraid to experiment along the way.

It's important to **vary your pace**. Working in time blocks helps you see the day as a series of short sprints rather than a marathon, but – as in sport itself – most of us can manage the latter better than the former. In an interview for *Harvard Business Review*, Tony Schwartz, a productivity expert who co-developed the idea of the 'Corporate Athlete', expands on this idea:

> *Most of us mistakenly assume we're meant to run like computers – at high speeds, continuously, for long periods of time, running multiple programs simultaneously. It's just not true. Human beings are designed to be rhythmic. The heart pulses; muscles contract and relax. We're at our best when we're moving rhythmically between spending energy and renewing it. We need to recognize the insight of athletes, who manage their work-rest ratios.*

The lesson? Work intensely, then take a break and recover. Work solidly all day and you may well find yourself consistently outper-formed and outdone by a colleague who works in short, intense stints with regular breaks in between. To adapt the fable, this is less a choice between being either the tortoise or the hare, and more a case of finding a way to be sometimes one and then the other.

Another aspect of time blocking involves grouping similar tasks together and tackling them all in one go. Known as **batching your tasks**, this technique reduces the amount of work your brain needs to do to switch tasks. Instead of entering one expense receipt, then reading one report, then answering one voicemail, the idea is that you save them up and do all the tasks in the same category together.

The last idea for helping create space to do involves **breaking things down**. It's easy to confuse a task with a project. Anytime you find yourself resisting or procrastinating on a task, try breaking it down into smaller components. Tree surgeons don't cut entire trees down, they tackle one branch at a time, then move onto the trunk, which sometimes gets chopped down in multiple pieces too. It's tempting to think that you need to create hours and hours of space to get something done and find yourself consistently not being able to do that; a solution might be to break the project down into various tasks and to create the space to tackle one of these at a time.

A personal example

If I am having a standard day in the office, my preference is to write first thing (assessment reports, proposals etc.) and then do other activities later in the day (meetings, admin etc.). I usually then have a mini-burst of energy in the late afternoon that allows me to get two or three smaller, but still significant, chunks of work done (a more complex email reply, revising a document etc.). My concentration will really start to flag after ninety minutes, so I then have a break, or at least a change in routine. Even a five-minute stretch and walking around can do the trick.

The crucial thing is to create the space that ensures your preferred schedule ends up being your actual schedule. Be bold in blocking out your diary and saying no, or at least push back strongly on requests that don't fit in with your plan. There will always be exceptions, but the aim is to keep these at a minimum. If I'm not delivering client work, a typical day for me might look like this.

Time of day	Activity	Note
9.30–11.30 am	Writing – an assessment report, proposal or other document. If I haven't got anything to write I invariably use this time for thinking.	I keep my to-do list open and jot down anything that occurs to me that I need to do later. I DO NOT look at my emails or answer my phone. I am not the Chief of a Fire Service. Not much can happen in my profession that can't wait for two hours. This is most likely true for your job too.
11.30 am–1 pm	Meetings, calls, admin, emails etc. (or on some days a coaching session).	
1–1.30 pm	Lunch break	It's important to have this break, ideally out of the office for a change of scene – and pace. It's called a 'break' for a reason.
1.30–3 pm	More meetings, calls, emails etc.	
3–4.30 pm	Coaching session etc.	
4.30–5.20 pm	Two or three longer pieces of work that require more steady concentration.	If I'm hot desking I will put headphones on at this point in the day in an effort to 'clear my desk' of those things that require a bit of concentration.

Time of day	Activity	Note
5.20 – 5.30 pm	Anticipate and plan tomorrow (and even a few days ahead).	I find this ten minutes the most vital of any day. I usually find I should send off a quick email so I am prepared for something that may come up in the next day or so. Napoleon said that the secret of his success was to be 'Five minutes ahead of himself.' I think they are possibly the wisest words about productivity ever spoken.
Just after 6 pm	Home with the family Twice a week I will get home even earlier than this (I may have been working at home) so that I can see the kids straight after school and have an early family tea. I never work after I have arrived home. I may shoot off a simple email if I see it on my phone, but I never sit down in my study and work. When I'm home, I'm home. The same is true of weekends.	

Of course, the demands of your own job and your own individual preferences will be different to mine. But what does your ideal day look like? Do you even know? If you don't know, or fail even to try and achieve it on most days, then you are letting everyone else decide for you. You've allowed them, literally, to steal your space.

ASK YOURSELF: *What is my plan for using my most valuable resource – my time? Could I experiment with doing it differently to see what happened?*

Relational Space

There are many ways in which other people will influence what you do, the way you do things and how you do them. This is an area that we explored in Part 2, where we looked at how the Spirits Team worked together; we will look at it again in the next story when we look at Space to Lead and delivering through and with others.

Psychic Space

It's very important that as well as doing all the aforementioned external things to create space to deliver you also create space internally, to nurture the right mindset. This involves three overlapping areas that you need to explore and master: prioritisation, accountability and expectations.

Prioritisation is the ability to decide – decisively and ruthlessly – what it is you are making space to do. It is linked to the choosing of goals, which we looked at in the last chapter, but it is more than just that. Most people's work involves more than their chosen goals and includes the multiple demands of others and having to deal with events as they unfold. **Accountability** is the mindset and behaviour that drives you forward, as you hold yourself responsible for persisting, and for overcoming obstacles. **Expectations** relate to how you manage the demands of others, while maintaining the space you need and preserving the trust of your colleagues.

Mastering prioritisation – the religion of success
The Labour Party politician Nye Bevan once asserted that: 'The language of priorities is the religion of socialism.' I believe that the language of priorities is the religion of success. Given our society's love of 'priorities', it's an interesting fact that when the word entered the English language in the 1400s it was used in singular form only, and stayed that way for the next 500 years. Only in the last couple of centuries did we start talking about having more than one priority, which led us to here – a time when we juggle multiple and often conflicting priorities. It is vital, if you are to truly lead, to create enough headspace to be able to distinguish what is important from what is urgent.

The former truly matters; the latter matters right now, but also leaves you on the back foot, working reactively instead of creatively, a passenger on the journey rather than the one behind the wheel.

Understanding and deploying your resources are the key here. I am assuming that you are not someone who has loads of spare time to fill up with new tasks but that, on the contrary, you already feel pushed and pulled in all directions. So the resources you allocate to your strategy come at a price; they have an opportunity cost. If you allocate more resources to your own personal goal, then you'll have less of those things – time, energy, freedom, money – to devote to something else. (I say money because sometimes it's possible to sacrifice immediate reward for longer term reward. For example, when I was writing this book, I made sure that the consultancy I founded was commercially successful, but I consciously accepted that we would only grow to an extent, putting our bigger business development and expansion plans on hold until the book was done. I would have loved to have done both, and was sorely tempted to delude myself that I could. But I couldn't. So I didn't. I made the sacrifice that David Ogilvy was talking about.)

Lying behind such prioritisation is something that people feel uncomfortable about, but which is important to name and address. I'm talking about the idea of being ruthless – even a bit selfish. Not all the time and not in the way you are with others, but some of the time, and with how you are with yourself. You need to see yourself as the 'CEO of you'. Your job is to deploy your resources in the way that adds most value.

ASK YOURSELF: *Have I got a clear sense of my priorities? Are they realistic or wishful thinking? Have I been ruthless enough?*

Once you have sorted your priorities you can think about how to itemise and track the elements of what you have to do. Here, again, a person's own preferences come into play. What is absolutely universal, however, is the need to have a clear, prioritised 'to-do' list. Keeping things in your head, or on different scraps of paper is doomed to let you and others down. I have tried various methods

Losing a third

I almost always use this simple exercise with clients. I start by suggesting that a full 15 per cent of what they are doing now should just be jettisoned. Why? Because they are almost always overworking, with a work-life balance that is out of kilter. Most need to reconnect with their family and, in many cases, themselves. Next I suggest an additional 15 per cent of what they *are* doing should be jettisoned to make time for reprioritising what they *are going to be* doing. Because this involves rejigging their ancillary goals a bit, and identifying and focusing on one BIG GOAL, we also plan how to actually execute on this, in particular identifying the required resources.

So that's 30 per cent in total. Gone. 'But that's a third of my life,' the mathematically adept coachee will exclaim, incredulously. 'That is just the start,' I reply. When you have really gone through the whole process of creating space for what really matters you'll have jettisoned a lot more than that. It's intentional shock therapy. I want them to see that we are talking about a major re-structuring of their working lives here, not just some tinkering and a deluded commitment to 'work even harder'.

Such radical change isn't always possible in practice, but by being so dramatic I am showing how much they need to push back and change the direction of travel. They need to be creating space not colluding in it being devoured. On a practical level, identifying what you can cut out follows on from the prioritising and strategising outlined previously. What are you doing now that – however enjoyable, useful or helpful it is – is not aligned with your goals?

(including apps), but find the simplest and most effective way to keep track of what I have to do is to put a TO-DO list in my calendar at the time when I will be doing such tasks. Critical tasks are coloured red, less critical ones orange. Anything not done at that time is carried over to a new slot.

The point of telling you all this is not that you should necessarily adopt the same system, but to illustrate the essential elements of whatever system you choose to use, which are: it's all in one place; it's easily accessible; it's easily amended; it involves a clear hierarchy.

To help you evolve a system that works best for you, here is the well-known 4D rule of time management that underpins my own process of prioritisation: DO, DEFER, DELEGATE, DROP.

Most people I begin working with allow far too many things to end up in the DO category. Indeed, many of them exist in a weird state where they never, ever actually DO all of the things they have supposedly 'decided' to DO. Now, in any other sphere of life this would be ridiculous. If you decided that a certain recipe needed ten ingredients you wouldn't just chuck half of them in and hope for the best. The bar for DO should be set very high. It should be the absolutely essential things that only you can do in order to realise your professional and personal strategy. Again, to stretch the cooking metaphor, you don't add extraneous stuff into your recipe either. You only have what really needs to be there.

Sometimes there are things that you need to do, but can't do now or in the near future, hence DEFER. But beware of this category, as it can be an easy option for avoiding tough decisions. There shouldn't be too many DEFER items and they should be regularly reviewed. If after, say, a fortnight, a particular item hasn't made it to your DO list then either DELEGATE it or DROP it (or put it on a separate long term ideas list). In short, don't pretend you're going to do something just because you don't feel comfortable dropping it. This is what makes this hard. If you were just culling stuff that is pointless or irrelevant that would be really easy. But those things don't tend to appear on even the longest to-do lists. In reality, we tend to have lots of things we'd like TO DO, but if they are not wholly necessary for your chosen goal(s), DROP them.

I assume you have some sort of to-do list even if it's on a scrap of paper at the bottom of your laptop bag. Get it out now and go through it. Mark each item DO, DEFER, DELEGATE or DROP.

Now look at those DOs and really ask yourself whether they need to be done immediately, because they are essential to your chosen goals. If not, re-categorise them. Now take another look at your list. There, at last you have an actual TO-DO list.

ASK YOURSELF: *Do I have a clear sense of what I need to do now? Next? This week? This month? This year? Am I driving what appears on these lists or is someone else, or even worse, no-one, I'm just on auto-pilot?*

Mastering accountability – it's my responsibility

Accountability comprises three things: taking complete ownership; communicating with clarity; being reliable and trustworthy.

This is such an important area that it is one of the twelve attributes that indicate high potential in the DEEP model of potential (discussed on p. 64). Being accountable is first and foremost about adopting a mindset in which you commit to taking absolute personal responsibility for yourself; your work; your contribution to the teams and projects you're involved in; as well as the overall business. This means working from a stance of internal personal leadership – regardless of your role or level of responsibility in any external hierarchy. Someone who's truly embodying accountability won't wait for it to come from another person.

There are a number of clear, observable behaviours that go along with accountability. Being accountable is about being trustworthy and reliable, and this happens over time, not overnight. In order to be accountable, you need to maintain ongoing awareness of what's on your plate, what's booked in your calendar and what others expect of you. It also requires making space to reflect, evaluate and plan ahead. Ultimately, it's about doing the right thing regardless of whether you're a lone voice in a crowd. When something goes wrong, accountability means 'me first'. Being truly accountable means looking at oneself before addressing the faults of others, especially when you're in a leadership position. You can't expect from your team what you won't deliver as a leader, and you can't take your team further than you've gone yourself.

ASK YOURSELF: *Do I do what I say I'm going to do, when I'm going to do it? Do I walk my talk?*

Mastering expectations – under-promise and over-deliver

A key aspect of execution involves setting expectations, especially in today's increasingly networked world. Very few of us are lone workers, and it makes a lot of sense to create clarity at the outset with clients, colleagues and other stakeholders. At the beginning of any project or task in which you are involved, initiate a conversation with the relevant person (or people) to formalise exactly what is expected of whom and by when. Set expectations around what you can do, and by when, that are realistic and take into account your other work and priorities. As and when things change, communicate this promptly and responsibly. If you don't have clarity, or suspect that there is an 'expectation gap,' then take the necessary action to close that gap. Take the reins rather than waiting for others to tell you what is required or expected of you.

These conversations become the basis of your accountability agreements with everyone you work with and will ensure that their hopeful and often unspoken expectations are converted into trust. If you are unsure or unconfident in how to broach this, practise by writing out a draft email or mentally rehearsing the conversation.

And beware of scope creep. Once you've said yes to something, watch out for people adding things on top of their original request. Just because you said yes to one thing doesn't mean you have to say yes to everything.

Before you negotiate deadlines, however, bear in mind the following: projects, commitments and tasks often expand to fill the amount of time available to complete them – even if we apply our best efforts to be disciplined. We tend to be optimists, underestimating how long something is going to take. Even if we are quite clear on what something requires from us, we often forget to factor in things beyond our control – other people, their schedules and level of involvement, and so on. We might end up needing to pull an all-nighter, or having to push back a deadline (which may have a knock-on effect on those around us), or submitting incomplete work. None of these are ideal, and they are all often (but not always) avoidable.

An executive I coached called Samira swears by the mantra, 'under-promise and over-deliver'. She estimates how long something will take and then adds another 30–40 per cent when negotiating deadlines. 'I felt uncomfortable when I started using this technique,' she told me. 'I thought it would make me look slow and lacking in drive, especially compared to colleagues who promise to get things done asap. But I soon realised it was better to set realistic expectations than have the horrible feeling of delaying delivery of a project. Plus I may finish earlier than my deadline, which makes everyone feel good and ahead of schedule.'

Think about the number of projects – in your workplace, your personal life and in the news – that have been beset by delays and setbacks. Whether it's a high speed railway service, home repairs or a product launch, delays are often so common that we sigh in unsurprised resignation, not acknowledging that by creating space at the outset, we could have created a different way of experiencing the situation, *even if none of the external circumstances changed*. The point is that we fail to factor in the unexpected, and by doing so, we set ourselves up to feel rushed and be late. Creating space in this way isn't just good for your reputation, it's also good for your physiology and health, since you end up being much less stressed.

Navigating your way around all this isn't easy. I work regularly with a FTSE 50 company that is known for pushing its people hard. A while ago I was working with two members of their high-pressure commercial team, let's call them Sally and Fiona. When I talked to their boss his feedback was brutal. First we discussed Sally.

'Sally's going to work herself into an early grave, I fear for her marriage. When does she ever see her kid for God's sake? If you ask her to boil the ocean she'd ask what you wanted her to do with the leftover salt. She's got to learn to say no.' We then moved on to Fiona. 'She'd better watch herself. She's getting a reputation for ducking hard work. She sent an email to the big boss last week saying I can do x and y but not z. Who the hell does she think she is?'

I knew the boss well enough to point out the contradiction: 'What you want, then, is a perfect mix of Sally and Fiona?' He at least had the good grace to laugh, but then he made a serious point. Sally was being too indiscriminate, but Fiona was being too discriminate. The balance was, truly, somewhere in the middle. 'Besides,' he added revealingly, 'who tells someone so senior you're not going to do what they want? You just nod and then do the important stuff and assume they'll forget the stuff that wasn't.'

ASK YOURSELF: *Did I communicate the expectations clearly? Did I include the right people in the conversation? What could I have done differently? Where were my blind spots?*

These three areas of mastery – prioritisation, accountability and expectations – take us neatly to the next area where we need to create space. If and when we become leaders, we have to take these skills on to a whole new level, so we can create the space to lead.

CHAPTER 9

Space to Lead

Yulia and Her Hungry Sea Lions

LESSON: *If you step back and make the space to deliver through others – in a way that empowers and inspires – then you will be able to deliver something really outstanding.*

YULIA WAS NEWLY APPOINTED to help head up a global cosmetics company's push for faster growth. She had worked for the company for over a decade, working her way up through the sales department to her new role as country CEO. She was bright, driven and intensely client-focused. Nonetheless, the company felt they were taking a risk with her appointment. Would she be able to adjust to being a manager of other business leaders rather than just a manager of managers? The company was organised on classic matrix principles. Finance, IT, HR and legal sat at the centre, under Yulia, but the company's brands were run by Brand MDs who reported to Yulia, but also via a 'dotted' line to the global head of each of those brands. Traditionally, these people were given quite a lot of autonomy.

This assignment was a little different. I had been asked to design some intense transition coaching for various people at Yulia's level who had been promoted to be country CEOs across Western and Eastern Europe in a shake-up driven through by the new Group CEO. In the desire to bring in fresh blood, there was a fear that some people had been promoted slightly prematurely. I put together a pro-gramme that built on the assessments they had all done a year or so before. Yulia was the first person to go through the programme, and I flew out to her offices to spend two days with her. On the first day we went through the existing report, updated it, and drew out her key strengths and development areas. After lunch we spent another two hours focusing those development areas into a couple of clear goals. Then, the next day, we spent another two hours working on how she could make the attitudinal and behavioural shifts necessary to achieve those goals.

What became quickly apparent during our first few hours together was that Yulia knew what she needed to do, she just didn't know how to make herself do it. Three months into the role, she was too involved in the detail of what was going on. Indeed, the first thing she told me was that she had spent most of the weekend before I arrived in the office working with one of her teams on a pitch to a national retailer. I went for the jugular:

'What would have happened if you'd been ill and couldn't have come in?'

She looked surprised.

'Look, I'm not saying you should or shouldn't. How do I know? But I want you to start questioning the use of your time.'

'Well, the team are a bit inexperienced and I have done that kind of thing for years, so ...' She trailed off.

'So?'

'I never really thought about it, I just did it.'

'So let's think, what would have been different ...'

She laughed. 'Not a lot actually.'

'Really?'

'Maybe the pitch was stronger. It's hard to say.'

'Why is it hard to say?'

'Well, I ... I don't know what would have happened if I hadn't been there.'

'Exactly.'

There was a pause.

'How do you think Erik (the Brand MD) felt about you being there?'

'He seemed OK with it.'

'He may have been, he may not. It doesn't really matter. Look, people will often like you being involved. They get your experience, your ideas, maybe they don't have to think too hard. They've got their backs covered, right? I mean, who's accountable for that pitch now? Whose fault is it if it goes wrong?'

'Mine, I guess.'

'Yes. Whose fault should it have been?'

'Erik's,' she said without a second's hesitation.

It was time to talk to Yulia about a key concept I use in almost all of my coaching assignments. It is a simple model that you can apply to all sorts of scenarios in your own life. I call it 'Third Space'.

Third Space

'Third Space' is one of the key models that I use in my leadership consulting practice. The idea is drawn from the work of two psychoanalysts. D. W. Winnicott wrote of 'potential space' as a place where inner and external realities mix, and where one can explore new ways of seeing and being. Thomas Ogden, a contemporary psychoanalyst and an admirer of Winnicott's work, writes about the 'analytic third', which builds on but is not the same as 'potential space'. Ogden defines the term as 'a third subject, unconsciously co-created by analyst and analysand, which seems to take on a life of its own in the interpersonal field between analyst and patient.'

I refer to the Third Space model in the vast majority of the assessments and coaching that I do. My colleagues joke about finding it scattered through our offices, endlessly scribbled on whiteboards, flip charts and even bits of scrap paper.

First I draw the simple diagram on the next page.

The 'other' can be a particular person we are discussing (e.g. one of your direct reports), a whole team or group, or even an entire organisation (e.g. your company). The space in between, which is co-created by you and the other, is not a simple mix of the two. It is

something entirely new. A non-work example would be a marriage. This third space, 'the marriage,' is something different from either partner, or a simple amalgam of both. That is why, incidentally, it is so hard to understand marriages from the outside, even if you know both people, as individuals, really well.

A business example would be those companies which were founded by complementary duos, the best example being the two Steves at Apple. Jobs – the tireless, demanding visionary – and Wozniak – the hands-on technically brilliant engineer. On a much smaller scale Darren and Tom in Chapter 7 are also examples of this complementarity. When this works, the 'third space' created is more than the sum of its parts. But it can work the other way, with the symbiotic relationship between two people ending up being less than the sum of the parts.

It therefore becomes vital to understand what role you have in creating this third space. Do you tend to fill the space? Are naturally dominant? Speak first? Get to the decision more quickly? What effect does this have on the other? Are they be grateful for such clear, decisive leadership? Relieved because they don't need to think as much? Feel pushed aside? Undervalued? Bored? There's no universal – or right or wrong – answer. The model allows you think about what is happening in any particular circumstance, and adjust accordingly.

In most cases, I use it in coaching to help a good leader see why they are not a *great* leader. People who are clever and quick, and, in a sense, natural leaders, will always underestimate the extent they fill the third space. While this can be welcome to others, it can also be off-putting and, ultimately, disempowering. What kind of people will you attract to work with you if you fill so much space? One key part of understanding all this is realising that the style of domination matters less than you might think. It's easier to see how an arrogant, loud, domineering (usually alpha male) type can eat up the space and leave others out. It's harder to see, but just as deadly, if it's done by someone who sounds gentle and collaborative. To make the point, I often joke to coachees: 'It doesn't matter if someone fills up your bed with dead rats or sweet-smelling roses – you still can't get in the bloody thing.'

When looking to create more space in your life, this is a key concept to bear in mind: you should be managing the third space around you in a thoughtful, self-aware and strategic way. Otherwise others will fill it for you. Or, if you are a leader, you will be filling it too much yourself.

★

In Yulia's specific situation, we needed to look at what was happening in the third space between her and Erik.

'There's you,' I told her. 'There's "the other" – Erik, in this example, but it could be anybody, right? Then there's this, "the third space" – which you filled. Without even thinking about whether you should be, or why.'

She stared at the board. Then she stood up and walked over to me, and took the marker out of my hand. She started to scribble all over the 'space'.

'It's what I do. All the time. I fill this space.'

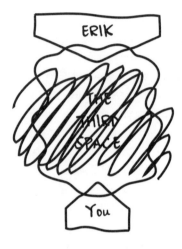

She stopped scribbling. The whiteboard was covered. She handed me back the marker, then showed why she was, in many senses, a natural leader. Staring me straight in the eye, she said: 'OK. Got it. Now, what do we do about it?'

The following coaching session was two hours of intense work. We covered several overlapping areas: how this ability – of taking charge, filling the space – had, up until now, been a huge strength for her and underlain her exceptional performance. I said I would send her a synopsis of *The Leadership Pipeline* by Ram Charan, Steve Drotter and Jim Noel, the book that best explains the notion of leaders constantly having to evolve.

We also talked about how she thought she might feel if she didn't take up the space. Was there a fear there? I asked her to imagine a situation where she hardly ever gave answers and, instead, asked questions, probing the other person, and coaching them to the answer.

This led us on to the next 'breakthrough' moment. We started to talk about what price she would have to pay for making this change. I think this is the most important moment in helping someone think through his or her behavioural development. It's too tempting to see it as all upside: the client will be freer to do more 'leadership stuff', which they'll thrive on, and their team will step up to the plate and exceed everyone's expectations. In reality there will be benefits, but there are also costs. What might these be for you? What were they for Yulia?

As we talked she suddenly blurted out: 'I'm going to be fucking bored.'

Jackpot, I thought.

'Tell me more.'

'Look,' she said, 'what I love is thinking, solving problems, fixing things, driving things forward. I see the benefits of stepping back and creating all this space for others, but what about for me? Not only is it hard, but it's cutting off what I'm best at – deciding things, telling people what they should do…'

What should a coach do in this position? Rush in to reassure her that it wouldn't be boring? Not in my opinion, or at least that's not my style.

'You know, you're right,' I said. 'It may seem boring. At least at first. You'll be having a meeting and you will be gently encouraging the discussion and some people – maybe people not as sharp or quick as you – will be mumbling and stumbling towards a solution, and you will have the answer, right there, on the tip of your tongue. But your job isn't to give that answer. It is to create the space for others to get to that answer.'

I then told her one of my favourite stories, about another CEO I worked with who was brilliant at all this stuff. He said to me that 75 per cent of the meetings he went to were a waste of time. He could have made the decision himself or he could have told the meeting what to do in the first five minutes, but he didn't. He sat there, exuding an enthusiastic and encouraging demeanour but keeping largely quiet while his team found their own way to the answer. Why? I remember his rationale clearly:

> *Because that's the way to build a team, to empower people to stretch themselves. Also, I may go to four meetings that bore me, where I have to bite my tongue and then in the fifth one, if I keep quiet, the discussion will lead to someone piping up with an idea or a thought that has the potential to be truly transformational. Someone who might not have spoken at all if I'd dominated or even led the meeting my way. That's the point of it all. To create the space for that one thought that your own style, unchecked, would have killed at birth.*

I also told the story of another senior manager who shared with me her agony when, on a Friday afternoon, she could see someone on her team struggling and where she knew she could leap in and solve everything. She had learned to resist doing that, living with her guilty feelings as she saw her colleague slouch off towards a weekend full of work and worry. Why? Because that process, of taking on the responsibility, of feeling it weigh heavily on your shoulders, is part of what develops people into strong leaders. Rescuing people, propping them up, may seem like kindness but it is actually – taken too far – disempowering and, ultimately, demotivating. My old psychotherapy supervisor in Berkeley, Peter Silen, had a great phrase for it: 'The helping hand strikes again.' Now, I should stress that both of these examples are slightly exaggerated to make a point. I often do this in coaching. Moving someone's pendulum is very hard, so I like to give it an almighty swing in the other direction so it might, when the developmental dust has settled, end up swinging back, but not entirely back to where it started from. I will often be explicit about this, and sketch out this diagram to show what I mean:

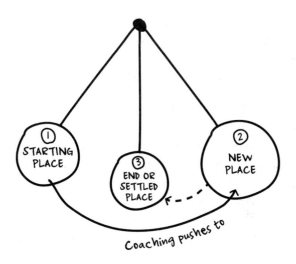

The Pendulum of Change

While I gave these examples, Yulia was listening carefully. She then got up and went to her desk and came back with a bound A4 notebook. She threw it down on to the conference table.

'It's all in here, look,' she said, pointing to the book. 'Before every meeting I write down what I think, and at the beginning of the meeting I will set it all out – before anyone even speaks!' She paused. 'Whoosh goes all the space. Gone.'

We sat silent for a minute.

'How do people seem to react to that?'

'Well, I've never thought about it, but actually, thinking of it now, I don't think they mind. In fact they expect it. They sit there ...' She paused, blushed a little and laughed quietly.

'What?'

'Well, it's a terrible thing to say but I just had an image flash into my mind.'

I waited.

'They sit in the meeting, like a load of sea lions, with their mouths open, like in the zoo, waiting for fish.'

'… and you are the zookeeper with your bucket.' I gestured to her notebook. 'Full of fish.'

Again, we sat in silence.

'You know, some people don't mind a boss who is always feeding them. It makes their life easier. But eventually the more talented people feel stuffed, and get sluggish, and yearn to feel a bit of hunger, and start wanting the buzz and challenge of going out to hunt their own fish.'

'Jan,' she said.

Again I waited.

'Jan, he's Erik's peer, manages the other big brand. That's what I can feel coming from him. A frustration. I didn't get it, but you're right. For some reason, Erik wants the fish; Jan, he has almost started to turn his mouth away. That's what it's felt like these last few months.'

She was pensive, maybe a little sad. I gave her some time.

'Well, that's the cost to Jan, what about the cost to you?'

'How do you mean?'

'What doesn't get done because you are doing all this other stuff?'

She laughed. 'Well, I know the answer to that. I don't get time to think, not really deeply, about the future, about the more tricky stuff. Plus, of course, I'm working all hours God sends.'

Her gaze went to the wall behind her desk where two childish drawings were pinned up. The only slight bit of scruffiness in her pristine, minimalist office.

'You don't see the kids enough?'

She sighed, 'No.'

'Well, a more sensible work-life balance should be a key part of what we create space for. But at work, here, as well as that time for strategic thinking, what else might you be losing?'

She thought a while.

'I'm not sure.'

'I think you are using up the space that you could actually use to develop your leadership skills across a wide range of areas.'

We took a look at the DEEP Potential Model (outlined on p. 60), to explore Yulia's own Personal Potential Profile. She was strong across the spectrum but she could use the space she created from delivering through others (rather than by herself) to develop each area further. She would have increased space, for example, to become more strategic or more creative. The area where she was weakest, though, and where she should prioritise her learning, was around P – People skills. She didn't have enough awareness about how her leadership style affected people and that made her a less empowering and inspiring leader than she had it in her to be.

By this time, we were near the end of our time together. I felt that Yulia had gained significant insight into how her overly directional, micro-managing style came at a heavy cost both to herself and her team. The remainder of our work that day consisted of drawing up these insights into clear goals. I left her for ten minutes to articulate these, in her own language, on the whiteboard. When I returned, she had written:

> *Yulia needs to go from a leader who is taking decisions to a leader who is giving directions on how to make decisions.*

> *Yulia needs to go from a leader who is conquering decision-making space to a leader who is creating decision-making space.*

Now, this wasn't exactly how I would have put it but it was how she saw it. Besides, it was 80 per cent there. I try to practise what I preach, after all, and it was definitely good enough. (I might have added something explicit about being empowering, but in the interests of doing exactly that for Yulia, I kept quiet.) We talked some more about how she could achieve these goals and came up with the following that she could try:

1. Not making any decisions for a whole week, but passing the responsibility on to others.

2. Not giving answers in her weekly meeting, but only asking questions.

3. Share what she was trying to do with her team, and ask for their support.

At the end of our time together we agreed next steps. We would speak on the phone in a month's time to see how she was getting on, and then again, a month after that, perhaps surveying her team, and others, to measure progress. Finally, three months after the session, we would meet again, review how things had gone and think about any further work we needed to do together.

As she tidied the room a bit and I gathered my stuff, we stopped for a moment and smiled at each other. Her PA opened the door to announce that my taxi would be here in ten minutes. We looked at each other. Was there a need to use up that time, to fill it? We both seemed to think not.

Enabling not doing – Creating Space to lead

'A leader is best when people barely know he exists, when his work is done, his aim fulfilled, they will say: we did it ourselves.'

Lao Tzu

Delivering, as outlined in the previous chapter, was Yulia's signature strength. But hitherto her executing had been centred on delivering by herself, rather than delivering through others. Left to her own devices she could fix any problem and drive any issue forward. What she wasn't so used to (or good at) was executing as a *leader* rather than as an individual contributor, and that is where her growth lay – in the vital lesson that for leaders, the heart of execution involves empowering others rather than doing things yourself – even if you're the 'best' person to do them.

Our work on her Personal Potential Profile and not filling the Third Space was about Yulia working out who she needed to become. For many people new to leadership positions, this can feel very daunting. Growing into this next version of herself required Yulia to go through an uncomfortable period of holding back and allowing mistakes to happen. She had to let go of the reins and of who she had been up to now, and that process is rarely comfortable.

In order to succeed in her new role Yulia *had* to let go of who she used to be and embrace a different version of herself. Her driven, detail-oriented and extremely thorough approach to her work were obviously assets, but they needed applying in a different way in order for her to thrive in her new role. Rather than using those skills to ensure her own work was of a stellar quality, she now needed to utilise her skills to empower the people she was leading. If she had kept on employing the behaviours that until now had served her well, she would have risked the very position they had enabled her to move into. Realising that what had brought her this far wouldn't take her any further was a bittersweet pill for Yulia to swallow. But if she hadn't faced that truth and acted on it, she would have risked stifling and, at worst, suffocating the very people she was supposed to be inspiring.

Yulia is not alone in struggling with the transition from doing to leading. High achievers are used to being in the spotlight, garnering praise for their accomplishments, but the shift into a leadership position, where others take centre stage, can be emotionally tough, like a prizefighter becoming mentor and coach to a brilliant protegé. Alan Mulally, the CEO of Ford, has said, 'Leadership is not about me. It's about them.' For Yulia this even meant biting her tongue when others made suggestions that she knew she could add value to. As a leader, the risk of adding value to others' ideas is that you will subtly kill their ownership for those ideas simply because you are in a more senior position – even if that is the furthest thing from your mind. As unfortunate as it is, when you add to your reports' ideas you run the risk of them no longer feeling the idea is theirs. So it must be done judiciously.

One of the coaching clients mentioned by Michael Bungay Stanier in his book *The Coaching Habit* said that he'd learned a very hard lesson about being a CEO of a big company: 'My suggestions became orders.' This echoes what Yulia experienced. Without meaning to, she took up too much of the space that should have been available for her team to grow into. In my experience, seeing this and stepping back is often the hardest thing leaders have to master. But to reach the top, master it they must.

Embracing delegating, avoiding monkeys and other suggestions that help create the space to lead

All of the qualities in the chapters so far – such as reflecting, deciding, relating and planning – are the bedrock of being a great leader. Mastering them is the pre-requisite of really succeeding.

The Third Space

You can use the 'Third Space' model to examine your own style of interacting with others and your wider team. Spend a few minutes sketching out the diagram as I did with Yulia and see what comes to mind. You can use this technique to bring clarity to how you manage the 'Third Space' in all your relationships. Try it for your colleagues, direct reports, peers and boss. You can even use it to shed light on your relationships outside work – with your wife, husband, partner, friends and even children.

ASK YOURSELF: *Who fills the space here? Is that how it should be? How I want it to be? How do I think the 'other' feels? What can I do to step back, or step up?*

ASK YOURSELF: *Before I set out to lead, have I created space for the basics of being successful?*

Meet Morov, Lessov, Tossin and Ridov

The simple 'My job isn't …, it's …' formula offers a practical yet powerful tool for assessing where your next growth spurt might come from. You might want to play with that, first asking yourself, 'What isn't my job now?' and writing down all of the things that you're good at but which you know your role requires you to let go of. Then consider, 'What is my job now?' If you get stuck, try to recall three pieces of feedback you have had in the last month – and if you haven't had any, stop what you're doing and go and get some. Ask a trusted colleague or mentor for some input. The goal is to pay attention to what you need to stop doing, keep doing and start doing in order to lead as effectively as possible. One great CEO of a luxury retailer I work with had a cute way of posing these questions, based on four imaginary Russians. He would ask people what they needed Morov and Lessov and what they could Tossin or be Ridov.

ASK YOURSELF: *What isn't my job now? What is my job now? What do I need to stop doing? What do I need to start doing?*

The Art (and science) of delegation

One of the key differences between being a manager or leader rather than an individual contributor is that you suddenly have direct reports who you can use to help you deliver. As Yulia found, there is huge potential in the power of real delegation. As leadership expert John C. Maxwell says, 'If you want to do a few small things right, do them yourself. If you want to do great things and make a big impact, learn to delegate.'

When thinking about *what* to delegate, consider the work that needs doing and who you'll be delegating to. If you tend to feel guilty about adding more to other people's workloads, reframe delegation in your own mind as an opportunity to help them grow and develop in their careers. Delegate tasks and even projects that will push your team members beyond their comfort zone. Delegation is designed to free up your own time so that you have the mental space to step back and see the bigger picture. It can also allow you to devote time to training and coaching your people. Trusting people to get on with the job at hand tends to bring out the best in them. Without delegation, we risk burning out and demoralising the people who we work with, as was beginning to happen to Yulia's team member Jan. By not showing our faith in our team, we are implying that we don't trust them enough to do important and meaningful work.

When working with newer managers (or the many experienced managers who still struggle with the idea), I have a simple four-step checklist that I use to help them think through what they should be delegating and how. Note that actually delegating is Step 4 not Step 1. Take what feels relevant and useful from the following as you hone and refine your skills.

Step 1: Decide whether and what to delegate

When considering whether to delegate, consider the following:

○ Can someone else do this task, or is it critical that I do it myself?

○ Will this task (or some form of it) recur in the future?

○ Could this task give someone else an opportunity to grow or develop?

○ Do I have sufficient time and resources to delegate effectively? As that could involve having to train, answer questions, check progress and, if necessary, rework.

○ Does the task have any timelines or deadlines?

○ What are the consequences of not completing the task on time?

Step 2: Be sure of objectives and outcomes

○ What are the essential and desirable outcomes of this task or project?

○ How important is it that the results are of the highest possible quality? Would 'good enough' be good enough?

○ Is this task critical for long-term success or can it afford some sort of failure? (i.e., does it need my attention rather than someone else's?)

Step 3: Choosing who to delegate to

○ Who has relevant experience, knowledge and skills for the delegated task?

○ Do they have capacity in their schedule / workload to take this on?

○ Will one or more of their existing priorities / responsibilities need deferring / delegating?

○ Who is closest to the task, with the most intimate knowledge of the detail of the work?

○ How much training is needed, and would the training be related only to this one-off task or could it be beneficial longer term?

○ Are there any issues to address in terms of the person's attitude or confidence that might hinder task completion?

○ What is their preferred work style? How independently are they able to work?

○ What are their long-term goals? Does the task support these in any way?

Step 4: Delegate

Start with a conversation where you clearly articulate the desired outcome of the task and project. Specify – or elicit from your colleague or employee – an expression of the desired results. Make sure that you are crystal clear about what needs to be done.

Clearly identify how much authority, responsibility and accountability you are delegating to the person and what you remain ultimately accountable for, particularly the first few times you delegate. Discuss whether they should wait to be told what to do before acting or take action and then check in. Depending on their level of experience, you might want them to provide updates regularly or periodically. Discuss in advance the extent of their authority and whether they should act, or ask for your or someone else's input if they get stuck.

Close any potential communication gaps by being clear and offering guidelines, instructions, deadlines and anything else – especially if you think it is obvious. Don't assume that the person to whom you're delegating knows what you know. What's obvious to you might not be to them.

Focus on the outcome not the method employed to get there – on the results not the process. Not everyone will work the way you do. Your way isn't the only or even the best way! Empower your colleagues. Resist the urge to interfere. If you do not trust the person you've delegated the job to, you have either chosen the wrong person, or you're not giving the right person a chance. Exercise self-restraint. As David Ogilvy once said, 'Hire people who are better than you are, then get the hell out of their way.' Or, in the words of US General George S. Patton: 'Don't tell people *how* to do things, tell them *what* to do and let them surprise you with their results.'

If support and advice is needed, you should resist the urge to offer answers; stay in coaching mode, ask questions and help your report find their own answers, even if this takes time. It is at this moment, when your report is struggling, that managers often become impatient (or feel guilty) and take back the task, figuring they may as well do it themselves. This is almost always a mistake. If it was worthy of delegation once then it still is, and if your report needs support then you should give it, not disempower them by taking away their challenge. Without realising it, managers doing this are falling prey to the phenomenon of 'taking back the monkey', as explained in Harvard Business Review's most downloaded article. The manager's task is to keep the monkey (i.e. the problem) on their report's back, not let it somehow scramble back onto theirs.

Lastly, give and ask for feedback at the end of a project. Creating the space to reflect on the process will, like delegation itself, save you time in future. Make sure you offer appropriate thanks and even rewards if possible.

ASK YOURSELF: *Have I delegated as much as I possibly can? To the right people? In the right way? What did we both learn?*

The fundamental change that occurs when you become a leader is exactly the one Yulia had to confront and master. Suddenly, the task is not just creating space for you but creating space for others. That, in a single, simple phrase, is the best definition of leadership I know.

Conclusion

In Part 3 we have explored three aspects of doing – planning, delivering and leading. I hope that this exploration will enable you to deliver what really matters in a more efficient and empowering way.

There are three key lessons. First you need to be crystal clear and disciplined about what you want to deliver – and not commit to delivering too much. Second you need a well thought through (albeit flexible) plan to get there. You then need to develop your own pOS (personal operating system) that brings out the best in you. What environment do you need, physically, mentally and emotionally, to be most productive? Don't be afraid of trying out new approaches. Sometimes what we think is 'our' way is only really our habit and actually other ways would be better for us.

Last, you need to make sure that as you increase in seniority you master the art of delivering through others rather than directly yourself. At the most senior levels, you need to be able to lead other leaders. Knowing what – and how – to delegate is crucial for this, as is consciously creating the space to develop yourself as a leader. We looked at the need for you to pursue twin strategies – your business strategy as required by your role, and your personal strategy as required by your career goals and desire to develop yourself.

Now that we have explored the three pillars of creating space for success – space to think, connect and do – we will step back a little and make some space to look at the more fundamental questions that arise out of our professional endeavours. Questions that relate to who we are, and what we need and want: our dreams and sense of purpose; our balance, sustainability and resilience; and our need to keep growing. In Part 4 we look at Creating Space to Be.

PART 4

Create Space to Be

A S WELL AS CREATING the Space to Think, Connect, and Do there is a more fundamental thing we need to create Space for – and that is simply to Be. We live in a world where someone, somewhere is always switched on, always accomplishing, shipping, launching, succeeding or striving. Even before you get up, people on one side of the world are busy working away, and when you finish, those on the other side have just started. For anyone with a lot of ambition, the temptation to just keep going and going is strong. But this mentality ignores one crucial fact: we are human *beings*, not human *doings*, and we are not designed to be permanently productive.

The truth is, if you are waiting for things to slow down before you finally give yourself permission to stop and just *be*, you're going to be waiting a very long time. We need to take care of ourselves, and work out who we are, what we want, and what we need, on a basic level, before we can try and master everything else. If we don't, we run the risk of existing but not really living, and we run the risk of feeling lost or overwhelmed – experiencing what one psychoanalyst called the 'nameless dread'. There are three areas where we need to take action to ensure that we are living worthwhile, happy and sustainable lives.

First, we need to **Create Space to Dream**. Too often we fall into things, or keep going out of habit or a lack of imagination. We feel the push to produce more, and don't make space to sit still, take stock and think, on a deeper level, about what it is that we want from life and how we might achieve it. As we will see with Oscar, doing this can save us from a depressing decline and free up all sorts of possibilities.

Second, we need to **Create Space to Balance**. We are all holistic human beings who require more than money and 'success'. Our health, inner contentment and our spiritual lives are important too. In the modern, busy world we can easily lose sight of these things. Trevone clearly did. He had a short, sharp shock that the rest of us will, with luck, avoid but that we can nonetheless learn from.

Finally, we need to **Create Space to Grow**. Not only do we need to feel we are learning and growing in our jobs, but that this is also happening in our lives. As we go through the phases of life what we want changes, and being open to experimenting and taking risks allows us to discover what that might be. As Almantas's story shows, leaving our comfort zone and making some tough choices can help us to move to the next stage of what life has to offer.

All three stories reveal how being open can help us to challenge BAU (business as usual). We must allow ourselves to dream, make sure we are taking care of ourselves and relentlessly question the path we are on. That way we will have the best chance of living life to the full.

CHAPTER 10

Space to Dream

Oscar and His Love of the Land

LESSON: *You need to create the space to look deep on the inside to know what you really want, and then have the courage to go after it.*

O SCAR IS THE CHIEF INFORMATION OFFICER of a big bank. He was hired for his energy and vision but he has lost his way. His boss, the bank's new CEO, wants to drive through big changes, making the bank more innovative and digital. He feels that Oscar doesn't seem up for the challenge ahead and, out of disappointment and frustration, he sent him to see me.

When talking to Oscar I was struck by how low his mood was. He seemed distracted, unenthusiastic and bored. Initially I thought he might be depressed. As a trained therapist I was able to explore this with him but it rapidly became clear that Oscar's mood only related to his work. When he talked about his family and his hobbies, he lit up and was full of energy and plans.

He told me his story, of growing up on a farm in Somerset, loving the outdoors, the animals, and even the back-breaking work. When he left for university he sorely missed the place. In his final year, his family's world was turned upside down when his dad got very ill and the farm went under. I could see that this had been pretty traumatic for Oscar but he hurried through the tale and started to talk about doing well at university and finding his first job. Interestingly, Oscar's mood stayed positive and lively as he talked about the early part of his career and the challenges he faced to get to the top of his department. Yet, when his story got nearer to the present day he became deflated again.

Something seemed to have changed, but what? We started to talk about his purpose. This means what you want to achieve in your professional life, beyond just delivering what the job requires. It is what gives you a sense of direction and helps you be energised and inspiring. It could be called, in relation to the 'work' part of your life, your 'reason for being' or 'what you live for'. Having a strong sense of who we are and what drives us is important, especially for those leading others.

The example I most often give is of a prison officer I met once whose job, frankly, was a nightmare: low pay, poor environment, and all topped off with the constant threat of violence. What he wanted was a job that he enjoyed, one that enabled him to be creative, was deeply fulfilling and offered the chance of some respect and admiration. All pretty unlikely if you looked at his job, but not if you asked him his purpose. That, he would explain, was to try to save the occasional young prisoner he had been able to bond with, and inspire them away from a life of crime. It didn't happen often, every six months or so on average he thought, and a promising case would often end in disappointment. But when he did manage it? Wow, he felt all the things he had listed and more.

Over the next few weeks Oscar and I did several things. First, we made the space for him to feel the loss, sadness and fear that he'd had back when the farm was broken up and sold. At the time, he'd felt he'd had to stay strong for his parents but inside he'd been totally broken-hearted. We spent a moving half-hour with him intermittently sobbing and remembering all the things the place had meant to him.

We also did an exercise I often use called 'Dual Life', which shed light on his underlying sense of purpose. It's something to try if you want to explore your own sense of purpose.

Dual Life

This exercise is deceptively simple but profound. First you imagine what you would spend your life doing if you had no constraints whatsoever, no family to provide for or worry about, no geographical ties, no need for money. Whatever you come up with (sometimes it's a dream job, other times something more adventurous), next write down the three words that come to mind if you had to say what describes that job or activity. I call these 'life-givers'. The obvious next question is how much of those three things – for example, the outdoors, freedom, autonomy – do you experience in your current life and job? This could lead to a fundamental re-examination of what you are doing and why (like it did with Oscar) or, less dramatically, inform a conversation about how you could get more of those three 'life-givers' in the job you currently have.

---

*

Finally, I deployed a tool I've developed called TELOS720 to get some outside perspective from Oscar's family and friends. This asks some simple questions such as 'When is Oscar most excited and inspired?' It also asks the respondents to suggest some images that sum up the person concerned. This results in a collage of images that brings to life what people thought Oscar was all about. Oscar's 'collage' was a colourful mix of the countryside, trees, animals, the sky and an expanse of fields and forests, alongside a big box of tools. This environment, according to his nearest and dearest, was where Oscar was at his happiest. It was a long way away from his glass-walled, minimalist office, stuffed with computer terminals, thirty-four floors up a skyscraper in Canary Wharf.

As we looked at the collage it became crystal clear to both of us what had happened. Deep down in Oscar there had always been the dream of living on a farm like he had done as a kid, but the pain of seeing his dad fall on hard times had scared him. That purpose had been repressed, only allowed expression when on holiday and through his hobbies. His core pathogenic belief was that he couldn't live the way he really wanted to and had, instead, to do corporate work in an office to feel 'safe'. His true purpose had been cloaked in a new purpose: building financial security for his family. What had changed in the last few years was that he'd achieved that purpose. His success meant that his previous belief no longer held true. His heart knew that, which is why his enthusiasm for his career had dropped away, but his head had yet to catch up. Now it had, and the consequences were profound and rapid. Within six months of our meeting he had left his job and moved back to Somerset. He found a working farm that made enough money to stay afloat, and subsidised his and his family's needs from his investments. Luckily his wife ran her own business and happily relocated – interestingly she'd always said that she wanted to move out of the city once the kids had gone to university.

Suddenly Oscar and his family were enjoying the life that had been conjured up by that TELOS720 collage. He had made the space to really examine what he wanted and why. Now, if you'll forgive me the cliché, he was living the dream.

But where does that happy ending leave the business? The CEO did joke when he heard Oscar's plans that he wanted his money back, but what could I have done? Tried to coach Oscar to repress his purpose again, to pretend to be enthused by his bank job? No. Even though it wasn't quite the outcome the business had desired – and it caused considerable disruption – this was the right answer. As it happened, Oscar's deputy was ready to step up and has been doing a great job.

Coming fully alive and Creating Space to Dream

'In the depths of winter I finally learned that within me there lay an invincible summer.'

Albert Camus, from *Lyrical and Critical Essays*

Oscar's experience of reconnecting to his lost dream was poignant and life-altering but painful. No wonder he had resisted going there before. We live in a society that is generally extremely pain-avoidant, whether that pain is physical, emotional or mental, yet we are fascinated with it too (we seem pretty obsessed, for example, with TV shows in which people suffer the most awful crimes, accidents and illnesses). Yet in our own lives we tend to numb or medicate emotional pain. We rationalise and repress it, doing whatever we can to avoid feeling it – yet, as Oscar's story demonstrates, pain often carries an important and even life-altering message, and sooner or later it *will* get our attention.

As hard as it was for Oscar to revisit the devastating loss and associated heartbreak from his childhood, I think of him as lucky. He was forced to confront himself at a relatively young age and deal with what some psychotherapists and philosophers call an existential crisis.

At its heart the 'dark night of the soul' that many of us go through at some point or another, is a response to the unpalatable but inescapable fact that everything is fundamentally impermanent and we are all going to die. It's tempting to start joking about how morbid this is, but it's actually just a fact of life.

It's pretty clear that we are a youth-obsessed culture, one consequence of which is that while we live in society with so many elderly people, we don't really have that many elders. (This is one of the starkest contrasts, incidentally, between our modern life and that ancient life on the Savannah, where elders were honoured, respected and expected to be leaders.) Nowadays, it's as if we collectively turn our eyes away from the inevitability of death by segregating older people to the periphery of our awareness. Yet as many spiritual teachers have emphasised, it is essential that we come to terms with death in order to truly live

One poignant echo of this comes from Steve Jobs' 2005 speech to the graduating students of Stanford University. Two years after his first cancer diagnosis and six years before the second (which would ultimately kill him), Jobs said that,

Remembering that I'll be dead soon is the most important tool
I've ever encountered to help me make the big choices in life.
Almost everything – all external expectations, all pride, all fear
of embarrassment or failure – these things just fall away in the
face of death, leaving only what is truly important … Death is the
destination we all share. No one has ever escaped it, and that is how it
should be, because death is very likely the single best invention of life.
It's life's change agent. It clears out the old to make way for the new.

Dan Howell's beautiful words, 'Embrace the void and have the courage to exist', also remind us that courage is at the heart of being truly alive – that really being here, being fully alive, can co-exist alongside a sense of meaninglessness. In fact, it is only by looking the anxieties of life in the eye and embracing the unknown that we can choose what we want things to mean. We do not need to deny our struggle in order for it to loosen its grip on us. In the middle of pain, there is great purpose to be found. A rock bottom of any kind, but particularly an existential crisis, can be a gift in disguise, one with enormous transformative power.

Oscar had to get to grips with all of this material during our work together. It's one thing to read about this stuff in a book; it's quite another to walk through this kind of experience in one's own life. Not only did he have to deal with all the anxieties involved in changing his world, but he had to turn and face the unfinished business from his past, which in itself was a mammoth undertaking. Dreaming begins in childhood, and if something happened back then to interfere with that process, we often need to give ourselves the time, space and support to really grieve over those losses so that we can move on. There's a lot of evidence, in both therapeutic and epigenetic circles, that unresolved trauma is transmitted from one generation to the next, compounding and intensifying with each new generation that has to deal with it. The loss of dreams – to economic crises, deaths, addictions and more – is a huge unspoken part of many families' histories. Patterns repeat, often until we acknowledge the pain and loss, and honour it in some way. It's like working with any form of denial; once you fully admit the truth, its silent grip over you lessens. In allowing himself to feel the bottled up pain and heartbreak from all those years ago, Oscar did something that might never have been done in his family before. It was a vital step in being able to reclaim the dream he had discarded when his dad fell ill and the family's farm went under.

In many cases, being able to dream well requires that we know suffering. Siddhartha Gautama would never have become enlightened if he had remained cut off from suffering behind the protective palace walls. He had to encounter *samsara*, the cycle of birth, life (much of it meaningless) and death in order to awaken. Only then could he become the Buddha. Many of the world's greatest businesses, projects and not-for-profit organisations were founded because of pain or suffering. As J. K. Rowling stated during a commencement speech, 'Rock bottom became the solid foundation on which I rebuilt my life.'

Another powerful emotional experience that can strongly connect us to our dreams or a sense of purpose is anger. When things make us livid, or outraged, or disgusted, or appalled, it's a sure sign that our inner compass is pointing towards something that really matters to us. Anger and passion share many of the same qualities – a fieriness and an absolute laser focus. If child exploitation, animal welfare or everyday sexism really get your hackles up, you have the opportunity to use that as a springboard towards doing something that feels meaningful and purposeful. I recently met a woman called Louise who spent twenty years running a children's care home for violent children and girls involved in the sex trade. Louise didn't dream of doing this as a child, but she saw injustice in the world and felt compelled to help. However, meaningful work doesn't have to look like Louise's work; we need principled and passionate artists and entrepreneurs, scientists and architects, farmers and accountants, managers and CEOs.

For some of us, 'finding our purpose' might look more like a shift in perception about our lives rather than an overhauling of life as we know it. Oscar clearly wasn't ultimately suited to working in Canary

Wharf, but many people thrive in such environments and wouldn't swap them for the world. Which doesn't preclude the search for more meaning while they are there.

A word of caution about trying to unearth your 'purpose': beware of thinking of it as a singular thing. I'd like to dispel that notion, which I find wraps people up in knots, especially those of us who aren't like Oscar. He was lucky in that he had a clear vision of the life he wanted; the childhood loss stood in the way, but once that was grieved for, he found it relatively easy to make the choice to go after what he really wanted. Some people are undoubtedly born with one great talent, passion or path, but countless people are multi-talented and, as importantly, multi-passionate. So when considering the space to dream, I love the simple, powerful suggestion of Elizabeth Gilbert – to follow your curiosity.

Think of purpose not as something elusive to pin down, but as something to explore and experiment with. Instead of searching for your purpose, try living the rest of the day purposefully. Instead of hunting for your purpose, pay attention to the sense of engagement and fulfilment in your life. If you are on purpose, life might feel engaging, satisfying, interesting, even effortless. If you're off track with living purposefully, life might feel empty, unfulfilling or even anguished, and that's often easier to notice. We all suffer in some ways, for certain periods of time, but *prolonged* emotional and psychological suffering is often a symptom that we are not living in alignment with a sense of purpose.

Also bear in mind that we might be living extremely purposeful lives for a period, but may feel the spark of inspiration going out as we enter a different season in our lives. That doesn't mean we've failed; it means we're human – evolving, growing and changing. Dreaming requires that we get into the metaphorical arena that Teddy Roosevelt first spoke of and that we 'dare greatly'. Along the way we may find ourselves in a similar position to Oscar, having to look back and deal with some unfinished (emotional) business in order to forge ahead.

Dreaming might seem frivolous, a pastime for the privileged few in a world where we're sometimes stretched too thin to even think straight, let alone really dream, but I see it differently. Without the dreamers, I think our world would be in a far worse state than it is. We need people to keep dreaming, to dare to believe that something more beautiful, or magical, or spectacular, or kind might be possible. The people I see as powerful dreamers are those with vision and perseverance. That combination is essential, and it's something that many leaders have a good blend of.

I was once privileged to meet George Lucas, the creator of *Star Wars*. The perseverance that he needed to get the original film made is almost beyond belief. The budget was cut, his choices were questioned, he had to scavenge and adapt props from old movies, and, even when finished, the powers that be gave the film a tiny release, expecting it to die a quick death. Forty years later it is the most successful film franchise in history, earning around $30bn and counting. Lucas's best advice? 'Always remember your dream determines your reality.' Not entirely true but not entirely untrue either.

We really are here for such a short period of time, and we only get to live each day once. In the speech I mentioned earlier Steve Jobs also said, 'Remembering that you are going to die is the best way I know to avoid the trap of thinking you have something to lose. You are already naked. There is no reason not to follow your heart.' You'll have to face the detractors, the doubters and the critics on the sidelines, laughing and mocking and pointing out where you've gone wrong, just as happened to George Lucas. You may be plagued by doubt, haunted by uncertainty and riddled with insecurity – but you might also find that creating space to dream and then challenging yourself to go after it is one of the most meaningful, bravest things that you've ever done. There's a wonderful Mary Oliver poem called 'The Summer Day', which closes with the line: 'Tell me, what is it you plan to do with this one wild and precious life?' The poignancy of the question leaps out at you when you read it, possibly because of how evocative the rest of her imagery is in the poem. A lover of nature, Oliver writes about a grasshopper that lands in her hand, eating a sugar cube from her palm before flying away. Just before the final line, Oliver asks, 'Doesn't everything die at last, and too soon?' reminding us once again of how transient and impermanent and therefore how incredibly meaningful things – especially this moment – are. In inviting us to consider what we 'plan' to do with our one life, Oliver is really encouraging us to create space to dream. Her use of the word plan is really describing living intentionally, recognising that while, on the one hand, we have a lot of life available, on the other, we'll never get to live this particular day or season of our lives again. In John Lennon's words, 'life is what happens to you when you're busy making other plans.' Our dreams are a vital part of what make us human, whether they are expressions of our wishes, hopes and fears (for ourselves and for the world) or an attempt to escape from our existing reality. As it was for Oscar, this is your one life. Will you give yourself the space to really live it?

Starting with why, dreaming of death and other practical ideas to help you create Space to Dream

There are as many ways to create space to dream as there are dreams. Finding what works for you might be a case of trial and error. Trust yourself and listen to your instincts. Here are four ways that may help you:

Start With Why

I often recommend that clients watch the great TED talk by Simon Sinek called 'How great leaders inspire action' – otherwise known as 'Start With Why'. He also wrote a book of that title and, as I mentioned in Chapter 5, presented a compelling case for exploring the 'why' at the heart of every business, project and venture. Creating the space to ask why you're doing something forces you to confront the conscious and unconscious reasons for your choices, and can be extremely helpful in bringing your values to the surface. Exploring questions related to your life purpose with someone who knows you well – a friend, loved one or mentor – will enable them to call you out whenever your core pathogenic beliefs seem to be running the show. For example, a client of mine wasted tens of thousands of dollars and many years of his life attending law school and practising law. When I asked him why, he said he did it because it was sensible – but 'sensible' wasn't a value that was anywhere near the top of his list of what mattered! He wanted a connected, creative, simple and adventurous life, and he knew it right from the word go. I don't believe that we should regret the life choices we've made, but I do think it was clear that my client knew deep down that his set of choices would lead to further choices, none of which he would find fulfilling. He just didn't act on what he knew.

ASK YOURSELF: *Do I have a clear sense of my professional purpose? Do I know my 'Why'? What would doing the Dual Life exercise mean for me?*

Dreaming of Death

Reflecting on death might not feel like a fun thing to do, but that doesn't mean it isn't worthwhile. Although none of us can possibly know what the experience will be like, we can at least attempt to imagine what Carl Jung called the second 'great mystery' of life. If you were dying with no regrets, what would you have done in the previous six months to guarantee that? This exercise can be quite confronting, particularly if, like Oscar, you feel somewhat trapped in the golden cage of a safe, comfortable, predictable life. It can also be incredibly powerful, cutting through the bullshit, excuses and amnesia about our impermanence, all of which stop us from truly living.

Bronnie Ware's research on the regrets of the dying found that people on their deathbeds were not wishing they had done more work. When you look back on your career you may well feel incredibly proud of your accomplishments, but the chances are that without conscious attention, you will come to regret the following, as the dying people Ware worked with did:

*I wish I'd had the courage to live a life true to myself, not the life
others expected of me.
I wish I hadn't worked so hard.
I wish I'd had the courage to express my feelings.
I wish I had stayed in touch with my friends.
I wish that I had let myself be happier.*

ASK YOURSELF: *If I had six months to live, how would I want to
spend that time? What would I let go of? What would I keep? What
would I do, give, try or be?*

How does it feel?

In her book *The Desire Map*, Danielle LaPorte highlights a profound
question – not what do you want to be, do or achieve, but how do
you want to feel? This question is deceptively simple, yet in allowing
ourselves the space to consider it, we often come face to face with all
of the choices we make that lead us to feel the exact opposite of what
we claim we want. This opens up some interesting lines of enquiry:
if we want to feel peaceful, why have we crammed our schedule
with wall-to-wall activities? If we want to feel connected, why do we
all sit looking at our phones over dinner? If we want to feel expansive, why haven't we booked that class we've long wanted to take? If
we want to feel focused, why are we on Facebook at 9.03 am? Clari-
fying how we want to feel also unhooks us from the constant tug
of consumerism, which pulls our attention in a thousand different
directions every day, telling us to buy this, own that, purchase that –
each shiny object holding out the unfulfillable promise of joy, a sense
of completion, harmony and success. By clearly stating the handful
of feeling states we value the most, we become more autonomous
and creative, harnessing the power of attention bias which notices
the things we have made a conscious effort to focus on.

ASK YOURSELF: *How do I want to feel in my life? In my body? My
home? My career? My finances? My relationships? My free time?*

Reconnect with your dreams

You may find it useful to revisit Oscar's story and use it as a jump-start for delving into your own. Do you remember what you dreamed of doing when you were younger? What did you love so much that you could spend hours doing it? Was it dancing? Building forts in the woods? Playing teacher? Taking things apart and putting them back together again? What happened to those dreams and first loves? Perhaps you received messages from significant people in your life, messages that would go on to become core pathogenic beliefs and perhaps influenced your life decisions. Maybe you were told – or thought yourself – that maths was too hard, even though you loved it, or the arts didn't pay, or something else. This is deeply personal work and there are only so many possibilities I can suggest. No one can do this work for you, but no one can take it away either. One thing that is certain is that we live in an age where the most unlikely careers are possible. Although it isn't as simple as 'If you want something enough, it will happen', there is a lot to be said for putting a stake in the ground and giving yourself a period of time to try. The law of attraction as set out in Rhonda Byrne's best-seller *The Secret* is too kooky for most of us, but I suspect there is something in the idea that if we want something strongly enough, then visualise it and the path to reaching it, our 'thoughts' will indeed have some effect on what happens.

There are countless excellent questions you can use to conduct an inquiry, which in coaching simply means to reflect deeply on a question rather than simply looking for one right answer. Here are some possible questions to help you explore your dreams:

ASK YOURSELF: *What is it to live well? What is it to dream? What do I want? What do I really, really want? What do I not allow myself to want? What would living fully in alignment with my values look like? What does real success look like? What am I building? What pain do I notice in the world around me that I feel compelled to help? If I were at my best, what would my next action be? Where am I settling? What am I tolerating? What would living bravely for the next (day/30 days/90 days) look like? What would a perfect day be? What would be so good, I can barely imagine it?*

CHAPTER 11

Space to Balance

Trevone and His Near-Death Experience

LESSON: *Work and life aren't in opposition, creating space to find balance between them will make you more successful at both.*

T REVONE IS THE CEO of a big hedge fund. He has always been a forceful, charismatic leader and driven himself and his employees hard. A few months ago, he had made an appearance in the financial news pages that shocked the City, and those who knew him well. It was announced that he had taken three months off work due to 'stress'. As well as being under medical care, the Chairman of the Board wanted him to have a coach to help him transition back to work as he recovered.

I had expected him to be resistant to my appearance in his life, but it was quite the opposite. He had been even more shocked himself at what had happened and was happy to get the help he needed. As we spoke, though, I began to get the first glimmer of a concern that was to grow stronger as the weeks wore on. For Trevone, it was about getting better so he could go back to how things were. A real change wasn't on his mind.

First, though, I had to get behind the label of 'stress'. It turned out that Trevone had been suffering from exhaustion, some panic attacks and a bit of low-level clinical depression. It further transpired that he'd actually been suffering like this for several years and it was only at the insistence of his wife that he'd sought help, at which point the company's insurance advisers had insisted he take time off and get properly treated.

Trevone's problem was more high profile then most, and more pronounced, but it was all too common in a milder form. When faced with stress or overwork I like to try and get a picture of the coachee as a whole, using a tool called the Wheel of Life. You can easily apply it to yourself.

The Wheel of Life

Draw a circle. Then fill it in, like a pie chart, with four aspects of your life – work, self, family and social, and spirituality – each one proportionately taking up the space it occupies in a typical month.

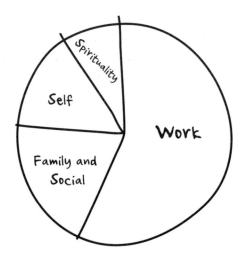

The Wheel of Life

It is amazing how much the modern executive's life is consumed by work; family and social life almost always come next, with self and spirituality a distant joint third. In fact, some people I have this conversation with barely know what I mean by each.

*

Trevone was typical. Work was around 80 per cent, his family 15 per cent, he barely saw his friends, other than the occasional golf game (which we agreed could go under 'self'), and he had no spiritual aspect to his life at all.

If it seems relevant, I will sometimes ask my coachees to have a full health checkup too. Even if they are given the medical all clear the doctor will almost always recommend some changes in lifestyle. A great read on this subject is 'The Making of the Corporate Athlete' by Jim Loehr and Tony Schwartz, which draws a parallel between athletes and executives, pointing out that we expect both to perform at their peak, but tend to ignore the physical body in the case of the executive. The authors make a strong case for addressing your physical health and wellbeing in order to fulfil your potential in a corporate environment.

Creating his wheel of life did shock Trevone a little. We moved to the next stage and I asked him to sketch out what he wanted the wheel to look like. It was very different, work had gone down to 60 per cent; family up to 20 per cent, with friends adding an extra 10 per cent to that, with 10 per cent left over for something a bit transcendental. He was talking about taking up mountaineering again, which he'd enjoyed in his twenties, but also confessed to wondering about going back to church. He'd been brought up a Roman Catholic and, to my surprise, told me he'd once considered going into the priesthood.

The week after we'd discussed all this, Trevone was clearly disgruntled as we began our session. 'I've been thinking about last week,' he began. 'It's all very well me saying I want to cut my work down from 80 per cent to 60 per cent, but how am I going to do that? We've got the merger, new regulation and Brexit to navigate.' Hearing these words, my heart sank. Just like Yulia – but more profoundly I felt – Trevone seemed to be a leader who assumed that, in the end, he had to do everything himself. Even when, as in his case, he had hundreds of people working for him, some of them paid, literally, millions.

When I raised this, Trevone seemed to get it, but I felt there was something blocking him. I got an inkling of what that might be as we sketched out what a new style of leadership might look like. In *The Psychopathology of Everyday Life* Freud wrote about how jokes can give away our true, unconscious feelings. On one occasion Trevone muttered about how what we were talking about sounded like semi-retirement. I asked what he meant. 'Well, it sounds like an easy life, doesn't it?' I tried to probe this but he brushed it off. I tried another way, asking him to draw the images that came to mind when he thought of going back to work full-time. He stepped up to the white-board and drew an old factory, then a treadwheel, then a storm – all black clouds and zig-zags of lightning.

As I explained earlier, sometimes my questions seem to come straight from the heart, and I found myself asking him, 'Do you enjoy work?'

He looked at me, and harrumphed.

'That's a stupid question.'

'What's the answer?' I persisted.

He slowly capped the dry marker and sat down. 'I've never really thought about it.'

'Well, now's your chance.'

We then spoke for an hour about the fact that he'd never really enjoyed work. We went all through his employment history and I got him to do just the 'work success and fulfilment' parts of the Lifeline exercise that you may remember from Yulia's story. While his success line was very high, his fulfilment line was pretty flat.

We had discovered Trevone's pathogenic core belief: work was supposed to feel like shit. It wasn't really clear where, in Trevone's upbringing or early life, this notion had taken hold or why. That mattered less than his attitude to it today. As soon as he'd articulated it he saw how absurd it was and expressed a desire to change.

As we worked on this we saw how this central, if hidden, motif had influenced his hard-driving management style (everyone else should be as miserable as he was) and even his health (why not look and feel like shit as well). Oprah Winfrey has a fantastically simple but profound saying that she uses when someone is talking about how awful their husband or wife is to them. 'Honey,' she will drawl, reaching out to place a comforting hand on their shoulder or knee, 'love ain't supposed to feel bad.' This isn't quite true of work. Good, fulfilling, challenging work will feel hard sometimes, but not all the time. Often, most of the time even, it should feel good. Once Trevone had realised this, it affected him on a deep level.

We pulled out the glimmers of enjoyment from his Lifeline and brainstormed how he could reinforce and expand these; we explored his sense of purpose, like I had done with Oscar; and we worked on the idea of him building in time during his working week for praise (of others and himself) and celebration.

Slowly but surely over the next year Trevone began to fundamentally change who he was as a leader and how he related to work. A few months after the coaching had finished I bumped into him at a City Awards dinner. He ran over, looking fitter than I'd ever seen him. After we had chatted for a bit he sighed and said he had to get back to his table, motioning over to a group of middle-aged guys in suits, all looking a bit worse for wear. He leaned in to whisper something: 'Some bits of work are still shit, eh?' before bounding back to his seat, slapping people on the back as he did so.

Bastard work again and Creating Space to Balance

'Better learn balance. Balance is key.'

Mr Miyagi in *The Karate Kid*

Trevone's belief, that work should be hard, long and feel like shit, is a particularly insidious cultural narrative, embedded deeply into our society. Perhaps that's why, in his coaching, we couldn't pinpoint where it had come from; it's such a given for so many people that it's hard to identify a specific starting point. One of my close relatives labels the Monday–Friday alarm on his iPhone 'Bastard Work Again'. It's the first thing he sees when he wakes up.

We wear our near-exhaustion as a badge of honour, taking pride in how busy we are. We're running on caffeine and quick fixes and very much live in an all-or-nothing, crash-and-burn society. Burnout is a near constant spectre, especially for those of us in leadership positions. The idea of an unstressed leader might reassure us on one level – after all, no one wants a headless chicken leading the way – but it also stirs up some subtle discomfort, too. How come *they* aren't stressed out when the rest of us are? Why do *they* get to work normal hours when everyone else is stretched to the limit? How come *they're* not answering their calls or emails immediately when we are expected to be available at everyone's beck and call? We're all caught up in a giant game of call my bluff, constantly teaching ourselves and each other how to treat one another.

Although Trevone's situation was serious – secret panic attacks, exhaustion and low level clinical depression – it was also, in a sense, unremarkable. I explained in an earlier chapter that evolution cannot keep pace with the rate of progress in our society, and the simple truth is that we are simply not designed to do life at such an intense, relentless pace. With burnout on the rise (it's estimated to cost around £255bn per year in the UK alone), it is for you to decide what balance means to you, using tools like the wheel of life to help you explore where you are and where you might want to be. 'A Type' personalities like Trevone typically feel allergic to the idea of slowing down – much of their identity and sense of self-worth comes from their achievements, and the treadmill of achieving needs constant updates. I introduced Trevone to the idea of being a corporate athlete, which will appeal to many people with that same A type leaning. The foundational principle of the corporate athlete mindset is that high performance in the business world has to address the whole person, as athletes do. If all we do is deal with the neck up, we're missing some vital aspects of what it means to be at your peak.

Achieving what Loehr and Schwartz call the Ideal Performance State (IPS) requires shifting back and forth between energy output and energy renewal – and this is where we often get it wrong. The whole premise of this book is that we are the first generation in a thousand that needs to create space rather than fill it. Athletes that do not create the space to recover do not reach their potential, and this applies equally to executives. Sooner or later, the well runs dry. Stress in and of itself isn't the issue – stress is actually what makes muscles grow stronger – but stress without disciplined, intentional recovery depletes us at best and is disastrous at worst.

The case for adopting the mindset of being a corporate athlete is pretty compelling. According to Loehr and Schwartz:

> The demands on executives to sustain high performance day in and day out, year in and year out, dwarf the challenges faced by any athlete we have ever trained. The average professional athlete, for example, spends most of his time practicing and only a small percentage – several hours a day, at most – actually competing. The typical executive, by contrast, devotes almost no time to training and must perform on demand ten, 12, 14 hours a day or more. Athletes enjoy several months of off-season, while most executives are fortunate to get three or four weeks of vacation a year. The career of the average professional athlete spans seven years; the average executive can expect to work 40 to 50 years.

When we think of it that way, it makes complete sense to build in the space and strategies to support ourselves in order to keep going, especially in such a competitive environment. Nearly twenty years ago I attended an intense residential workshop called the Hoffman Process, which I sometimes recommend to clients who are in need of some deeper personal work beyond the remit of coaching (I believe a week on the Hoffman is equivalent to a year's very good therapy). The process incorporates many valuable ideas but at its heart is the notion that we are all 'quadrinities', that our self is made up of four parts – the intellectual, emotional, physical and spiritual, or the mind, the heart, the body and the 'source'. Parts 1 and 2 of this book focus on the first two parts of the quadrinity – the intellectual and emotional self, and how we can create the space for each of these to be expressed best – the space to think and connect.

By looking at balance and the idea of the corporate athlete we have explored the third part of the quadrinity, the physical self. It is worth noting how the physical often gets neglected when working in an office, thanks to many corporate cultures which assume that we'll come in, sit down at our desks and – aside from making a quick cup of coffee – hardly move about at all. Since knowledge and information work – even creative work – basically involves our brains, eyes, mouths and hands, the rest of the body is sort of just *there,* a tool to be used but not something that warrants paying much attention to. Many workplaces are addressing this, offering gym membership and the opportunity to get involved in sport, but with the UK's obesity rate rising faster than in the USA, and research showing that half of adults walk less than a mile a day, it's clear that we are not taking brilliant care of our bodies.

One of the most unaddressed aspects of our physical selves involves how much rest and sleep we get. There's a lot of material out there about how successful leaders sleep less (they're sometimes called the 'sleepless elite'), and that doing so will make you a better leader too. However, there is even more information available about how many people are already feeling sleep deprived, and that their energy levels and the quality of their decision making suffer as a result. For this reason I often carry out a sleep audit with clients. I'll return to this later.

Matthew Walker, a neuroscientist and author of *Why We Sleep,* tackles the prevailing cultural attitude where sleep machismo is prized. There's a narcissism of busyness in our lives today that precludes true balance, where a balanced life would include lots of downtime, screen-free time, unscheduled white space. We equate busyness with importance, and use how little sleep we get as evidence of how important we are. 'Sleep,' as Walker puts it pithily in an interview, 'has an image problem.' Our society has created an unhelpful and inaccurate yet fairly stubborn association between sleep and laziness. Eight hours of sleep seems slothful. 'Every disease that is killing us in the developed world has significant and many causal links to insufficient sleep,' Walker states. Studies have found a 40 per cent increase in the risk of cancer in people who sleep less than six hours a night. Poor sleep is associated with Alzheimer's, and research

shows that treating sleep disorders in adults can delay the onset of
the disease by years. Poor sleep is connected to obesity, diabetes and
weight gain. One study restricted the sleep of healthy adults to four
hours a night, and in just one week their blood sugar had reached
levels that were pre-diabetic. A study of half a million people found
a 45 per cent increased risk in developing heart disease due to inadequate sleep. In our black-and-white culture, we often prefer to do
extreme things – such as attend a boot camp or do a seven-day juice
cleanse – rather than simply pay attention to the quality and length
of our time asleep, despite the science showing that even a small
adjustment to our sleep routine can be really beneficial.

Finally, there is the fourth aspect of our 'quadrinity': the
neglected, and often disavowed, spiritual self. I recognise this is going
to be a controversial part of the book, so let me lay my cards on the
table. I went through a spiritual awakening when I was around thirty
years old. This involved yoga, Reiki, and a flirtation with Buddhism
before I eventually found a spiritual home in the High Anglican tradition of the Church of England – a tradition replete with ritual and
ceremony, but also liberal and mystical.

I recognise that overt spiritual practice and, in particular, organised religion are not for everyone. Many people see their spiritual
self as being expressed through their relationships, good deeds or
their connection with nature. For Loehr and Schwartz, our spiritual
aspect is 'the energy that is unleashed by tapping into one's deepest
values and defining a strong sense of purpose.' For people in recovery from a multitude of addictions in twelve-step fellowships, it is
the 'all things to all people' higher power.

Others believe that the word spirituality implies something more
transcendent, mystical or even supernatural. Pia Mellody, one of
the great recovery therapists defines it like this: 'Spirituality is the
experience of being in a relationship with a power external to you
and greater than self that provides acceptance, guidance, solace and
serenity.' An allusion, I guess, to God, arguably the most mysterious
space of all. My work with hundreds of people over the years leads
me to strongly believe that having some sort of spiritual belief and

practice – however you choose to define it – is an important part of staying grounded and balanced.

Taking an audit of your own quadrinity, seeing how you fare on the intellectual, the emotional, the physical and the spiritual, will help you gain and retain a good balance. Creating space for the parts of your quadrinity that are currently underserved won't take away from what you achieve at work. On the contrary, as Trevone found, it will provide the foundation for a richer, deeper and more sustainable form of success.

Your five a day, daily six, three buckets, and other practical ideas to help you create space for balance

The 2016 Health Survey for England found that our desk-bound work culture is contributing to more than eight out of ten middle-aged adults being dangerously unhealthy. How are you doing? Have you drunk the recommended two litres of water a day over the last few days? Do you get your five-a-day fruit and veg? Are you moving every couple of hours? How often do you get your heart rate up through exercise? How is your sleep? These things sound obvious and they are, and my intention isn't to patronise. I know how easy it is to grab a coffee and croissant for breakfast, power through till lunch, take a quick afternoon break for cake to celebrate a colleague's birthday, and round it all off with a takeaway, supermarket pizza or eating out for dinner, hydrating mostly through caffeine and alcohol while spending eight hours a day staring at a screen. Going against the grain and really taking care of ourselves requires effort and a bit of planning, and until it becomes a habit – which the evidence tells us is likely after about thirty days – it can be really hard. But, as the advert says, you're worth it!

In addition to taking care of the physical, here are three more psychological suggestions for how to create space to inspire a more balanced life:

Your daily six

The search for balance should be about progress not perfection. And it should be personal. Hannah Massarella, the Founder of Bird, a consultancy that focuses on resilience, has a simple method for keeping track of her self-care practices. In the back of her notebook she writes out her 'daily six', a list of six small but significant well-being habits. These change depending on what she wants to focus on. When I last spoke to her, they were: go for a run, drink a smoothie, gratitude, meditate, yoga and no booze. Interestingly, her goal isn't to do them all: 'It's *fine,* absolutely fine, not to tick all of them off,' she says. 'It's far worse to do five things and then beat yourself up for the one that you missed than it is to do four and feel good about those four things. Plus, I usually get something additional done each day that isn't on my list, such as a walk, a nap or laughter.' By aiming to do a few small things consistently, there's much more chance that these habits will become ingrained and part of your daily life.

ASK YOURSELF: *What would be on my 'daily six' list? How many of them are already part of my life? Which could I focus on over the next few days?*

The Three Buckets

As well as taking an audit of your 'space for balance' using the wheel of life, you could also explore a simple framework created by entrepreneur, author and podcaster Jonathan Fields, called 'the three buckets'. The three buckets are for Vitality, Connection and Contribution.

If a bucket is full, life will feel wonderful. If a bucket is empty or nearly empty, there will be pain – and if two buckets are running low, pay attention to the red flashing warning sign. The **Vitality** bucket looks at the state of your mind and body, and Jonathan lists mindfulness, sleep, exercise, diet, gratitude, getting comfortable with the unknown, nature, slowing down, authenticity and a growth mindset as the main levers of this bucket.

To fill your **Connection** bucket, Fields suggests the following:

figuring out your social orientation (are you more introverted, extra-verted or an ambivert – a mix of the two?); finding 'your people' – people who speak the same 'language' about life as you and with whom you can deeply connect; having clear boundaries; knowing who and what fills you up and makes you come alive; doing a digital detox; and looking at the different ways that love and connection are present in your life. You could also try using some of the tools from Part 2 of this book.

Work naturally fits into the **Contribution** bucket – since this bucket is all about what you add or contribute to the world – but so do such things as volunteering, looking at your strengths, figuring out your values, mentoring someone, and doing acts of kindness for others.

The simple premise is that the fuller our buckets, the better our lives – and it is up to us to keep them filled, plug any leaks and, above all, keep the idea of a well-balanced life simple.

ASK YOURSELF: *What does my wheel of life tell me about my balance? What might I want to change? How are my three buckets? What can I do to fill the one(s) that need filling?*

A good night's rest

Finally, I want to return to the issue of sleep. I have found, again and again, that it is an underlying factor in all sorts of performance issues. Without adequate rest, and a feeling of being refreshed, you won't be able to make use of any space that you create to think, do or connect because you will not have the energy or presence to do so. If you are wired, and pushing on through exhaustion you will think poorly, not deliver to your best and neglect and let people down.

I worked once with a high-flying executive called Philippe who felt that one thing holding him back was that other people were able to get into the office before him, so were more visible and able to deliver more. He had tried getting up really early, but after a few weeks had felt shattered and had gone back to his usual sleeping habits.

First I outlined to him the consensus research on sleep – most people need a good eight hours sleep but some need a little more and others less. Some very rare people need a lot less. The former UK Prime Minister Margaret Thatcher, for example, famously slept only four hours a night, and it didn't seem to dim her focus or productivity. However, most of us aren't like Maggie and, in the long run, having less than your own, individually required quota of sleep is unsustainable. It isn't about 'will power' or tricks and techniques, it's about what *your* body needs.

Philippe said that he felt he needed to sleep until 7.30 am at the latest. He said he went to bed 'around 11 pm'. I asked him to keep a detailed sleep diary. I also asked him to let himself sleep in at the weekend and wake up naturally. (His wife wasn't so pleased about this but she agreed to help in the end, for the purposes of research.)

Overall, he said he felt OK, but was a bit tired by Friday, and actually quite refreshed by the end of the weekend. So as not to draw conclusions based on just one example, I had him repeat the experiment for the next three weeks. The results were basically the same.

I suggested that the diary indicated that he needed about 8½ hours of sleep. This was how long he slept at the weekend if he didn't set his alarm. If we added up his sleeping time during the working week he was getting about 15 per cent less sleep than he needed. Some experts say that sleep is as important as breathing to our metabolism. Imagine if you were getting 15 per cent less oxygen than you need. If you've ever climbed up a really high mountain you'll know the effects of altitude sickness – symptoms akin to flu, carbon monoxide poisoning, or a bad hangover.

We talked a bit about how he spent his time before going to sleep, and he recognised that it was less about what he needed to do, or even enjoyed doing, and more about what he was used to doing. His night-time routine was not a choice he had consciously made; it was just a habit.

This exercise provided the space Philippe needed to become aware of what he was doing and to rethink things. He set out to create a new habit. First he needed a clear goal. He decided he

Philippe's sleep diary

Night	Went to sleep at?	Woke up at?	Activity before sleep?
Monday	11.45 pm	7.30 am (alarm)	Half watching TV, looking at social media
Tuesday	12.10 am	7.30 am (alarm)	Watching TV, on the phone to friends
Wednesday	11.55 pm	7.30 am (alarm)	Checking emails, looking at social media
Thursday	12.15 am	7.30 am (alarm)	Watching a film on TV
Friday	1 am	9.30 am	Went out, came in late, watched TV
Saturday	12 am	8.45 am	Watched TV
Sunday	11.35 pm	7.30 am (alarm)	Checking work emails, watched TV

wanted to get up a full hour earlier so he could extend his working day. He also accepted his need to have 8½ hours sleep a night. Seemingly impossibly conflicting goals? Not really. He committed to switching everything off and going to sleep at 11 pm every night. This meant that he still had two hours after the kids were settled down to do some tidying, look at Facebook and watch a TV show, or even a movie. It took about a month for him to get used to this new routine but with perseverance and discipline he did it.

Some other strategies are: establish a regular bedtime and routine, and try to go to bed and wake up at a similar time each day; lower the temperature of your room by a couple of degrees (the ideal room temperature is thought to be 20° Celsius); acknowledge that caffeine interferes with REM sleep so monitor the effect that it has on you (lots of people find it messes with their sleep if drunk after 3 pm, but figure out what works for you); finally, consider turning screens off an hour before bed – not only is this good for your mind (giving it time to wind down so you won't go to bed so wired), but you also lessen exposure to the blue light from the screens which inhibits the release of sleep-inducing hormones. If you must look at a laptop screen in the evenings, install a red light removal app, such as f.lux.

When I spoke to Philippe a few months later he said his new routine now came completely naturally and he felt more refreshed and energised at work. He could even go out late one night in the week and still get up at his usual time without feeling too bad. Just by becoming aware of his patterns and habits, and committing to a quite small change in behaviour, he had literally created significantly more space in his life.

ASK YOURSELF: *Did I sleep well last night? Deep down, in my bones, how tired am I right now? What is my night-time regime – and why? What would I like my sleep goals to be? How am I going to make that happen?*

CHAPTER 12

Space to Grow

Almantas and His Gladly Missed Targets

LESSON: *There is always an opportunity cost to creating the space to grow. You need to recognise this and be willing to pay the price.*

I WAS WORKING WITH TESSA, the MD of the EMEA (Europe, Middle East and Africa) division of a FTSE 50 FMCG company. The region contributed more than a third of the business's global profits. Tessa had a complicated structure beneath her: thirty countries all at different stages of development, and each with its own particular challenges. Some smaller countries were clustered together, meaning that there was a total of twelve managers under Tessa, either running big countries or a group of small ones. I was working with Tessa herself, the team as a whole, joining their quarterly meetings, but also with each of the twelve 'market' MDs. It was a big, engrossing project, but one in which I felt I could make a real contribution.

Almantas ran the Baltics area – Estonia, Latvia and Lithuania. As we worked together, he began to open up and share some of his frustrations. In particular, he thought he was being overlooked for promotion to one of the company's bigger markets in Western Europe. Deep down he felt there was something prejudicial going on, that people regarded him as different and thought he wouldn't fit in culturally elsewhere.

For the last three years he'd tried to offset this by working harder and harder, driving his team remorselessly and exceeding his targets. The more we talked, the more it became clear that whatever the truth of his suspicions, he himself had a real concern about whether his approach and style would be successful outside of his home market.

After some discussion, we agreed that he would do three things over the next twelve months. First, he would take an advanced business English course, to improve his confidence in communicating. He found an intensive three-month course that took place on three evenings a week. He also found a mentor in the country he most wanted to work in who generously agreed to meet him socially and help build his cultural awareness. They got on so well that Almantas, his wife and young sons were invited to stay with his mentor, and so got the chance to see what living – not just working – in this new place would be like. Finally, his manager, impressed by the commitment he was showing, agreed that he could undertake a three-month secondment in the country. This was a serious sacrifice family-wise, but Almantas took the plunge.

The secondment was a great success and resulted in the permanent posting that Almantas had desired for so long. He and his family uprooted themselves, moving across Europe for a bold new chapter of their lives. It was a huge upheaval, as they had to pretty much start all over again. His sons spoke the language of their new country (but not fluently), and had to settle into a new school and make new friends. Almantas's wife probably struggled most, having to navigate a new language, culture and country.

There was a cost for Almantas in achieving his goal of promotion: he only just made his target that year, in stark contrast to his team's exceptional performance of the previous three years. There had always been an awareness that this might happen, but all that really mattered was that Almantas hit his targets – he wasn't duty bound to exceed them as he usually did. Nonetheless this still carried a risk: there might be comments from the Board about why his numbers had dropped so significantly, his reputation for smashing his targets would be injured, and he would no longer receive the accolades for having the largest year-on-year growth.

This 'opportunity cost' was, though, a price Almantas was willing to pay, because although it might invite raised eyebrows from elsewhere in the company, he and Tessa had discussed his plan in detail and had both agreed that if the secondment went well, it would be worth it. At the meeting where he was offered the transfer, Tessa made it clear that she hoped he would soon go back to exceeding his targets in his new environment, but that this year's 'blip' was something she was willing to live with. Almantas had chosen a powerful 'big goal' and had executed it in a ruthless and determined way. He reaped the reward. As, eventually, did the company, because the following year – you guessed it – he was back smashing his KPIs.

The opportunity and the cost of Creating Space to Grow

'And the day came when the risk to remain tight in a bud was more painful than the risk it took to blossom.'

attributed to Anais Nin

Almantas's story is less dramatic than the life or death situation that faced Trevone or the existential angst felt by Oscar. On the surface it is just about a manager getting a promotion involving a relocation. This is intentional. While the drama of the preceding stories, with their major upheavals and core pathogenic beliefs are truly representative of the work I do with senior leaders, the work is also, sometimes, more prosaic. It is no less life-changing for that. For Almantas and his family what happened that year was a big change.

When we grow we may have to give up a part of our identity to which we've become very attached, as Almantas did when he sacrificed his reputation for 'smashing' targets. This kind of exchange, of one benefit for another, is known as an 'opportunity cost' – the giving up of something beneficial or positive that you *could* have received by choosing an alternative course of action. One way of thinking of it is as a trade-off. In Chapter 9 we discussed the trade-off that takes place during delegation: the certainty of knowing exactly how a task or project would be executed if you did it yourself is exchanged for the benefit of not having to do it, and the freed-up time and energy that that creates. In a sense, everything in life requires us to trade one thing against something else; if, for example, you decide to eat out less, you get the benefit of saving the money and calories, but in return you have to buy, prepare and cook your food (oh, and wash up). Go to the gym and you have that less time to do those things that are arguably more fun than going to the gym, but you gain good health and in all likelihood, increased longevity. Opportunity cost is everywhere, and as the CEO of your own life, you have to weigh these kind of decisions up against each other on a daily basis. There's an opportunity cost of pursuing a new career versus staying in our familiar one, an opportunity cost of a sabbatical, an opportunity cost of really focusing on one area of growth rather than another. Everything we say yes to requires that we say no to something else.

Sometimes, growing requires that we all but relinquish one identity for another. Huge changes like these can swiftly strip away layer upon layer of self that we've acquired over the years, compelling us to let go and to experience ourselves and life anew. This is rarely comfortable, but once again, we have a choice about how we ride the rollercoaster. We can cling on for dear life, becoming rigid and brittle, or we can do our best to breathe and surrender to the ups and downs.

In effect, this entire book has been about creating the space to grow. Doing this means facing the parts of us that don't want to grow, but that prefer coasting through life and taking the easy path. Growing doesn't mean that we have to get rid of this part of ourselves; ease is a beautiful energy, and I actually think it's a vital energy to touch base with on a regular basis. In business most of us often force things too much, pushing for results without allowing ourselves and our teams time and space to recharge and take stock.

We might live in human-built metropolises, disconnected from much of the natural world, yet even the most cursory of glances at nature will remind us that growth is cyclical rather than constant, and that winter is an essential and unavoidable part of the cycle. In the commercial world, it's easy to ignore this and buy into the story that growth is linear and constant. The corporations we work within may set year-on-year targets in a consistent, predictable way, always aiming, say, for a 10 per cent increase in profits. Our countries do the same, seeking consistent growth in GDP year on year. However, as Anais Nin states (in Volume 4 of her diaries), 'We do not grow absolutely, chronologically. We grow sometimes in one dimension, and not in another, unevenly. We grow partially. We are relative. We are mature in one realm, childish in another. The past, present, and future mingle and pull us backward, forward, or fix us in the present.'

The poet David Whyte has observed that human beings are the only life force on the planet with the capacity to stop themselves from flowering. In your own unique way, and via your own meandering path, make sure you always create the space to let whatever is within you bloom.

Your No.1 meetings – a practical suggestion for Creating Space to Grow

There is one idea that I use religiously to ensure that I am keeping my plans for growth at the very forefront of my mind, and as a clear priority for action.

We rarely stop to question the usefulness of quarterly and annual business reviews, but when was the last time you created space to systematically review your personal development? Pressing pause to reflect on where you have grown, plus looking at any major struggles, challenges or areas for development that have arisen, can give you a lot of perspective. It can also remind you that whatever you're facing right now, you've already achieved a lot. So how do you make sure that your strategy for growth, your development plan – for want of a better phrase – is on track?

You have to create space to review and refresh what you are doing. I suggest doing so in what I call your 'No.1 Meeting'. For me, this is a meeting that rarely gets cancelled. Sometimes it has to be done on the hoof, in the back of a taxi or in an airport lounge, but in some way I almost always honour the commitment. Ideally, this No.1 meeting should be scheduled for half an hour. Who are the attendees for this meeting? Just the three of us, as the De La Soul song goes – 'Me, Myself and I'. Yes, a half hour a week of reflection time is one of the most crucial building blocks of creating and sustaining the space to keep your plan on track. How you do it is a matter of personal style. I need a notepad and pen in my hand, even if I don't write anything down. A friend I know has his while swimming. Another friend every Friday evening on her long commute, with headphones on and eyes closed against the distractions of the packed train. The agenda? Draw up one that works for you, but something like:

1. How am I feeling this week? Has it been a good week or a bad week? Why?

2. How are my weekly objectives going? Do I need to review them?

3. How do I see this next week shaping up?

4. How am I doing on my big goal?

Now, this sustained level of setting aside proper time for reflection should be replicated throughout the year. I recommend to clients that they undertake a personal monthly, quarterly and annual review too. Some suggested areas to review, which I encourage you to tailor to your own needs, are:

○ Your accomplishments, including what you've learned and how you grew as a result.

○ Your failures, including what you've learned and how you grew as a result (like many entrepreneurs, you may find that you learn and grow far more from your failures than your successes). Where did you fall short?

○ Any opportunities you missed or turned down, and why.

○ Any learning curves you've been on. Have you started to develop a completely new skill? What are the top three challenges and lessons you've gained from this?

○ Key lessons learned by 'category' and overall (categories could be specific and project- or accountability-oriented, or you could use the four sections from this book: Think, Connect, Do and Be).

○ What feedback have you had? Feedback is a powerful tool for discovering where we have (or haven't) grown, and where our key areas of development may be.

To summarise, this is how your No.1 meetings schedule might look:

Weekly	Focused on this week and next	½ hour
Monthly	Reviewing the month and looking forward	90 mins
Quarterly results	Checking progress against the plan for the year	½ day
Annual retreat	Reviewing and setting next year's goal	1 day

On the date of each long meeting, you miss out the shorter meeting; for example, you don't have your monthly meeting when that month is a quarterly review.

The quarterly half day may seem like a lot, but if it involves a thorough review of where you are and what might need to change going forward it isn't, especially if some of that time is spent having a heart-to-heart with your 'goal mentor' (see p. 168). I tend to spend an hour preparing this meeting, then treat my mentor to a nice lunch, before spending an hour capturing thoughts and planning. Boom! Half a day gone, but spent so productively, centring me back on what I want to be achieving, not what the world has been demanding.

When it comes to my 'annual retreat' I take it quite literally. I go off on a 'business trip' where I am the client I'm visiting – somewhere that's a short train ride away, where I won't be disturbed by work, family or friends. Last year I went to stay in a B'n'B at Dungeness, a bleak but beautiful stretch of the English south coast where, if you try hard enough, you can hear the constant low-level hum of the neighbouring nuclear reactor. I arrived in time for an enjoyable dinner, then had an early night. The next day, I woke up refreshed and took a long walk followed by a few hours pondering and scribbling things down. Then a light lunch, another stroll along the endless shale beach before some more focused thinking and planning. I then had dinner and another early night, getting up the next morning to catch an early(ish) train back to 'civilisation'. In my backpack there was a notebook full of if not the right answers then certainly the right questions, ready to guide me through the next twelve months.

Now, as you may have already noticed I am a particularly structured person. I completely accept that others may want to do all this in a less routine way. However, while you are welcome to jettison the more finicky parts of what I'm proposing, differences in style or personality don't preclude the need for discipline of some sort. It can be less process driven, not as systematic and more laid back, but it must be done.

When clients complain that they can't afford to spend time in this way, I not only make the obvious (if slightly facetious) point that they can't afford not to, I also ask them what percentage of their time they could see themselves re-allocating without it materially affecting their performance? If I say 10 per cent, they usually say that's too much. If I say 5 per cent, most say it might be possible. In fact, the time I am suggesting setting aside for these No.1 meetings is actually about 2.5 per cent of your working time per year (this assumes a total of 50 hours out of 2000 worked).

ASK YOURSELF: *What's my way of reviewing how my plan is coming along? Do I do this in a disciplined, open, honest way? Am I growing in the way I want to?*

Conclusion

In Part 4 we have looked at three parts of being: dreaming, being in balance, and growing. These all raise big questions that transcend the day-to-day demands of work and ask us to think about things from first principles. Why am I doing this? Who for? Who do I want to be? And ultimately, how do I want to live – even, how do I want to die?

The idea of being brave seems to stand out as the key lesson. Have the courage to ask the hard questions, make the change, take the risk. As Renton says in the film *Trainspotting*, 'Choose life.'

PART 5

The Three Gateways to Creating Space

I N THIS FINAL SECTION of the book I want to pull together and summarise the key themes woven through the previous twelve stories. These will then act as a 'checklist' for you as you seek to apply these ideas to your own life. I call them the 'Three Gateways to Creating Space'. That is because without having these three overarching elements in place it will be harder to implement the specific lessons from the stories that you feel apply to you. Prior to embarking on the process of creating space, you need to work on each of these. They are the foundation for everything else you will do. Without them you run the risk that any space you do create will be squandered. They relate to your strategy, your productivity and your mindset:

The Three Gateways are designed to set the psychological and practical conditions which allow you to begin creating space. First, you must set your overarching goal and formulate the strategy that will get you there; second, you need to reach a baseline of efficiency that will speed up and simplify all that you do; lastly you need to get into the right mindset and let go of any false and destructive assumptions.

Gateway 1: Set Your Personal Strategy

You need to know where you are going, how and why. This involves setting your personal strategy and sticking to it, unless you have good reason to change it. Your personal strategy is your opportunity to identify and commit to the things that require your focus. Discarding the things that don't helps you create the space you need to develop. It consists of three elements:

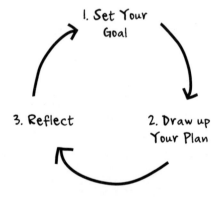

Set your goal

This seems elementary, but if you don't know where you are going how on earth will you end up there? Nonetheless, it is amazing to me how few people actually have clear, specific, articulated goals. Exactly what are you trying to achieve and by when? You need to be ruthless. Don't have too many goals, or ones that are ambiguous or shifting. Make a decision and stick with it.

Draw up your plan

Once you have your goals, you need to draw up a plan of how to get there. What resources are necessary? What are your key stages or mileposts? Even when people do have clear goals, I find that many fall down at this stage. They don't turn their vision and hope into something tangible – a roadmap of getting from here to there.

Reflect

The third key element of setting your strategy is reflection. As you make progress, be open to how things are unfolding – what you think about it, and what you feel. Ask yourself, is this what I expected? What I wanted? Do I need to adjust things? Radically think again? Setting aside ring-fenced time to do this reflection is vital, otherwise other things will crowd it out and your goal will slip further and further out of your consciousness.

Gateway 2: Raise Your Personal Productivity

As well as setting your strategy and goals – and sticking to them – you need to make sure that you are working as productively and efficiently as possible. It doesn't make sense to apply what you've learnt from this book to create more space, if inefficient ways of working then eat up that space. Here are summaries of the four key areas which we have covered in different places throughout the book:

Sleep

Make sure you are getting enough rest. It is the foundation to having the energy – both physical and mental – to do everything that you want to do in your waking hours.

Rhythm

Sleep is linked to the body's circadian rhythms, as are our energy cycles throughout the day. Make sure that you are tuned into your own rhythms, and, to the best extent possible, organise your working day around these. Be tough about this and set firm boundaries with your boss and colleagues.

Single task

Whenever you can, devote yourself to discrete pieces of work in a disciplined way. Try and minimise switching from one task to another and avoid distractions like social media.

Manage Time

Have a clear plan of what you are doing when and why, and a way of tracking your work and regularly reviewing it. Delegate wherever possible.

If you address these four personal productivity areas – sleep, daily rhythm, multi-tasking and 'to-do' organisation – you will work more productively. Without having to do anything else, you will free up more time and space to work on your priorities.

Gateway 3: Adopt the Space Mindset

Once you have a sense of your big goal and personal strategy, and are committed to it, it's time to adopt what I call the 'space mindset'. The need for this – and how to achieve it – is discussed throughout the book. At the end of this section, I itemise the five central points it is vital to hold in mind as you begin to try and create more space in the ways we have looked at.

First, though, we need to step back and think a little about what 'mindset' really is. You will see it is closely linked to the idea of core pathogenic beliefs that features in most of the twelve stories. Another way of describing it is as your 'psychic space' or 'inner world'.

Welcome to Your Inner World

In his talk 'The Concept of a Healthy Individual' (1967) the psycho-analyst D. W. Winnicott said:

> *The life of a healthy individual is characterised by fears, conflicting*

feelings, doubts, frustrations as much as by the positive features. The main thing is that the man or woman feels he or she is living his or her own life, taking responsibility for action or inaction, and able to take credit for success and blame for failure … it includes the idea of tingling life and the magic of intimacy. All these things go together and add up to a sense of feeling real and of being, and of the experiences feeding back into the personal psychical reality, enriching it and giving it scope. The consequence is that the healthy person's inner world is related to the outer or actual world and yet is personal and capable of an aliveness of its own.

By 'inner world' Winnicott means the world that exists inside our minds, as opposed to the 'external world'. It is comprised of thoughts, beliefs, ideas, memories and fantasies, and is sometimes referred to as the internal world or internal reality. Some of it is conscious, some unconscious. In his book *Dream-Life* (1984) Donald Meltzer wrote of the psychoanalyst Melanie Klein that she had: '… made a discovery that created a revolutionary addition to the model-of-the-mind, namely that we do not live in one world, but in two – that we live also in an internal world which is as real a place of life as the outside world.'

This internal world is not just our private thoughts and day-dreams. It is a very powerful construct that is influenced by the external world, but also, in many ways, influences how we see it. This is summed up by the recurring line in Lars Saabye Christensen's 2004 novel *The Half Brother*: 'It doesn't matter what you see, but what you think you see.' We all know someone who thinks the world is out to get them, or someone else who believes that things always work out for the best. Behind such differences of outlook lies a whole mindset, which sets the stage for our intra-psychic and interpersonal relations. In the same way that a set provides the backdrop for a movie's action, transforming the blank soundstage into a frightening gothic cityscape or a sun-filled village square. The same characters could walk into each scene, but we will experience them very differently within each, even before they say or do anything. For most of

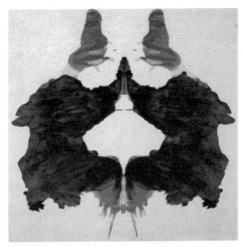

An image from the famous Rorschach or 'ink-blot' test

us, thankfully, the architecture of our inner world lies somewhere in between dark foreboding or naive optimism.

It is an insight into our inner worlds that psychological tests like the famous 'ink-blot' or Rorschach test are designed to discover. When you gaze at the mysterious shape and say what comes to mind, you are projecting your inner world onto something which is actually open to an infinite number of descriptions.

When I was being trained to administer this test I gave it to two women. One saw a series of horrific images: witches with machine guns, gushing blood, dead animals and monsters. The other, looking at exactly the same image, saw clowns throwing flowers, butterflies and playful children. Both were high functioning, successful and intelligent women. Later, when I was walking with the first woman, we saw a cardboard box lying on the pavement beside an empty car with its passenger door swung open. 'Look, someone is stealing everything out of that car,' she exclaimed. To me and to most people, and certainly to the second woman, that's not how it would have appeared – it looked like someone was loading or unloading the car. The first woman's inner world coloured her perception of events fundamentally, in a way that I am sure is echoed throughout all her experiences and personal relationships.

These are simple examples to illustrate my point. Our internal worlds are full of complexity and contradiction. Indeed, psychoanalysis believes that the most influential parts of our inner worlds are not even known to us, except by derivatives e.g. the consequences they wreak on our lives. It is the unconscious aspects of our psychic structure that compel us to do things we don't understand, such as attempt relationships with the wrong people, engage in self-destructive behaviour, fail to live up to our best intentions. We think that some of the things we do don't make sense, given what we know of ourselves; but to our internal, unconscious world there is method to the madness.

By increasing our self-awareness, either through coaching or therapy, or by following some of the ideas set out in books like this, some of that miasma may dissipate. In the words of psychoanalyst Adam Phillips (2004), 'we might be better able to know what we think about what we think.'

Philosophers and psychologists have debated endlessly how these internal worlds come to be. Are they genetically determined; formed in the first few months of interaction between mother and child; or the result of the more drawn-out experiences of childhood, adolescence and adult development? Common sense suggests that our characters, and the 'internal worlds' that underpin them, are a result of a complex interaction of all three, and, although there are still purists and evangelicals for each of the three theories, that is the consensus that holds today.

The importance of the concept of the 'inner world' is that it elevates what we might mistakenly think of as 'mere' thoughts and beliefs into a sort of permanent, solid psychic structure, which, like the external world, will be resistant to change.

D. W. Winnicott describes 'potential space' as a place where inner and external realities mix, and where one can explore new ways of seeing and being. This place, on the fringe of our imagination, is where great artists roam, but it is also where the simplest of children's games reside. 'Grown-ups' in 'grown-up' jobs are rarely able to let themselves float away from 'reality' into that nether world. But it is where truly great breakthroughs come from. Thus our task becomes one of ridding ourselves of the everyday and the prosaic (for a while at least) and practising being in that 'potential space' of ambiguity, wonder and creativity.

Take the example of thinking more strategically or innovatively. If your mind is full of insistent bits of tactical detail, how will you have the clear space to come up with anything truly transformative or profound? That requires a broad, initially empty canvas, which you begin filling after reading, thinking, conversation, but that might require a long time of apparently fruitless pondering before you suddenly have your Eureka moment. If you are endlessly consumed by smaller thoughts and tasks, you will never create the space to have your big idea – and then make it happen.

So how can we break this down and start to build a psychic space or inner world for ourselves that frees us up to reach our potential? I believe that such a mindset comprises five interlocking assumptions or beliefs, which I present below, alongside their opposing assumption/belief. It is important to note that these beliefs are not necessarily fully conscious, you may not have really considered them before, or at least with such clarity.

SPACE MINDSET	CREATING SPACE vs DEVOURING SPACE	OPPOSITE OF SPACE MINDSET
Yes, I'm sticking to my ruthless goals	←→	No, I have to do this instead or as well
Yes, this can be 'good enough'	←→	No, it has to be perfect
Yes, that can wait	←→	No, it must be done now
Yes, it's OK to get things wrong	←→	No, I cannot make any mistakes
Yes, I have faith in myself	←→	No, I am crippled by self-doubt

Getting into the 'Space Mindset' means consciously dragging yourself to the left-hand side of these polarities. There will always be occasional exceptions – sometimes things do have to be perfect and sometimes they have to be done right now. But the demands of the modern workplace and our own ingrained habits all too often make these 'exceptional' demands the norm.

Each and every time you consider a task, step back (create space) and ask yourself is this really an exception? Do I have to step out of the space mindset? Doing so requires a really compelling reason and should happen rarely. Very rarely.

1. Yes, I'm sticking to my ruthless goals

This is the first element of the space mindset and it underpins all the others. The importance of creating the right goals, and sticking to them was explained in Chapter 7. Obviously a major part of this is learning the ability to say no. Some people are more temperamentally disposed to do this than others, but we must all, politely yet firmly, be able to say no if saying yes would take us out of the space mindset. I find that explaining your reasons can work wonders, even to bosses. 'I'm sorry, I can see you want me to do that but right now I have set a firm priority of X and I really need to stick to that.'

2. Yes, this can be 'good enough'

The opposite of this mindset is being a perfectionist. Sometimes, of course, perfection is vital. You might be a brain surgeon, or a jeweller cutting a diamond for the Queen's crown. But for most of us in most situations good enough should be just that – good enough. D.W. Winnicott coined the phrase in the context of the 'good enough' mother in an attempt to allay the anxieties of mothers who think they have to be perfect. On the contrary, he argued, trying to be perfect (or even being so) would be bad for the baby. The developing child needs a mother who is good enough and who will make mistakes. The child learns to tolerate these mistakes and will eventually come to rely on and fend for itself.

In business, this mindset was best summed up by a Steve Jobs quote, 'real artists ship'. This was a dig at certain artistic types who spend so long tinkering with their work that they rarely finish it. He was also claiming that, despite being a very pragmatic, commercial guy, he too was an artist. In other words, he was saying don't wait for it to be perfect – beautiful, yes, but not perfect. Get it out of the door and deliver (or ship) it into the shops. What today's tech world calls an MPV, or Minimum Viable Product.

3. Yes, that can wait

A close cousin to the need to say no, this is about putting off things that you can't say no to until the time is right for you. Again, some people find this easier than others but we all have to practise it. Sometimes, when my PA tells me that a client needs something 'right now', I respond 'Tell them I can get it to them the day after tomorrow, and if that's a problem they can call me on my mobile.' Nine times out of ten they never call, because it wasn't really that urgent.

4. Yes, it's OK to get things wrong

The close cousin to the mistaken belief 'I must do it perfectly' is the belief that 'I'm not allowed to make mistakes', which is just as limiting. The fact is everyone makes mistakes, and it is in the crucible of making mistakes that we can develop best, as in the Samuel Beckett line 'fail better'. On joining one company I was told that the culture was one where it was better to ask forgiveness than permission. Again, within obvious constraints, that's a great corporate culture to have. From my experience, the great cost of resisting anything that might end up being a mistake is that you grievously constrain what you might attempt, and therefore the learning that flows from success – and failure. To draw from Steve Jobs once more – anyone remember the Apple Lisa? Thought not. One of his many 'mistakes', which included the belief that people would never want phones bigger than the original iPhone, 'no one's going to buy … a phone you can't get your hand around,' he declared. A mistake of his that Apple has corrected, I am glad to say (as an avid user of an iPhone plus). None of that makes Steve Jobs a failure, and neither does making mistakes make you one.

5. Yes, I have faith in myself

This underlies the other beliefs, but is also important in other contexts too. In order to make the call that 'this is good enough' and to tolerate making mistakes, you need to have an underlying faith in yourself. This is one of the clearest dividing lines between the people I see in psychotherapy and the people I see in executive coaching. In the former people's self-confidence and self-esteem is often shot to pieces, usually by something that's happened to them recently but more often by a difficult childhood, the traumatic consequences of which are triggered by something happening to them as an adult. The business people I see generally wouldn't get to the levels they are at without a strong sense of self-confidence. It may wax and wane, it may be enshrined in quite a lot of reflection and self-doubt but, at their core, it will be there. If you feel that you don't have enough faith in yourself to make the calls that this book is constantly urging you to make, then take a look at your underlying levels of self-esteem. Seeing a therapist could help, or you could try working through Patrick Fanning and Matthew McKay's book *Self-Esteem*. You can also find a short e-book, *Break Free From Your Past*, at www. derekdraper.net, which lots of people have used to great effect.

These, then, are the five rules of the 'Space Mindset'. Every day, until it's sunk in, go back to the chart and remind yourself to stay on the left-hand side. That way you help create the space you need. If you find yourself on the right-hand side, be brutal about asking yourself why – and do your utmost to move back.

Conclusion

This book grew out of the work I do on a daily basis to help people create more space for what they believe is important to their lives, and for what they want to achieve and become. My experience is that most people know what is important to them – they just don't always act on it, and that they need help to think through exactly what and why they want to achieve, and how best to do that.

Helping people in such a way is a great privilege and I feel blessed to have found a professional life that is so interesting, fulfilling and rewarding. But, of course, there is a limit to how many people I, or my colleagues, can work with. My hope is that this book will act as a 'proxy' coach, stimulating you to have an internal discourse that won't be too different from the one we'd have if we were sitting in my office together.

At the beginning of this book, I outlined the two ideas that underlie my belief that everyone in today's world, but particularly leaders, need to 'create space':

We have become the first generation in one thousand generations of human beings who, rather than having the need to fill space, have the need to create it.

and

Before you set out to grow as a leader, you must first create the space that you will grow into. Creating space is the a priori task that unlocks optimal personal performance and development.

We looked in depth at four domains where creating space will serve both us and the people around us. These were:

1. Space to think. All of the things that make our human-made world so incredible – the inventions, skylines, books, practices and art – emerged from thought, from human beings who dared to encounter white space or a blank page.

2. Space to connect. We are fundamentally relational beings. A life replete with achievements and activity would, for most of us, be utterly worthless without someone to share it with or to connect with along the way.

3. Space to do. Whether you call it executing, delivering or plain old getting things done, 'doing' makes up a large part of our lives, particularly our work lives. In a world stuffed to the brim with distractions, creating space to 'do' sets you apart.

4. Space to be. Despite what I just said about doing, we are human beings. Making the space and time for the 'being' part of our lives is vital to having a life well lived.

As the book progressed, we explored twelve key lessons, brought to life by characters inspired by the brave, curious people I have had the honour of coaching.

1. From Raku we learned that making the space to reflect on your decisions, carefully exploring what you are doing and why, frees you to contribute to the very best of your ability.

2. Rachel's story taught us that in today's fast-changing world you must operate with genuine humility and create the space to be curious and open to constant learning.

3. Hans's story showed us that if you want to be a creative, visionary and strategic leader you must create the space to be clear about what you think; make bold decisions; communicate these with confidence; and be known for being decisive.

4. Nick's story about his deadbeat dads illuminated how being aware of what you're feeling, and why, will stop you being

driven by buried emotions from the past and allow you to create the space to live fully in the here and now.

5. Beata's story about her team reminded us that, if you are to have real, rich relationships, it's vital to be in touch with – and brave enough to share – what is really going on for you. Even in a leadership role.

6. Amir's hard won lesson showed us that however many strengths you have, you also need good Emotional Intelligence and the ability to build rich relationships to be truly successful.

7. Tom and Darren's tech company dilemma showed us that having a clear goal (what you want to do) and a clear plan (how you're going to get there) are the prerequisites of executing successfully.

8. Tamsin's busyness and ultimate failure to deliver reminded us that if you try to do too much, you will fail to create the space to think about and deliver what really matters.

9. Yulia's story showed us that stepping back and making the space to deliver in a way that empowers those around you, means you can deliver something outstanding and truly transformational.

10. Oscar's powerful story about his love of the land, highlighted how there are times when you need to look deep on the inside to know what you really want, and then have the courage to go after it.

11. Trevone's story of near collapse served to demonstrate that work and life really aren't in opposition; finding balance between them will make you more successful at both.

12. Almantas taught us that there is always an opportunity cost to creating the space to grow. You need to recognise this and be willing to pay the price.

As well as highlighting the power and vitality of space, I spoke a lot about core pathogenic beliefs. In the middle of each person's struggle to make space to think, connect, do or be, there was a belief running in the background that was the real source of what was

going on. The lack of space in that person's life, whether it mani-
fested as Tamsin's incessant busyness, Trevone's 'stress', or Amir's
refusal to acknowledge his and others' emotions, was a symptom of
something deeper. We looked at where CPBs come from, why we
have them and how they can get in the way of our leadership and our
lives. I presented a number of strategies for working with and transforming your CPBs into healthy, enriching beliefs which, when given
the space to take root in your life, can create lasting positive change.

We also explored numerous tools, strategies and shifts in perception that might open up more space in each of the twelve areas.
Obviously it's not possible to do all of this at once. I would go as far
to say that you could spend a month focusing on each and still have
some way to go. As we near the end of the book, my sincere hope
is that it is not the end of your time with this material. I urge you
to make this not just a book that you read and put away, but that
you use it as a manual or handbook that will serve and support you
for many years to come. Think about two or three changes you'd
really like to make in your life over the next twelve months, and use
those particular chapters or essays within the chapters to coach and
support you as you make those changes, one shift at a time. Then
next year choose a few more.

*

Almost all of this book addresses the world of work. Implicit,
though, is the idea that the need to create space also applies to the
rest of our lives: our intimate personal relationships, our parenting,
our friendships. In particular the lessons contained in Part 2 on Space
to Connect and Part 4 on Space for Balance contain insights and
ideas that you can apply in your personal and family life as well as at
work. For almost all of us, family and friends are the most important
things in our lives but, alas, for almost all of us, we don't always act
like it.

This book has set out multiple ways to help you create the space
to consider – carefully and deliberately – what you want to do, how
you should go about doing it and, on a deeper level, who you want

to be and what kind of life you want to live. I send good wishes for
whatever comes next. Thanks for creating space to read *Create Space*.
I hope you've enjoyed it and found it useful. I'd love to hear from
you: derek@cdp.consulting.

List of tools and models

All intellectual property and other rights in and to the ideas and models in bold belong to Derek Draper. While permission is granted for one-off personal (non-corporate or commercial) use by a purchaser of this book, any other use whatsoever requires permission, and the payment of the appropriate licensing fee.

CDP and our partners use the insights and models outlined in this book in our leadership consultancy work. Our purpose is to transform business performance by working at the deepest level to unlock potential. We offer:

O In-depth individual leadership audits for selection, promotion and development

O High-performance executive and transitions coaching

O Team effectiveness interventions (including Board effectiveness)

O Organisation Development and cultural change support

O High-level leadership and talent consultancy at CEO and HRD level

CDP Leadership Consultants
21 Bloomsbury Square, London, WC1A 2NS
+ 44 (0)20 3900 4010
mail@cdp.consulting | www.cdp.consulting

Appendix

An analysis of the concept of Space in 1000 randomised global Leadership Development Reports

To test the real-world value of this model, I wanted to compare it to leadership frameworks used by consultancies such as CDP, Korn Ferry and Egon Zehnder. More importantly, I wanted to compare it to the actual leadership frameworks used by global companies. I therefore conducted an analysis of over fifty different leadership frameworks, including those of various FTSE 100 and Fortune 500 companies and of organisations such as the British Civil Service and the US Army. On the right of the table below you will see the key elements from these leadership frameworks (they tend to be, unsurprisingly, pretty similar) and how they fit under each element of the 'Space' model.

Create space to ...	Is linked to these leadership capabilities ...
Think	Decision making, problem solving, strategic thinking, creativity, innovation
Connect	Collaboration, inspiring, motivating, developing, influencing, connecting, self-awareness, self-satisfaction, parts of drive, EQ, teamwork
Do	Executing, parts of mobilising, high performance, managing change, transformation, delivery
Be	Better work-life balance, personal meaning and purpose, sustainability, resilience

This table illustrates the power of this book's central insight. Most business people want to get better at the capabilities listed in the right-hand column. Indeed, companies spend nearly $10bn a year trying to help their employees improve these. However, unless you first help create the space for people to do the things on the left-hand side you will not have enabled them to grow the capabilities on the right-hand side. Again, creating space comes first; the development this unlocks comes later.

My old consultancy had assessed over 50,000 leaders in the last twenty-five years and has an unrivalled database of the results. This allowed them to benchmark how each person compared to their leadership framework in comparison with various norms (e.g. senior leader). While working there, for example, I was helping a FTSE 100 construction company assess people who might step up to be their next CEO. We were able to compare the individuals concerned against other people at their level in the FTSE 100, and also against their peers in the construction and building industries. I also helped one of Europe's biggest telecoms companies to identify and develop their most likely next CEO. Again, we were able to compare the person to hundreds of 'successor CEOs' that the firm had assessed over the last two decades.

The problem I faced was that the framework that we used there didn't draw out space as a discrete area. Instead it looked at more traditional leadership capabilities such as strategic framing etc., so I had no alternative but to go back to the raw data – the assessments themselves. I therefore examined 1000 random reports that had been written by around fifty consultants from all over the world, about leaders in every region – Europe, the Americas, Africa, Asia and the Middle-East – within the last five years.* As well as containing a psychological profile of the assessee, each contained approximately half a dozen strengths and roughly the same number of development

*I am grateful to the then Chairman of YSC, Gurnek Bains, for allowing me access to the reports he had analysed for his own book, *Cultural DNA – The Psychology of Globalisation.*

areas. The reports were anonymised (all names and identifying information removed) and I sat down for several days of reading. I noted where any report's development areas contained words and phrases relating to space, including the word 'space' itself as well as related concepts such as 'stepping back…' or 'making room to…'.

Here are some examples of relevant actual development areas, written by a wide range of different assessors.

Space to Think:

> *He could take time to **step back** and think about the business from a long term, macro perspective.*

> *She needs to **find the space** to reflect and learn from her experiences.*

> *Going forward he will need **to create space** to focus more on longer term strategy and how he can have an impact that goes beyond his formal remit.*

Space to Connect:

> *She is encouraged to consider the discretionary commitment she might inspire in her team if she allowed herself **to identify and express her feelings more overtly** rather than trying to control them.*

> *He would benefit from **taking the time** to build richer, deeper relationships with people, rather than approaching others with what tends to be a tactical and transactional style which limits true connection.*

> *He needs to find the time and willingness **to step back** from his own preoccupations and really connect with his team, so he understands their potential to take things off his shoulders …*

Space to Do:

> *She is adept at plate spinning but it risks distracting her attention from the really **key, longer-term** deliverables.*

*It will pay him to more consciously give [his team] a bit **more space*** *and see his own role as supporting their success.*

*She would benefit from **standing back** from being quite so involved* *in day-to-day actions and, instead, getting herself more organised* *around/thoughtful about how she sets up her work agenda and how* *she manages people and responsibilities over the longer term.*

It is worth noting that there were few references relating to 'Space to Be' in the assessments, although there were some to work-life balance and resilience. It is also worth noting the very low frequency of words and ideas relating to space in the strengths section of the reports. In my view this is because space acts as the prerequisite for strengths to flourish, therefore it is the consequent strengths that are noted by assessors (rather than the space that enables these to happen).

In total the reports contained more than 4,500 development areas. An examination of the data derived from them led me to conclude that the issue of 'space' is an issue across all types of businesses, in every culture and at all senior levels. Indeed virtually all (93 per cent) of the individuals assessed appear to have had a development need related to creating space in some form or another. The number of people with at least one development area relating to each theme broke down as follows:

Theme	Percentage of reports highlighting this area
Space to think	46%
Space to connect	75%
Space to do	32%
Space to be	11%
None of the above	7%
At least one of the above	93%

So three-quarters of all global executives assessed (and, by implication, all global executives *per se*) need to create more space to connect. Nearly half need to create more space to think, a third space to do and roughly 10 per cent the space to be. I was glad to find this evidence for my ideas.

As I was finishing my analysis I was involved in a programme assessing executives working for one of Europe's biggest operations/ facilities management companies. I had assessed the UK leadership team and my colleagues had assessed the teams in other countries. When the aggregate analysis of all the executives came through, which I had had no involvement in preparing, lo and behold, the main recommendation was that the executives needed to learn to step back and create space for deeper, more strategic thinking.

Further reading

The following were all consulted in the writing of *Create Space*; in addition, I have included material for readers wishing to investigate further some of the issues raised in the book. Nearly all the articles listed are available online.

Introduction

Books and articles

Thomas Ogden, 'The Analytic Third: Working with Intersubjective Clinical Facts', *International Journal of Psychoanalysis*, vol. 75, 1994, pp. 3–19.

Henri Lefebvre, *The Production of Space*, Oxford, Blackwell, 1992.

Gurnek Bains, *Cultural DNA: The Psychology of Globalization*, Hoboken, Wiley, 2015.

Robert Kegan and Lisa Laskow Lahey, *An Everyone Culture: Becoming A Deliberately Developmental Organization*, Boston, Harvard Business Review Press, 2016.

Studies and resources

Alison Coleman, 'Over half of UK workers have experienced burnout in their job', Virgin.com, 15 April 2015. virgin.com/disruptors/over-half-of-uk-workers-have-experienced-burnout-in-their-job

Alex Matthews-King, 'GPs left to burn,' *Pulse*, 4 June 2015. pulsetoday.co.uk/your-practice/battling-burnout/gps-left-to-burn/20010166.article

'Research into UK workers stress levels', Skillsoft, 2015. nypolfed.org.uk/assets/uploads/PDFs/100331.pdf

PART 1: Think

Chapter 1: Reflect

Books

Stephen Grosz, *The Examined Life: How We Lose and Find Ourselves*, London, Vintage, 2014.

Ian Leslie, *Curious: The Desire to Know and Why Your Future Depends on It*, New York, Basic Books, 2014.

Nancy Kline, *Time to Think: Listening to Ignite the Human Mind*, London, Cassell, 2002.

Jeremy Holmes, *Exploring in Security: Towards an Attachment-Informed Psychoanalytic Psychotherapy*, Hove, Routledge, 2010.

Daniel Kahneman, *Thinking, Fast and Slow*, London, Penguin, 2012.

David A. Kolb, *Experiential Learning: Experience as The Source of Learning and Development*, Englewood Cliffs, New Jersey, Prentice Hall, 1983.

Articles

Giada Di Stefano, Gary P. Pisano, Francesca Gino & Bradley R. Staats, 'Making Experience Count: The Role of Reflection in Individual Learning', *Harvard Business School Working Paper* 14-093, 2014.

Jon M. Jachimowicz, Bradley R. Staats, Francesca Gino, Julia J. Lee & Jochen I. Menges, 'Commuting as Role Transitions: How Trait Self-Control and Work-related Prospection Offset Negative Effects of Lengthy Commutes', *Harvard Business School Working Paper* 16-077, 2016.

Oriana Bandiera, Luigi Guiso, Andrea Prat & Raffaella Sadun, 'What Do CEOs Do?', *Harvard Business School Working Paper* 11-081, 2011.

Linda Lawrence-Wilkes and Lyn Ashmore, 'Art of Reflection Quiz' in *The Reflective Practitioner in Professional Education*, London, Palgrave Macmillan, 2014. Also available at businessballs.com/freepdfmaterials/reflective-practice-self-assessment.pdf

Selma Fraiberg, Edna Adelson & Vivian Shapiro, 'Ghosts in the Nursery: A Psychoanalytic Approach to the Problems of Impaired Infant-Mother Relationships', *Journal of the American Academy of Child Psychiatry*, vol. 14 (3), 1975, pp. 387–421.

Studies and resources

'Talking Partners: The first circle of safety', *NextJump*, 22 September 2016. nextjump.com/longpost/talking-partners/

Martin Reeves, Roselinde Torres & Fabien Hassan, 'How to Regain the Lost Art of Reflection', *Harvard Business Review*, 25 September 2017. hbr.org/2017/09/how-to-regain-the-lost-art-of-reflection

U.S. Workplace Survey Key Findings, Gensler, 2013. gensler.com/uploads/documents/2013_US_Workplace_Survey_07_15_2013.pdf

Chapter 2: Learn

Books and articles

Martin Covington, 'Self-Worth Theory: Retrospection and Prospects', in Kathryn R. Wentzel and David B. Miele (eds), *Handbook of Motivation at School*, New York, Routledge, 2016.

Carol S. Dweck, *Mindset: Changing the Way You Think to Fulfil Your Potential*, London, Little Brown, 2012.

Gurnek Bains, *Meaning Inc: The Blueprint for Business Success in the 21st Century*, London, Profile, 2007.

Shelley J. Correll, 'Constraints into Preferences: Gender, Status, and Emerging Career Aspirations', *American Sociological Review*, vol. 69, 2004, pp. 93–113.

Studies and resources

'Research Reveals Fear of Failure Has Us All Shaking in Our Boots This Halloween: 1 in 3 Admit They Are Terrified of Failure', Marketwired report of Linkagoal study, 14 October 2015. marketwired.com/press-release/research-reveals-fear-of-failure-has-us-all-shaking-in-our-boots-this-halloween-2063788.htm

Donna J. Kelley, Benjamin S. Baumer, Candida Brush, Patrica G. Greene, Mahnaz Mahdavi, Mahdi Majbouri, Marcia Cole, Monica Dean & René Heavlow, *Global Entrepreneurship Monitor 2016/2017 Report on Women's Entrepreneurship*, Babson College, Smith College and the Global Entrepreneurship Research Association (GERA), 2017.

University Of Toronto, 'Old Brains Can Learn New Tricks: Study Shows Older People Use Different Areas Of The Brain To Perform Same "Thinking Task" As Young,' *Science Daily*, 25 October 1999.

Lee Mwiti, 'Back to School with Africa's Oldest Learners,' *The Guardian*, 5 February 2015. theguardian.com/world/2015/feb/05/back-to-school-with-africas-oldest-learners

Jeanine Prime & Elizabeth Salib, 'The Best Leaders Are Humble Leaders,' *Harvard Business Review*, 12 May 2014. hbr.org/2014/05/the-best-leaders-are-humble-leaders

Dr Brené Brown, *The Power of Vulnerability*, Houston, TED Talk, 2010. ted.com/talks/brene_brown_on_vulnerability

Chapter 3: Decide

Books and articles
Michael Maccoby, *Strategic Intelligence: Conceptual Tools for Leading Change*, Oxford, OUP, 2017.

Malcolm Gladwell, *Blink: The Power of Thinking Without Thinking*, London, Penguin, 2006.

Peter Senge, *The Fifth Discipline: The Art and Practice of the Learning Organisation*, London, Random House, 2006.

Studies and resources
Susan S. Lang, '"Mindless autopilot" drives people to dramatically underestimate how many daily food decisions they make, Cornell study finds', *Cornell Chronicle*, 22 December 2006. news.cornell.edu/stories/2006/12/mindless-autopilot-drives-people-underestimate-food-decisions

Archy O. de Berker, Robb B. Rutledge, Christoph Mathys, Louise Marshall, Gemma F. Cross, Raymond J. Dolan & Sven Bestmann, 'Computations of uncertainty mediate acute stress responses in humans', *Nature Communications*, 29 March 2016. nature.com/articles/ncomms10996

Kathleen D. Vohs, Roy F. Baumeister, Jean M. Twenge, Brandon J. Schmeichel & Dianee M. Tice, 'Decision Fatigue Exhausts Self-Regulatory Resources', *Psychology Today*, 2006. psychologytoday.com/files/attachments/584/decision200602-15vohs.pdf

Shai Danziger, Jonathan Levav & Liora Avnaim-Pesso, 'Extraneous factors in judicial decisions', *National Academy of Sciences*, 2011. pnas.org/content/108/17/6889.full.pdf

Charlie Munger, 'The Psychology of Human Misjudgement', lecture at Harvard Law School, 1995. youtube.com/watch?time_continue=15&v=pqzcCfUglws

PART 2: Connect

Chapter 4: Check In

Books
Paul Brown, Joan Kingsley and Sue Paterson, *The Fear-Free Organization: Vital Insights from Neuroscience to Transform Your Business Culture*, London, Kogan, 2015.

Daniel Goleman, *Emotional Intelligence: Why It Can Matter More Than IQ*, London, Bloomsbury, 1996.

Melanie Klein, *Love, Guilt and Reparation and Other Works 1921–1945*, New York, Free Press, 1975.

Tara Mohr, *Playing Big: Find Your Voice, Your Mission and Make Things Happen*, London, Arrow Books, 2014.

Studies and resources
John Cooper, 'How EI can improve your bottom line – dealing with the cost of defensive behaviours', JCA Global, 12 June 2017. jcaglobal.com/blog/ei-and-your-bottom-line/

Dr Kristen Neff, Self-Compassion Test, 2017. self-compassion.org/test-how-self-compassionate-you-are/

Chapter 5: Share

Books and articles
Bruce Tuckman, 'Developmental sequence in small groups', *Psychological Bulletin*, vol. 63 (6), 1965, pp. 384–399.

William Halton, 'Some Unconscious Aspects of Organizational Life: Contributions from Psychoanalysis', in Anton Obholzer & Vega Zagier

Roberts (eds), *The Unconscious at Work: Individual and Organizational Stress in The Human Services*, Hove, Routledge, 1994.

Patrick Lencioni, *The Five Dysfunctions of a Team: A Leadership Fable*, San Francisco, Jossey-Bass, 2002.

Simon Sinek, *Start with Why: How Great Leaders Inspire Everyone to Take Action*, London, Penguin, 2011.

Simon Sinek, *Leaders Eat Last: Why Some Teams Pull Together And Others Don't*, Penguin, London, 2017.

Amy Edmonson, 'Psychological Safety and Learning Behavior in Work Teams', Administrative *Science Quarterly*, vol. 44 (2), 1999, pp. 350–383.

Studies and resources

Charles Duhigg, 'What Google Learned From Its Quest to Build the Perfect Team', *New York Times*, 25 February 2016. nytimes.com/2016/02/28/magazine/what-google-learned-from-its-quest-to-build-the-perfect-team.html

Rob Cross, Reb Rebele and Adam Grant, 'Collaborative Overload', *Harvard Business Review*, Jan/Feb 2016. hbr.org/2016/01/collaborative-overload.

Chapter 6: Relate

Books

Duane and Catherine O'Kane, *Real: The Power of Authentic Relationships*, Clearmind, USA, 2016

Bronnie Ware, *The Top Five Regrets of the Dying: A Life Transformed by the Dearly Departing*, London, Hay House UK, 2012.

Studies and resources

Mental Health Foundation's mental health statistics mentalhealth.org.uk/statistics

Ray Dalio, 'How to Build a Company Where The Best Ideas Win', TED Talk, Vancouver, 2017. ted.com/talks/ray_dalio_how_to_build_a_company_where_the_best_ideas_win

Gallup, State of the Global Workplace report, 2017. gallup.com/services/178517/state-global-workplace.aspx

PART 3: Do

Chapter 7: Plan

Books and articles

Verne Harnish, *Mastering the Rockefeller Habits: What You Must Do To Increase the Value of Your Growing Firm*, London, Select Books, 2002.

James Collins and Jerry Porra, *Built to Last: Successful Habits of Visionary Companies*, London, Random House, 2005.

Michael Porter, *The Competitive Strategy: Techniques for Analyzing Industries and Competitors*, New York, Free Press, 2004.

George A. Miller, 'The magical number seven, plus or minus two: Some limits on our capacity for processing information', *The Psychological Review*, vol. 63, 1956, pp. 81–97.

Studies and resources

Michael Mankins & Richard Steele, 'Stop Making Plans; Start Making Decisions', *Harvard Business Review*, January 2006. https://hbr.org/2006/01/stop-making-plans-start-making-decisions

E. J. Masicampo & Roy F. Baumeister, 'Consider It Done! Plan Making Can Eliminate the Cognitive Effects of Unfulfilled Goals', *Journal of Personality and Social Psychology*, Online First Publication, June 20, 2011. users.wfu.edu/masicaej/MasicampoBaumeister2011JPSP.pdf

Chapter 8: Deliver

Books and articles

Larry Bossidy & Ram Charan, *Execution: The Discipline of Getting Things Done*, London, Random House, 2002.

Roberta M. Gilbert, *Extraordinary Relationships: A New Way of Thinking About Human Interactions*, New York, Wiley, 1992.

Steven Kotler, *The Rise of Superman: Decoding the Science of Ultimate Human Performance*, London, Quercus, 2014.

Brené Brown, *The Gifts of Imperfection: Let Go of Who You Think You're Supposed to Be And Embrace Who You Are*, Minnesota, Hazleden, 2010.

Greg McKeown, *Essentialism: The Disciplined Pursuit of Less*, Virgin Books, 2014.

Mihály Csíkszentmihályi, *Flow: The Psychology of Happiness: The Classic Work on How to Achieve Happiness*, London, Rider, 2002.

Brigid Schulte, *Overwhelmed: Work, Love and Play When No One Has the Time*, London, Bloomsbury, 2014.

Simon Parkin, *Death by Video Game: Tales of Obsession From The Virtual Frontline*, London, Profile Books, 2015.

Dan W. Kennedy, *No B.S. Time Management for Entrepreneurs*, Entrepreneur Media, 2004.

Erik M. Altmann, J. Gregory Traftan and David Z. Hambrick, 'Momentary Interruptions Can Derail the Train of Thought', *Journal of Experimental Psychology*, Vol. 143 (1), 2013, pp. 215–226.

Studies and resources

David J. Linden, 'The Neuroscience of Pleasure', *Huffington Post*, 6 September 2011. huffingtonpost.com/david-j-linden/compass-pleasure_b_890342.html

Daniel J. Levitin, 'Why the modern world is bad for your brain', *The Observer*, 18 January 2015. theguardian.com/science/2015/jan/18/modern-world-bad-for-brain-daniel-j-levitin-organized-mind-information-overload

Ian Barker, 'Millennials prefer to deal with companies by text', *Beta News*, 2017. betanews.com/2016/09/15/millennials-companies-text

Susan Weinschenk, 'Why We're All Addicted to Texts, Twitter and Google', *Psychology Today*, 11 September 2012. psychologytoday.com/blog/brain-wise/201209/why-were-all-addicted-texts-twitter-and-google

Martha C. White, 'Your Cell Phone Is Killing Your Productivity, but Not for the Reason You Think', *Money*, 20 July 2015. time.com/money/3956968/cell-phone-alert-productivity

Daniel McGinn, 'Being More Productive', *Harvard Business Review*, May 2011. hbr.org/2011/05/being-more-productive

Chapter 9: Lead

Books and articles

Thomas Ogden, *Psyche Matters*, Northern California Society for Psychoanalytic Psychology, 1999.

Marshall Goldsmith, *What Got You Here Won't Get You There: How Successful People Become Even More Successful*, London, Profile Books, 2008.

Ram Charan, Stephen Drotter & James Noel, *The Leadership Pipeline: How to Build The Leadership Powered Company* (2nd ed.), San Francisco, Jossey-Bass, 2011.

Michael Bungay Stanier, *The Coaching Habit: Say Less, Ask More, and Change the Way You Lead Forever*, Toronto, Box of Crayons Press, 2016.

William Oncken Jr & Donald L. Wass, 'Management Time: Who's Got The Monkey?', *Harvard Business Review*, December 1999.

PART 4: Be

Chapter 10: Dream

Books and articles

Viktor Frankl, *Man's Search for Meaning: The Classic Tribute to Hope from the Holocaust*, Reading, Ebury Publishing, 2004.

Bronnie Ware, *The Top Five Regrets of the Dying*, ibid.

Simon Sinek, *Start With Why*, ibid.

Danielle LaPorte, *The Desire Map: A Guide to Creating Goals with Soul*, Colorado, Sounds True, 2014.

Natan P. F. Kellerman, 'Epigenetic transmission of Holocaust trauma: can nightmares be inherited?', *The Israel Journal of Psychiatry and Related Sciences*, vol. 50 (1) 2013, pp. 33–39.

Studies and resources

BBC Radio 4's Loneliness and Solitude archives. bbc.co.uk/programmes/ p020xzbx

Campaign to End Loneliness campaigntoendloneliness.org/ threat-to-health/

Chapter 11: Balance

Books

Tim Laurence, *The Hoffman Process: The World-Famous Technique That Empowers You to Forgive Your Past, Heal Your Present, and Transform Your Future*, Bantam Books, 2004.

Matthew Walker, *Why We Sleep: The New Science of Sleep and Dreams*, London, Penguin, 2017.

Jonathan Fields, *How to Live A Good Life*, London, Hay House, 2016.

Julia Cameron, *The Artist's Way: A Course in Discovering and Recovering Your Creative Self*, London, Pan Books, 1994.

Pia Mellody & Lawrence S. Freundlich, *The Intimacy Factor: The Ground Rules for Overcoming the Obstacles to Truth, Respect, and Lasting Love*, San Francisco, HarperSanFrancisco, 2004.

Brené Brown, *Braving the Wilderness*, London, Vermilion, 2017.

The Mountaineers, *Mountaineering: The Freedom of the Hills*, Shrewsbury, Swan Hill Press, 2003.

Studies and resources

Jim Loehr & Tony Schwartz, 'The Making of A Corporate Athlete', *Harvard Business Review*, January 2001. hbr.org/2001/01/the-making-of-a-corporate-athlete

Rachel Judith Bretland & Einar Baldvin Thorsteinsson, 'Reducing workplace burnout: the relative benefits of cardiovascular and resistance exercise', *PeerJ*, vol. 3, 2015. ncbi.nlm.nih.gov/pmc/articles/PMC4393815

Lizzie Dearden, 'UK named most overweight nation in Western Europe as obesity rate rises faster than US', *The Independent*, 11 November 2017. independent.co.uk/news/health/uk-obesity-rate-rising-overweight-worst-country-western-europe-world-us-ranking-oecd-research-a8049451.html

Sarah Marsh, 'Unhealthy Britain: half of adults walk less than a mile a day – survey', *The Guardian*, 26 May 2017. theguardian.com/society/2017/may/26/unhealthy-britain-half-of-adults-walk-less-than-a-mile-a-day-survey

PART 5: Three Gateways

Books and articles

Matthew McKay & Patrick Fanning, *Self Esteem: A Proven Program of Cognitive Techniques for Assessing, Improving and Maintaining Your Self-Esteem*, Oakland, New Harbinger Publications, 3rd edition, 2000.

Resources

Derek Draper & Cecilia d'Felice, *Break Free From Your Past*, 2017. derekdraper.net

Index